LET ME TELL YOU A STORY

ALSO BY JOHN FEINSTEIN

LET ME TELL YOU A STORY

A Lifetime in the Game

RED AUERBACH *and*
JOHN FEINSTEIN

Little, Brown and Company

New York   Boston

Little, Brown and Company
Time Warner Book Group
1271 Avenue of the Americas, New York, NY 10020
Visit our Web site at www.twbookmark.com

First Edition

Library of Congress Cataloging-in-Publication Data

Auerbach, Red.
   Let me tell you a story : a lifetime in the game / Red Auerbach and John
Feinstein. — 1st ed.
      p. cm.
   ISBN 0-316-73823-9
   1. Auerbach, Red. 2. Basketball coaches — United States — Biography.
I. Feinstein, John. II. Title.
GV884.A8A26 2004
796.323'092 — dc22   2004013000

10 9 8 7 6 5 4 3 2 1

Q-FF

Printed in the United States of America

This is dedicated to the memories of
Dorothy Auerbach and Zang Auerbach . . .
who knew every one of these stories

Contents

Introduction

IT BEGAN WITH an extremely awkward situation.

I had been asked by a local TV station to discuss the upcoming NCAA basketball tournament on its weekly sports show. Years of experience have taught me that television people never tell you when they are actually going to put you on the air. They ask you to arrive early so they don't have to worry that you might be late. The conversation usually goes something like this:

"What time will I be on?"

"Well, we'd like you there by seven o'clock."

"That's not what I asked. What time will I actually be on?"

"Well, the show starts at seven-thirty."

"And I'll be on at what time?"

"It could be as early as seven thirty-five."

"Or as late as?"

"I don't know."

This was one of those deals. The producer told me he was almost certain I would be in the show's second block at 7:35. He suggested I get to the station no later than 7:00, although they preferred 6:45. I said I'd be there by 7:20.

I arrived on time and was taken to the greenroom. "You're the first one here," the makeup woman said to me. "The first guest is running a couple of minutes late."

"First guest?"

"Yes, someone named Red Auerbach."

Great. Not only was I not in the second block, but the absolute last person I wanted to share a greenroom with was Red Auerbach. It wasn't because I had grown up in New York, living and dying with the Willis Reed–Walt Frazier–Dave DeBusschere–Bill Bradley Knicks, and as a result hated the Boston Celtics. It wasn't even my filmy little-kid memories of him lighting up that damn victory cigar.

It was something he had said a few years earlier to my friend Dan Shaughnessy when Shaughnessy was writing a book about him. When Shaughnessy first approached Red to ask his permission, Red had said to him, "Okay, I'll do it. But just don't do to me what that SOB did to Bobby Knight."

That SOB would be me. Shaughnessy, after gleefully reporting the line to me, used it in the book. I figured Red's line to Shaughnessy still accurately summed up his feelings about me.

I was sitting on a couch, pretending to read something, trying to think of what to say, when Red walked into the room. I rarely get nervous meeting people. I'm too old and have met too many people for that. Now I was nervous. I stood up, offered my hand, and said, "Hi, Coach. I'm John Feinstein."

Would he refuse to shake hands? Would he call me an SOB? Red is legendary for many things, one of them being his bluntness.

"Hey, John, how're you doing?" he said, smiling and shaking hands with surprising firmness for someone who was eighty-one. "You on the show too?"

He then began apologizing for being late. I felt myself relaxing. Maybe, I thought, he's forgotten who I am. Red went in to get made-up. The producer came in to tell him they'd be ready for him in ten minutes. "Yeah, yeah, fine, whatever," Red said.

Red came back into the greenroom, sat down, lit a cigar (of course), and gave me another smile.

"So," he said, taking the cigar out of his mouth, "you talk to your buddy anytime recently?"

"My buddy?"

The grin was now what I would later understand to be wicked, when he's about to nail someone.

"Yeah, your buddy, Bobby Knight."

Oh Christ, he hadn't forgotten. Now I was nervous again.

"Coach, we don't exactly speak too often," I said.

Now he was laughing. "Yeah, no kidding. Don't worry about it. He hates a lot of people."

"He loves you, though." I had spent a good deal of time listening to Knight talk about Auerbach's genius and generosity.

He puffed on the cigar. "That's just 'cause I never wrote anything about him."

Now I was laughing too. We spent the next few minutes talking about the upcoming tournament and how overrated he thought number one–ranked Duke was (he was proved correct by Connecticut in the championship game). By the time they came to take him to the set, I was hoping the show might be delayed for another hour.

He smoked the cigar the whole time he was on the air. Naturally, no one dared to tell him there was no smoking in the building. When it was my turn to go in, Red paused on his way out. "It was good to see you," he said. "Keep up the good work."

The wicked grin returned. "I'll tell your buddy you said hello."

Knowing Red, he probably did just that.

Jack Kvancz, the athletic director at George Washington, and I have been friends since his days as the basketball coach at Catholic University in the early 1980s. Jack got out of coaching in 1983 and became the AD at George Mason, and then in 1994 got the job at George Washington. Whenever I went to GW games, it was impossible not to notice Red, the most famous GW grad of them all (class of 1940), sitting ten rows up from the floor.

"He never misses a game," Kvancz had told me one night when I asked how often Red came to see his old school play.

"Getting to really know him has been one of the great perks of this job."

"You spend time with him?"

"I go to lunch with him every Tuesday. Not just me, a group of guys. Morgan Wootten [the legendary DeMatha High School coach] goes most weeks; Sam Jones goes; some of Red's buddies from Woodmont. It's a whole crew. He sits there and tells stories the whole time. It's unbelievable."

"He still remembers stuff?"

"Remembers stuff? Are you kidding? He remembers *everything.*"

Driving home from the TV show that night, I remembered what Jack had said about the Tuesday lunches. At the time, I was writing a column for the *Washington Post Magazine.* If, in fact, Red didn't think I was an SOB, maybe he would allow me to sit in on one of the lunches and write a column about it. If nothing else, it would be fun to listen to him.

So I called Jack. I told him what had happened at the TV show Saturday night. What about lunch? I wondered.

"I don't know," he said. "I can ask him, but that lunch is a pretty closed society."

Just as I was about to write off the idea, Jack added a thought. "You know, if Morgan were to ask him, I'll bet he'd say yes. Me, he might say no to. Not Morgan."

So I called Wootten, a longtime friend dating to my early days at the *Post,* when I had covered high school ball. "I'd be delighted to ask," Wootten said. "The worst thing he can do is say no. I'll ask him at lunch tomorrow."

I was actually nervous about this now. If Red said no, it would make me think that our entire conversation Saturday night, which had felt so warm and real, had just been him being courteous. "Don't push it," I said to Morgan. "If he seems uncomfortable at all, let it go."

"Don't worry," Morgan said. "Nobody pushes Red."

The next night he called back. "You're on," he said. "Be at the China Doll at eleven o'clock next Tuesday."

"Eleven o'clock?" I said. "I thought this was lunch."

"It is," Morgan said. "Red starts ordering at about eleven-oh-five. Don't be late. Oh, and one more thing: whatever you do, don't try to pay for yourself or pick up the check. That's the one way to guarantee you'll never be invited back again."

I wasn't planning on being invited back, but I made a mental note of Morgan's warning anyway.

The China Doll is on H Street in Northwest Washington, between Sixth and Seventh Streets. It is in the heart of Washington's Chinatown, a two-block stretch that must have a dozen Chinese restaurants on it. I had eaten there a couple times before games after the MCI Center, two blocks away, had opened late in 1997. I walked in on the stroke of 11:00.

The restaurant was dimly lit, with what appeared to be a bakery counter to the right of the door, then a small bar. There were a few tables along the wall to the left, and then, at the end of the bar, the room widened out. Directly behind the bar was a round table. It was the only one that was occupied at that hour, a dozen men seated around it.

There were, I was pleased to see, five familiar faces: Red; Morgan Wootten, who sat on Red's left; Jack Kvancz, who sat next to Morgan; and Tom Penders and Joe McKeown, the men's and women's basketball coaches at GW, respectively. I remembered Jack telling me that Red always invited the GW basketball people to come to lunch when they were free.

The chair on the other side of Red was empty.

"Here, kid, sit down," Red said, indicating the chair. The man sitting to the right of the chair was small, wearing thick glasses and a Celtics baseball cap.

"Zang Auerbach," he said, putting out his hand. "Hard to believe a good-looking guy like me is Red's brother, huh?"

I was introduced to the rest of the table, but none of the names registered. There were two guys dressed in dark suits who looked like they had been cast as Secret Service agents in a movie. Their names were Pete Dowling and Bob Campbell. It was only later that I would learn that they *were* Secret Service agents. Most of the others were older men, in their seventies and eighties. One, whose name I heard to be "Hymie," began screaming at me soon after I sat down.

"Look at that notebook," he said when I took one out. "He brought a goddamn notebook. As if this sonofabitch" — he pointed at Red — "has anything to say worth hearing. Most unbelievable thing I've ever seen. Son, if this is the best you can come up with to write about, your career must really be going badly."

I looked at Red to see his reaction to all this. He was

cracking up. "Don't mind Hymie," he said. "He's still recovering from his war wounds."

I looked at the man again. He appeared to be almost as old as Red.

"Which war?" I asked.

"World War Two," Red said.

"Which war?" Hymie roared. "The Civil War. Which war? Seriously now, someone pays you to be a reporter?"

On the other side of me, Zang was yelling at Hymie. "I told you to behave yourself today. Why do you insist on ruining lunch every week?"

"Shut up, you old geezer," Hymie responded.

It was 11:05. "Emma," Red said as an attractive Asian woman walked over to him, "let's get this show on the road."

The next ninety minutes were as entertaining as the first five had been. While waiting for the food to arrive, everyone chatted about topics of the day, from Monica Lewinsky to Rick Pitino. Larry Bird's name came up. He was doing very good work as coach of the Indiana Pacers.

Morgan turned to Red. "What was a better move by you — Bird or the McHale-Parish trade?"

Red smiled. "McHale-Parish," he said, referring to the 1980 deal in which he acquired future Hall of Famers Kevin McHale and Robert Parish in return for the less-than-immortal Joe Barry Carroll. "Anyone tells you they knew Bird would be as good as he turned out — including me — is a liar."

I started writing furiously. Hymie glared. Red talked at length about Bird and McHale and Parish. "But the Russell deal was number one," Morgan said, doing my job for me.

"Oh yeah," Red said. "You know how I got Russell, don't you?" he said to me.

Before I could answer, Zang elbowed me. "Whatever you do," he said softly, "don't tell him that you know."

I knew something about it, knew it involved a trade with the St. Louis Hawks for Russell's draft rights in 1956.

"You traded two great players for him, right?" I said, not wanting to appear ignorant despite Zang's warning.

"Yeah, but that was the easy part," he said. "I gave St. Louis [Ed] Macauley and [Cliff] Hagan to move up to number two in the draft. But Rochester still had the number one pick."

"So how'd you get them not to take Russell?"

Red smiled. I had set him up perfectly.

"The Ice-Capades," he said.

"The Ice-Capades?"

"Sure. Walter Brown [the owner of the Celtics] was president of the Ice-Capades. I had him call Les Harrison, the owner in Rochester, and tell them he'd send the Ice-Capades up there for a week if they didn't draft Russell."

"So you got Bill Russell for the Ice-Capades?"

"You got it."

Never in my life have I written an easier column than that one, or a more enjoyable one.

❖   ❖   ❖

As the lunch was breaking up that day, two people approached me. The first was Zang, holding a piece of paper. "You ever want to come back," he said, "just call me on a Monday night to make sure we're on for the next day."

I thanked him, assuming that I would not be returning to the lunch anytime soon — if ever.

Right behind him was Hymie, who I had by now gleaned was Hymie Perlo, a name I was familiar with since he had worked in community relations for the Washington Bullets for many years.

Hymie looked at Zang, and I wondered if they were going to get into a fight.

"You coming to the Legion tomorrow?" Zang asked.

"I have no idea," Hymie answered. "Who knows if any of us will be alive tomorrow."

He turned to me. I girded for another diatribe. He put his hand on my back and leaned in close, dropping his voice to a whisper. "Remember one thing," he said. "Red Auerbach is not only the smartest basketball coach who ever lived, he's the best man you'll ever meet."

He pulled back. "And if you quote me on that, I'll hunt you down." With that, he walked away.

The column's headline was LUNCH WITH A LEGEND. The entire column, for all intents and purposes, was Red telling stories. Soon after the column had run, my phone rang on a Monday night. It was Zang.

"Red wants to know how come you haven't come back to the lunch," he said.

"Oh, well, I didn't know I was invited."

"I *told* you you were invited."

He had. I had thought he was just being polite.

"You free tomorrow?" he asked. I wasn't, but the date I had could be changed.

"Sure," I said.

"Eleven o'clock," Zang said.

This time I came without a notebook. Hymie yelled at me nonetheless for (among other things) not being familiar with someone who had played at GW *before* Red played there. I felt completely at home in this group of men I barely knew. A couple times when I ventured an opinion on something, Red shook his head and nudged me.

"Kid," he said, "let me tell you why you're wrong about that."

Then he told me.

Walking out, Zang said to me, "Call you next Monday?"

"Yes," I said. "Please do."

For the next four years, my Monday night was not complete until the phone rang and a now familiar voice said, "Is that Danny and Brigid's dad?" And then, what became my five favorite words of every week:

"We're on. Eleven o'clock tomorrow."

Only later, when I began writing this book, did I come to understand that everyone in the group feels exactly the same way. Tuesday. Eleven o'clock. China Doll.

Don't be late.

And don't try to pay.

LET ME
TELL
YOU A
STORY

1

The Club

"DID I EVER TELL you about Chamberlain?"

The old man leans back in his chair, a smile creasing his face at the memory. Someone sitting at the round table has said something about Wilt Chamberlain and, as always, memories and stories flood back to him.

"Chamberlain," he says, once the table has gone silent, "was the most unbelievable physical specimen *ever*. There wasn't anything he couldn't do on the basketball court. One year he scored fifty points a game. Another year he led the league in assists. He was so strong it was frightening."

He pauses. "But there was one thing he couldn't do. He couldn't beat us. Just couldn't do it. Russell wore him out, running up and down the court, and you" — he points across the table at one of his listeners — "you drove him crazy. Remember how we ran that pick-and-roll play, where Russell would feed you the ball and Chamberlain had to switch? He'd always get there just as you released the shot, and you, you sonofabitch, you'd say in that high-pitched voice of yours, *'Too late.'* And you made the shot every time."

The man he is pointing at is Sam Jones, who, like Bill Russell, is in basketball's Hall of Fame. Jones is cracking up at the story, at the memory, and at the shrill imitation of his taunting of Chamberlain.

"Remember the night he chased me?" he says.

"Oh yeah." Now the old man is laughing too. "You ran down the court, grabbed a stool from one of the photographers, and used it for protection."

"Protection?" Jones says. "I told Wilt, 'Now I've got a chance. You come near me, I'll swing the thing at you.'"

"He'd a still killed you."

"No way. He'd never catch me."

A dozen men are now convulsed with laughter.

"I ever tell you about the night Wilt tried to get at me?" the old man says.

For the next twenty minutes he talks about Chamberlain and all the times his Boston Celtics brought him grief, first as a Philadelphia Warrior, later as a San Francisco Warrior, then as a Philadelphia 76er, and finally as a Los Angeles Laker. "I actually liked the guy," he says when he is finished. "He flew all the way across the country to come to my eightieth birthday party. After all those years, that meant a lot to me."

For a split second, he is silent. Then he pushes back from the table. "Gotta go."

A dozen men stand up as if the old man is a judge walking out of a courtroom. Red Auerbach is now eighty-seven years old, but there aren't many down moments in his day. When it is time to leave lunch and get to his afternoon card game, he doesn't linger. For everyone else at the table it is different. Most of them have jobs to get back to.

None of them are in any hurry. They would prefer to linger. But when Red says, "Gotta go," no one argues. Arguing with Red is about as easy as beating his Celtics was for Chamberlain.

Outside, it is a midwinter Tuesday in Washington DC, and a cold rain is spitting down, the midday temperature hovering around freezing. On the sidewalk outside the China Doll, the twelve men who had been sitting at the round table in the back corner of the restaurant are now standing in groups of two and three, engaged in conversation. There is a good deal of contact between them: arms around shoulders; repeated handshakes; the occasional hug.

To those walking by, they must be a strange sight. Some of the passersby pause or even come to a halt when they get a glimpse of Auerbach, who is the only one in the group in any sort of rush to move from the spot anytime before dark.

"Come on, gotta go," he barks again, walking slowly in the direction of the silver Mercedes convertible parked in front of him. A glance at the license plate will quickly dispel any doubt about who the car belongs to. It says simply, CELTIC. Those riding with him know from his tone that this is last call, that it is time for one more handshake, a promise to call later in the week, a reminder to stay safe on the road.

Even so, as Auerbach starts easing himself into the driver's seat, his passengers are still lingering just a tiny bit. There may be one more story to tell, one last laugh to be had before departing. Only when he is seated, engine running, and looks up one last time and says, "Hey, how 'bout it?" do they finally break away and start to get into the car.

No one, except the old man, really wants to go.

By now, inevitably, some of those walking by or walking into the restaurant have stopped to stare. "Is that who I think it is?" they ask. Or they may just call out, "Hey, Coach, how's it going?" Auerbach waves in response, accustomed to the notion that there are very few places he can go without someone recognizing him.

One man dressed in a suit, walking rapidly with a cell phone to his ear, stops in his tracks when he sees him. He looks at no one in particular among those still on the sidewalk and says, "It's him, isn't it?"

Yes, he's told, it's him; it's Red Auerbach, the man who, for all intents and purposes, invented professional basketball.

"What the heck is he doing here?" the man asks.

The answer to that question is simple: it's Tuesday.

It began with two brothers who looked up one day and noticed that their grandchildren were either grown-up or on the verge of becoming grown-ups. They were, like most men, always busy with something: work, their own families, travel, friends. It wasn't as if they never saw each other; they did, but there was no consistency to it. Neither can remember who broached the subject or exactly why it came up, but they decided it was time to make a conscious effort to spend more time together.

"Let's go to lunch," the older one said.

"Chinese, I assume," said the younger.

"Of course."

Throughout his nomadic life as a basketball coach, Red Auerbach had always eaten Chinese food after games. His reasoning was simple: in almost any NBA city, there was always a Chinese restaurant that had late-night carryout. He would call ahead, pick the food up on his way back from the arena, and eat it in his room. What's more, because he always asked for the food steamed, it didn't sit heavily in his stomach the way some other food might. He slept easily and woke up feeling fresh and ready to make the trip to the airport and on to the next city. This was back in the NBA's Dark Ages, when teams still flew commercially, waking up at the crack of dawn to catch the first available flight to the next city. No charters; no five-star hotels. Most nights on the road for Auerbach, the most celebrated NBA coach in history, were the same: a game, Chinese food before bed, a predawn wake-up call, and a flight that left for somewhere with the rising sun. Auerbach grew to like Chinese food so much that for several years he was part owner of a Chinese restaurant in Boston.

Some time later, retired from coaching and mostly retired from general managing the greatest dynasty in the history of basketball, Red Auerbach told his brother, Zang, four years his junior, to meet him for lunch the next Tuesday at a restaurant in Washington DC's Chinatown called the China Inn. Most basketball fans don't realize that Auerbach has lived almost exclusively in Washington, except for a stint in the navy, since 1937, when he enrolled at George Washington University. Even when he coached the Celtics, his wife and two daughters lived in Washington. Red had an apartment in Boston during the season but sneaked home whenever the schedule allowed. And he spent the off-seasons — which were much longer back then — in Washington.

"Let's just agree," he told Zang that day, "that we'll meet here every Tuesday for lunch unless one of us has something else to do."

Zang, who had been a cartoonist at the *Washington Star* and had done magazine portraits of famous people throughout his career, was retired. His most famous piece of work can still be seen whenever the Celtics play a home game — Zang designed the Celtics logo that first appeared on the parquet floor at the Boston Garden and is now on the floor at the Fleet Center. Zang promised his brother, who still traveled to Boston at times for meetings and was often out of town to give a speech or do a clinic, to call him every Monday night. If both were in town and healthy, they would have lunch the next day.

"It became something we both looked forward to," Zang said. "But it occurred to me at one point that we had some close mutual friends whom it would be nice to see too. So I suggested to Red that we invite a couple of them to join us."

By this time, the lunches had moved from the China Inn to the China Doll next door. New management had come to the China Inn, and the restaurant stopped serving chow mein. Red likes chow mein. He had eaten at the China Doll in the past — he has eaten at every restaurant in DC's Chinatown at some point in his life — and enjoyed the food and the chow mein. So, when Hymie Perlo, who had known the Auerbach brothers since he and Zang had been in high school together in 1940, and Morgan Wootten were invited to come to lunch, it was at the China Doll.

Soon after, Red began occasionally inviting a couple of his friends from Woodmont Country Club. Red joined Woodmont, which is in Rockville, Maryland, in 1946 when the initiation fee was $500. These days the initiation fee is a bit higher: $90,000. Red has never played golf but did play tennis there for years. Nowadays, he spends five afternoons a week at Woodmont playing gin with a group of seven or eight men, almost always walking away from the table with a tidy profit for the day. "It's his other pension," jokes Jack Kvancz. "That's why he's the one guy who always has to get going after lunch. The more time he spends at lunch, the less time he spends playing cards at Woodmont."

Kvancz was invited to lunch soon after he became the athletic director at GW in 1994. "Back then, Red came in and played racquetball most days," Kvancz said. "I think he's the only guy in the history of the school to have a parking spot in the lot right outside our door who didn't have to pay for it. He'd come to my office after he played and we'd talk hoops."

Kvancz was a very good player at Boston College in the 1960s, on teams coached by Bob Cousy, another of Auerbach's legendary Celtic players. So the notion that Auerbach was sitting in his office several days a week talking basketball with him was almost overwhelming.

"One morning, it's like ten-thirty, and he says, 'Come on. We're going,'" Kvancz said. "I said, 'Where are we going?' He says, 'China Doll.' I looked at my watch to make sure it wasn't broken or something. But he said we were going, so I went. It's eleven o'clock in the morning when we get there, and I walk in and there's this round table and sitting there are Zang and Hymie and Morgan and Sam Jones and Alvin Miller [a Woodmont friend]. Right behind us, walking in, are Aubre Jones [Sam's son, who is GW's intramural director] and Mike Jarvis [then GW's basketball coach].

"Now, if something comes up on a Tuesday and I can't go to lunch, I'm really upset. I do everything I can to keep my calendar clear on Tuesday mornings, not because Red wants me there, which I know he does or I wouldn't be invited, but because I want to be there."

By 1999 the group also included Pete Dowling and Bob Campbell, Secret Service agents Red had become friends with, and Rob Ades, a local labor lawyer whom Red had met at Woodmont.

"I had been a member at Woodmont since 1980," Ades said. "But I never dared introduce myself to Red. I mean he was, after all, *Red Auerbach*. I've been a basketball fan all my life. I played, I went to summer camps, I ran summer camps, I thought I might coach someday. I'm also Jewish. Here's the guy who lived *my* dream and became the greatest coach ever. He's just not the kind of person you wander over to casually and say, 'Hey, Red, I'm Rob Ades. How's it going today?' "

In 1989, though, Ades had a reason to introduce himself. Ades's firm represents unions — not to negotiate contracts but to help union members who need legal services. "In other words, a cop needs a will written, we do it for him," Ades said. "A teacher has a son stopped for DUI, we represent the son. The kind of thing that isn't covered for them the way, say, medical insurance is."

In working with the DC Teachers Union, Ades had become friends with John Wood, who was then the basketball coach at Spingarn High School. Wood had a player in the mid-1980s named Sherman Douglas, a gifted point guard who desperately needed guidance in order to get him out of Northeast DC and into college. "I'll never forget the first time I went to his apartment," Ades said. "There was no door. Someone had stolen the door to his family's apartment."

Ades helped Douglas to eventually land at Syracuse, where he became a star, a surefire first-round draft pick. Douglas wanted Ades to represent him, but Ades had no experience as a sports agent. He agreed to help Douglas pick one. "So we're down to two guys," Ades said. "One is Bob Woolf, the other is Larry Fleischer. I'm at Woodmont and there's Red sitting there playing cards, a guy who knows more about the NBA and about agents than anyone. I owed it to Sherman to at least ask his opinion.

"So I walked over to the table and, kind of gingerly, said, 'Excuse me, Coach, I don't mean to interrupt —'

"*'Well, you are interrupting! Can't you see I'm playing cards here?!'*

"I ran, I cowered, I hid. A minute later, he comes over to where I'm standing, shaking like a leaf, and says, 'What can I do for you?' Thank God he had won the hand. So I introduced myself, told him I was friends with Sherman Douglas and that we were down to Woolf or Fleischer as an agent. Did he have any advice?

" 'Woolf has too much on his plate,' he says. 'Get Fleischer.' He turns around and walks away."

Douglas and Ades did get Fleischer, and Auerbach kept tabs on Douglas's progress. Eventually he landed with the Celtics, and periodically Auerbach would make a point of telling Ades how pleased he was with Douglas. Then one day he took the conversation a step further.

"Next Tuesday," he said. "We're having lunch at the China Doll. Be there at eleven."

Ades was nonplussed. First, he couldn't believe Red Auerbach was asking him to lunch. Second, he couldn't believe that lunch was at eleven o'clock in the morning.

"But it was Red, so I didn't ask questions," he said. "I showed up dressed in my best suit. I told everyone, 'I'm having lunch with Red Auerbach.' I walk in and there are ten other guys there. Okay, so it was still nice to be asked. We're finishing and I figure I'll be a mensch and pick up the check because I'm honored to be invited. I start to say something and Erv Lewis [a Woodmont friend] puts his hand on my arm and says quietly, 'Don't do it.' But I want to do it. 'You'll be insulting him. Don't do it.' I kept my mouth shut."

The following Tuesday evening Ades was getting ready to leave his office when the phone rang. He picked it up and a voice said, *"Where the hell were you?!"*

Ades's exact response as he remembers it was, "Huma, huma, whaaa?"

"Some lawyer you are," the voice said. "I'd feel great having you defend me."

"But, whaa?"

"Next Tuesday. Be there at eleven." SLAM.

Ades has been there Tuesday at 11:00 ever since.

The rules of participation are simple. After ten years, word of the lunches has spread among people in Washington and among basketball people. To get invited, one has to have, in effect, a sponsor, someone in the group who asks Red if it is okay to bring a friend.

Red almost always says yes to any group member who asks if he can bring someone, in part because there is a general understanding that these lunches are not for everyone. Unofficially, this is a men's club, if only because the language and the stories are frequently bawdy and because Red is old-fashioned enough to feel uncomfortable speaking that way or having stories like that told in front of women.

Being invited once does not mean you get to come back.

There have been numerous onetime guests, some because they only wanted to come once, others because they weren't asked to return.

Among those who have come once or come only on occasion are Marvin Kalb, the longtime NBC correspondent who came mostly to talk to Red about the old days of basketball as part of the research for his autobiography; Eugene Istomin, the late classical pianist, a huge sports fan who asked a mutual friend from Woodmont if he could come just once to meet Red; Mike Brey, the Notre Dame basketball coach who played and coached under Wootten at DeMatha; Joe Wootten, Morgan's son, now a successful high school coach himself; Jimmy Patsos, then Gary Williams's top assistant at the University of Maryland and now head coach at Loyola College in Maryland; Lefty Driesell, the great college coach who has been a friend of Red's for years; and Peter Vecsey, the longtime basketball columnist and TV commentator.

Vecsey and Red had had more than their share of battles through the years. It was Ades who asked if it would be okay for Vecsey, who is a client of his, to come to lunch.

"He's a friend of yours, right?" Red said.

"Yes," Ades said.

"Then it's okay."

The day Vecsey came was a miserable rainy day in Washington. Ades, soaked to the bone, walked in a few minutes after eleven.

"Where's Vecsey?" Red asked.

"He's outside," Ades said. "He wanted to be absolutely sure it was okay with you that he be here."

"He got an umbrella?"

"No."

Red leaned back in his chair and smiled. "Tell him to wait a few more minutes while I decide."

Vecsey was eventually rescued, and he and Red sat and exchanged war stories for the next ninety minutes. Clearly, Vecsey thought it was well worth the wait.

Until the fall of 2003 when retired *Washington Post* sports editor George Solomon and ex–Bullets general manager Bob Ferry joined the group, the only newcomer in the last four years had been Chris Wallace, the former ABC News correspondent and newly minted Fox anchor, who, even though he has carved out an extremely successful career in his own right, will always be looked upon by Red and the other octogenarians as "Mike Wallace's kid."

Wallace's sponsor for initial entry into the group was me — then the newest member of the club. When I asked Red if it would be okay for Wallace to come, he asked if he was related to Mike Wallace.

"His son," I said.

"Mike's a good guy," Red said. "He can come. Tell him he can bring his father too if he wants to."

Chris didn't bring his father but showed up the next week, nervous as a cat. "It was funny," he said later. "I've covered summits, I've interviewed presidents and heads of state, I've been on live national television more times than I can count, and I can't remember ever being quite as nervous as walking into the China Doll that day.

"Part of it was Red, knowing who he was and what he meant to sports, but the other part of it was feeling a little bit like I was being invited up to the tree house for the first time by the other kids. I didn't want to mess up."

Like all first timers, Chris spent most of the lunch listening. Red is often at his best when there is a newcomer in the group. It is as if he wants to be sure they enjoy themselves as much as they had expected to when they got themselves invited.

"I ever tell you about Letterman?" he said, perhaps thinking of Chris as a CBS person because of his father.

"One day they call me and want me to come up and do the show. I tell 'em okay and we set a date. The day I'm supposed to go up they call and say, 'Oh, we're sorry, something's come up. We need to reschedule.' I tell them that's fine, I know these things happen. They give me another date, we agree. Next date comes, they call again. Something else has come up. They want to reschedule again. I say, 'Absolutely not.' The woman says, 'But, Coach, last time you said you understand that these things happen.'

"I said, 'Right. These things happen. *Once.*'"

"She says [he is imitating a high-pitched female voice], 'Oh, but Coach, David will be so upset. He's such a big basketball fan.'

"I say, 'Apparently he's not *that* big a basketball fan.'"

Wallace laughed as Red finished and said, "Well, I'll be certain never to cancel an interview with you."

"Don't be so sure I'd schedule one with you," Red answered.

Wallace didn't know it, but he had just been given his initiation.

When it was time to leave, he thanked Red for lunch. Then, timidly, he looked at him and said, "Can I come back?"

Red glanced at Zang as if pondering his answer.

"What do you think, Zang?" he asked.

"He seems okay," Zang said, "for a kid."

Wallace is fifty-six.

"Okay then," Red said in his best trying-to-sound-gruff manner. "You can come back."

Since that day only Saddam Hussein has kept Wallace away. "Which is reason enough," he pointed out once, "to hate the man."

2

From Brooklyn to DC

"I EVER TELL YOU about the time we didn't want to pay Alan King?"

Red rarely reminisces about his childhood. Often, to get him going on the early days, it would take Zang bringing up someone from the old neighborhood in Brooklyn or someone asking him a specific question about his boyhood.

One day, though, the subject of tennis — probably Red's second-favorite sport — made him think about Alan King, the late comedian who was such a big fan of the sport that for years he sponsored an event in Las Vegas and always had not only a front-row box at the U.S. Open but also his own locker in the players' locker room.

"We needed uniforms for our basketball team," Red said. "We had a neighborhood team called the Pelicans. We traveled around Brooklyn and played kids from other neighborhoods in different school yards. Some of them had uniforms. We wanted uniforms too. We found out it would cost seventy-five bucks for eight uniforms. So we had to figure out how to raise the money.

"No one ever used the YMHA, where we played all the time, on Sunday afternoons. We decided to have a game day and a dance; play some games people could watch, then hire a band and have a dance on the gym floor. It cost us twenty-five bucks to rent the place. We hired a seven-piece band for fourteen dollars. Then we charged people twenty-five cents a ticket and sold five hundred tickets. That meant we made one hundred twenty-five dollars, which was more than enough since after we paid for the uniforms, the rental, and the band we were still going to have eleven dollars left over.

"At the end of the day, one of the guys says, 'Hey, let's not pay the band. They weren't any good.'

"I said, 'You gotta pay 'em no matter how lousy they were. We said fourteen dollars to play, not necessarily to play good.'

"We took a vote. I got outvoted five to three. So we went and told this little guy who was the band leader that we weren't going to pay him. He got mad and went and told the guy who ran the building, who came and told us if we didn't pay the band we could never play basketball there again. So we paid the band.

"Fifty years later, I'm at a tennis tournament and I run into Alan King. We start talking about the fact that we both grew up in Brooklyn. He tells me he had his own band when he was thirteen years old. I say, 'That's funny, reminds me of a story.'

I tell him the story and he looks at me and says, 'The YMHA. You guys tried to rip me off for fourteen bucks!'

"I told him I'd voted to pay him even though my friends didn't think his band was any good.

"And he said to me, 'They were right. We weren't any good.'"

Arnold Jacob Auerbach was born on September 20, 1917, in the Williamsburg section of Brooklyn, not far from the East River and the bridge named for his neighborhood. He was Hyman and Marie Auerbach's middle son, arriving three years after Victor and almost four years before Zangfeld.

Hyman Auerbach had emigrated from Minsk at the age of twelve along with two brothers, arriving on Ellis Island shortly before the turn of the century. He didn't talk very much about his life in Russia or what led to his parents' decision to send three of their six children to the United States. Red did learn that his father was the only one of the children in the family who had learned to read and write while still in Russia. It cost a penny each way on the train to get to the school nearest his family's home, and no one had that kind of money. But Hyman Auerbach talked the conductor into letting him ride each day without paying.

"That's the way my dad was," Red said. "He was an absolute charmer. Very outgoing, friendly. People always liked him. He was the kind of guy who could walk into a convent and make all the nuns fall in love with him. The funny thing is, none of us —

not Vic, not me, not Zang — were like that. We were all kind of introverted."

"Introverted" may be a bit of an overstatement when it comes to the younger Auerbachs. Red can be quiet at times, but when he has an opinion on something, which is often, he is more than willing to express it. Zang was always the dry wit in the family, someone with a knack for making people laugh almost anytime he opened his mouth.

"Vic was the student," Red said. "He worked hard in school, got good grades, stayed out of trouble. He was good enough to make the basketball team but was never a star. I was the athlete, biggest in the family. When something went wrong with the clothesline at home, I was the one who had to climb out the window and fix it. Zang had the highest IQ of all of us. Never worked in school and had the best grades."

Hyman Auerbach was in the restaurant business early in his life. He met Marie Thompson while working in a Manhattan restaurant called Rosoff's, and he later ran a delicatessen. "The guy who owned the building where the deli was came to my dad one time and offered to sell him the whole building for ten grand," Red said. "My father thought it was too much. Years later they tore the building down — and built Radio City Music Hall on the site."

Eventually Hyman Auerbach went into the cleaning business with his brother Sam. All the Auerbach sons worked for their father in high school, and Vic eventually became a partner in the business. Red carried bundles of clothes on deliveries for his father, and when he was in college and came home on break, he would work the overnight shift pressing suits. "Ten at night until eight in the morning," he said. "I'd get myself a pastrami sandwich and a cream soda and go to work. I did one hundred suits a night. Kept me from ever getting a swelled head about being a basketball player."

Red remembers his father as a savvy businessman, someone who knew a lot of people — some important, some not so important. "One time someone stole a bundle of suits," Red said. "The suits were worth three hundred, maybe four hundred dollars. If my father couldn't get them back, he'd have to pay for them, and that would have killed the business. He went to a guy he knew and said, 'Can you help?' The guy said, 'Cost you twenty-five dollars.' So Dad gave him the twenty-five and the next day he gets the suits back. A few years later this guy was executed at Sing Sing.

"My dad always told me never to buy anything from someone I didn't know. Always be suspicious. One day I'm on the subway and this guy is selling socks. It's a dozen pair for thirty cents. I figure that's too good a deal to turn down, so I come up with the money and buy a dozen. I get home and no two socks matched.

"Another time a guy on the street was selling these Indian head rings. I wanted one. He said three bucks. I went to my dad and said, 'Look, I never ask you for anything. I always help out at work. How about giving me three dollars so I can get one of these rings?' He looks at me and says, 'Are you going to spend your whole life getting taken by people? No. You can't have it.' A week later I'm in Manhattan helping out and there's another guy selling the exact same rings I had wanted — for a quarter. Taught me another lesson — the first thing you're offered is almost never the best deal you can get."

As a kid, Red played a lot of basketball and some handball. No baseball, no football. "There wasn't a blade of grass to be found for miles where we lived," he said. "We played some stickball on the streets and punchball, but that was pretty much it. Most of the really good athletes from the neighborhood took the trolley to go to Boys High or Hamilton High. I stayed where I was and just played basketball."

At Eastern District High School, Red was the best player on decent basketball teams and a good, if not great, student. His claims of being an introvert aside, he ran as a senior for president of the school and won. "We put in five bucks each to buy blotters and made up posters that said, VOTE FOR AUERBACH, RIZZO, AND RABINOWITZ. Put 'em up all over the school and we won."

By the time he was a senior, Red knew exactly what he wanted to do with his life: get a basketball scholarship to college; play ball while getting a degree in teaching; and then teach PE and coach high school basketball. This was the mid-1930s. Professional basketball didn't exist except for a few teams that barnstormed, and college basketball was still a regional sport, not a national one.

There was very little recruiting. In fact, most schools simply held tryouts. Players would go to the school, work out for the coach, and then a chosen few would be offered scholarships. *The* power in New York at the time was Long Island University, coached by the legendary Clair Bee. Red was invited to try out at LIU — and declined the offer.

"They had like one hundred fifty kids trying out for two, maybe three spots," he said. "I didn't want to go through that. There were a lot of very good players in New York in those days. I made second team all-Brooklyn as a senior. Now, you might think that's no big deal, but it was back then. I used to tell Russell and Cousy and Heinsohn and those guys that there was no way they could understand how tough it was to be second team all-Brooklyn. Of course I was right: they *didn't* understand it at all."

Having turned down the chance to try out at LIU, Red was invited to tryouts at City College, also a power at the time, and at New York University. He made it through the first round of cuts at NYU but opted not to go back for the next round when he learned that all basketball players at NYU had to major in business.

"What did I want with business?" he said. "I was going to teach and coach. It would have been a waste of time."

Nat Holman wanted Red to play for him at City College. The only problem was grades. CCNY was the Harvard of public schools in those days. Red had an 88 average in high school, was president of the school, and was a star on the basketball team. Not good enough. CCNY required a 93 average — minimum — to get in. Holman told Red he could go to night school for a semester, get his grades up, and then transfer in. Red didn't want to do that either.

"I figured CCNY was for smart kids," he said. "I didn't think I'd be comfortable there even if I got in out of night school.

Remember, I was making all these decisions on my own. My dad had never seen a basketball game. We played in the afternoons and he was always working. Same with Vic. So I had to do all this by myself."

He finally heard that one other local school was holding try-outs — Seth Low Junior College in Brooklyn. The best part about Seth Low was that it was a feeder school for Columbia. If a player did well there, he was likely to end up at Columbia. Gordon Ridings, the coach, had to choose between Red and another player for the final scholarship. He eventually offered it to Red.

"The tuition was two hundred fifty dollars a year," he said. "They gave me a scholarship worth one hundred fifty bucks. I had to work to come up with the other hundred."

Red was the first in his family to attend college. While at Seth Low, he finally convinced his father to come see him play. "I was the point guard," Red said. "I had a good game that night. Didn't score much because I didn't need to. I probably had about ten assists, maybe one turnover, and we won. I was very happy with the way I'd played.

"After the game I see my father and he says, 'Well, I'm sorry, son, you didn't do too good.' I explained to him that actually I'd had a good game, that my job was to pass the ball and set the other guys up. He just shrugged and said, 'The way it looked to me, all the action was in the kitchen and you were out in the living room.'"

Gordon Ridings had played his college basketball at Oregon, which had been coached at the time by Bill Reinhart. From

Oregon, Reinhart had gone on to coach at George Washington University. While Red was playing at Seth Low, Reinhart brought his team to New York to play in Madison Square Garden. The team practiced at Seth Low and, at Ridings's request, Reinhart hung around to watch Seth Low practice. Soon after that, Ridings called Red in to talk about his future.

"You got two options," he told him. "Bill will give you a scholarship to go down to Washington and play for him. Or, I can set you up to play out at Oregon. Up to you."

Red had been hoping that Ridings might get the Columbia job and take him there with him. But GW was the next best thing as far as he could see. It wasn't far from New York, it had a reputation as a good school, and Ridings, whom he respected, swore by Reinhart as a coach. "In the end," he said, "it wasn't a very tough decision."

He packed his bags and headed for Washington, the plan still very much intact. He had his scholarship, he would play basketball, and he would become a teacher and coach. His father wasn't so thrilled with the plan. He had never completely understood why Red spent so much time playing basketball, but as long as he was just a kid, it was fine. But now it was time to decide on his future. Teaching? Coaching? Like so many Jewish immigrants, he wanted his son to have a real profession.

"Doctor or a lawyer," Red said. "He just didn't see how you could go wrong with one of those jobs. He was probably right."

✽   ✽   ✽

The Washington DC of 1937 was a different world than the Washington DC of today. Schools were still segregated. So were many parts of the city. It wasn't the kind of strict segregation that existed in the Deep South. There weren't separate drinking fountains or anything that blatant, but it was very much a city divided by color.

George Washington had black students, but none were on the basketball team. When New York teams traveled below the Mason-Dixon Line in those days, they didn't bring their black players with them because they knew they wouldn't be allowed to play in segregated cities — Washington among them.

Red was a brand-new sophomore on a team filled with talented sophomores who had played together the previous season on an undefeated freshman team. The newcomer had to prove his worth and battle for playing time. "Needless to say," he said, "there were more than a few fights in practice."

Red was never one to back down from a fight, and, little by little, he earned the respect of his teammates and his coach. He had only one major setback, a game at Ohio State where he started and was assigned to guard the Buckeyes' leading scorer. "The guy ate me up," he said. "He had moves I'd never seen in my life. I couldn't do anything right the whole night. The next three games, I never moved off the bench.

"Then we went to Army and they had another guy who was a stud scorer. Reinhart comes to me before the game and says, 'You got him. Do a job on him.' Well, I did. He never said a word about what had happened at Ohio State. After that I was back in the starting lineup for good."

As planned, he majored in education and PE, graduating in the class of 1940. But the most important parts of his education came outside the classroom. One key place was in the gym, listening to Reinhart and observing him. "I would make the case that he was as good a coach as anyone," Red said more than sixty years after playing for him. "He was an innovator. He was one of the first coaches to use the fast break, to talk about passing lanes, things like that. But the most important thing, at least for me, was watching the way he handled his players.

"You see, he *didn't* handle them. Players are people, not horses. You don't handle them. You work with them, you coach them, you teach them, and, maybe most important, you listen to them. The best players are smart people and a good coach will learn from them. Sometimes when guys came to me with ideas, I knew they couldn't possibly work. But I didn't just say no, because they would see that as a sign that I didn't respect them.

"Once, [Bill] Sharman came to me and said that everyone knew our plays. We'd been running six basic plays for a long time and, sure, he was probably right that if we called, 'One,' a lot of teams knew what we were going to do. But that didn't mean they could stop us. So I listened to Bill and said, 'Okay, here's what we're going to do. We're changing all the numbers. From now on, number one play is number two. Number two is number three.' And so on up the line until the six play became the one play. We worked on it before the next game.

"Game starts, I remind them that all the plays have new numbers. They say they understand. Then we go out and we're totally messed up. Cousy calls, 'Two!' and half the guys are running our old two play — which is now the three play — and half the guys are running our old one, which has now become two. We look like Keystone Kops out there. I let it go until we were down ten and then I called time and I said, 'Forget everything we've done the last two days in practice. From now on, a one is a one, a two is a two, and if they can stop us, good for them.'

"Reinhart always listened to people. He was always learning. If he had coached at a place with a higher national profile, he'd have gone down as one of the great coaches. As it is, when people ask me about great coaches, he's one of the first names I bring up."

The other key learning center for Red during college was the National Training Center for Boys, which was located just across the district line in Bladensburg, Maryland. Each year, sixteen local seniors — four from GW, four from Georgetown, four from American, and four from Maryland — were given internships to work at the training center.

"It was, basically, a very tough reform school," Red said. "It was for kids who were federal offenders. They had stolen cars and taken them across state lines or committed crimes that involved guns. Some of them weren't kids either because birth certificates weren't all that easy to track down in those days.

"The place was segregated. There were four white companies and two black companies. I worked there twenty hours a week. I don't think I ever learned more about leadership, about discipline, about dealing with people than I learned there.

"One of the men in charge of one of the black companies

was Mr. Burns. I don't think I ever knew his first name. He was unbelievable. He was tough, so tough that when he took time off they had to bring in three guys to sub for him. But he understood people. He knew when to get in their faces and when to reason with them. He told me that the best way to get your job done wasn't to intimidate — which I couldn't have done anyway — but to earn their trust. If you said something was going to happen — good or bad — make sure it happened. I tried to remember that.

"One time, I caught a bunch of my guys with a still out in the back. They'd found a bunch of dandelions out there and had managed to brew up some awful, cheap alcohol. They were drunk as could be. I got 'em back inside, sobered 'em up, and put 'em to bed. Didn't turn 'em in. Who could blame them for wanting to get drunk in that environment? They remembered that.

"Another time, we're getting ready to go out for exercise and I realize that one of the master keys is missing. This is a big deal because someone has that key, they can get in any place on the complex, steal just about anything they want to steal. I get my guys together and say, 'We're not going out until I get that key. I don't care who took it. I'll turn my back and whoever has it just throw the key on the floor.' Nothing. So finally I take this guy named Frenchie aside. He was the leader. That's another thing Mr. Burns had taught me: every group has a leader and that guy knows everything. So I said to him, 'I don't want any information at all, but I know that you know who has the key, and we aren't going anywhere — today, the next day, whenever — until I get the key back.' I told him he had five minutes or I had to go to the higher-ups.

"Frenchie goes back into the room. I wait. A minute later, I hear the key clattering on the floor.

"I'm not going to sit here and tell you they were all good kids who'd had bad luck. But some of them were. I'd bought a car that year, finally got my dad to give me a hundred bucks to get one. It was a Ford convertible [to this day Red drives a convertible]. The radio broke. One of the kids said he could fix it for me, so I said fine.

"I go over to see how he's coming and the engine's running. He says, 'I didn't want to run your battery down so I just hot-wired the engine.' He also fixed the radio.

"A lot of those kids got out during the war by volunteering for the service. Years later, I still heard from some of them. If I learned nothing else from Mr. Burns it was when to trust people and when not to. You look a guy right in the eye and he doesn't look right back at you, you can bet he's lying. He looks back, he's either telling the truth or he's a damn good liar." Red has another theory on lying: "If a guy talks with his palms turned up, he's almost always lying."

After graduation, Red enrolled in a master's program in education. But he was no longer on scholarship, so he needed to work. He got his first coaching job at the prestigious St. Albans School in Northwest Washington. When he arrived, he learned that St. Albans had been very good the previous season — with five senior starters. He would be working, in effect, with a brand-new team.

"So we start practice, and for about three days it is just awful," he said. "I mean, they couldn't do anything. So finally I'd had enough. I stopped practice and brought them all to the center jump circle. I took a ball and I said, 'Okay, fellas, we're starting all over. This round thing I'm holding in my hands is called a ball. The goal of this game is to take this ball and to get it into one of those two things with a net on it — that's called the basket. Then, when the other team has the ball, you try to stop them from getting the ball into the other basket. Are you with me so far?' "

The team ended up having a very successful season, winning eleven of twelve games. Red is a little hazy on the details of the eleven wins. Not the loss. "We're playing Episcopal," he said. "Big school, good team. We've got 'em beat. We're up seventeen to sixteen with five seconds left and we've got the ball under their basket. All we have to do is get it inbounds, let them foul us, and even if we miss, they aren't going the length of the court to score. It just didn't happen in those days.

"Some kid, I swear I've blocked out his name on purpose, but I remember he was a congressman's son, takes the ball out of bounds for us. All of a sudden, he throws a pass *behind his back*. No one did that in 1941. Hell, no one does that on an in-bounds pass *today*. But he does it. He throws the damn ball right to a kid on the other team and he makes a layup at the buzzer and we lose eighteen to seventeen.

"I wanted to kill the kid. But you couldn't do that at St. Albans. Couldn't even yell at him. If he walked in here today, my first question would be, 'What in the world were you thinking about?!' "

Does the loss in this high school game still bother him more than sixty years later?

"Worst loss of my life."

It wasn't all bad.

Red had met a beautiful young woman named Dorothy Lewis when both were undergraduates at George Washington, and they were married in 1941, during his year at St. Albans. She later told Red's biographer Joe Fitzgerald that Red had struck her as very serious about getting things done in life. "I was impressed by his stick-to-itiveness," she said. "He was very goal oriented. He'd set one goal, meet it, move on to another goal."

Red stayed at St. Albans for one year while he finished his master's degree. He then got a job teaching and coaching at Roosevelt High School, a public school in Northwest DC. By this time he and Dorothy had a tenant in their small apartment — Zang.

"I had called home one day and my dad told me Zang had dropped out of school, that he wanted to go to vocational school. Apparently he hadn't been going much to begin with because he didn't need to. They said he'd show up five, six days a month and he had a ninety-four average or something like that. He was bored. He wanted to be an artist, always wanted to be an artist of some kind.

"I remember when he was ten, he took an old orange crate, cut it up, put some shellac on it, and painted John L. Sullivan, who had been the heavyweight champion, on the wood. It was beautiful. Looked just like the guy. I liked it so much I offered him five bucks for it, which at fourteen was a lot of money. He told me he'd already been offered ten by a guy and he'd said yes. He took the money, went out and bought paints and brushes, and taught himself how to paint. I've always said he was the one in the family who had real talent."

When Red heard from his father that Zang had dropped out of school, he asked him to convince Zang to move to Washington to live with him. When Zang balked at the idea, Red told him if he didn't come to Washington, his big brother would come up to Brooklyn and drag him to the train station himself.

Zang came.

"Red was about the only person Zang would ever really listen to," Zang's son-in-law, Stanley Copeland, said years later. "The two of them may be the most stubborn people I've ever met in my life. Zang would listen to absolutely no one. But Red he would listen to . . . sometimes."

Zang enrolled at Roosevelt High School, which was where Red was teaching and coaching at the time. Since Zang was living with Red, the big brother made sure the little brother made it to school — on time — every day.

Red quickly made an impression at Roosevelt. Gym class was generally looked upon with disdain by most students at the high school. They didn't like getting out of their clothes, getting sweaty, taking a shower, and then putting their clothes back on to go to class, all in less than an hour. So many of them — most — would show up with notes from home saying they had a sore throat, a cold, a back problem — anything to be excused from gym class.

"I had one class with fifty kids in it and forty of them had notes excusing them," Red said. "There was nothing I could do. If they had a note, they had a note.

"One day, though, before class started, I sat all the sick kids on a bleacher and I said, 'Hey, when you guys are at home, which do you take, a bath or a shower?' Just about all of them put their hands up and said they took a shower. I said, 'Good, fine. So if you aren't too sick to take a shower at home, you aren't too sick to take a shower here. With ten minutes left in class, I want you all to take your clothes off and take a shower.'

"Within a week, I had exactly one kid still sitting out. [Apparently he *was* sick.] They all figured if they had to shower anyway, they might as well get dressed for class."

It was while Red was at Roosevelt that he and Zang met Hymie Perlo, who had been an all-met basketball and baseball player at the school. Perlo was trying to figure out exactly what to do with his life — college, a job, the military — but spent a good deal of time hanging around the playground that Red was in charge of in the afternoons once basketball season was over and he didn't have any practices to run.

Red quickly picked Perlo out as the best athlete around, and the two of them began engaging in high-intensity one-on-one games at the end of the day. "Hymie was one of the best young athletes I ever saw in my life," Red said. "I don't mean he was good for the neighborhood or good for Washington. He was good — period. He could have really done some things if he hadn't been wounded in the war."

This was before all three young men — the two Auerbachs and Perlo — went off to fight in World War II. Perlo, who tries to come off as caustic and sarcastic most of the time, rarely allows people to see how deeply he cares about the Auerbachs.

"What's Red ever done for me?" he likes to say. "Bought me a few lunches. Big deal." Then he will pause and go through the litany of favors Red did for him in later life. But his first memories are of their one-on-one games in the playground.

"Anyone tells you that Red isn't a tough, mean competitor, send them to me," he said. "I think I've still got bruises from our games sixty years ago. He wasn't as good a player as I was, but he was good enough to make the games plenty close because he'd claw and scratch and do whatever he had to do to win.

"I remember one afternoon I'd brought my younger brother with me. I was babysitting. He was about six at the time. We're playing and he comes over and tells me he feels sick, that he wants to go home. I told Red I had to go because my brother was sick.

"He just looked at me and said, *'Finish the game!'* He meant it too. I finished the game. If Daniel had really been sick, throwing up, or if he'd gotten hurt, it would have been different. At least I think it would have been different."

Red's teams at Roosevelt, like his teams at St. Albans, were successful. But, as at St. Albans, they broke his heart.

"We were pretty good both years I was there," Red said. "One year we were undefeated during the regular season, another year we lost one. First year we're in the play-offs and we're up one with a couple of seconds left. Kid gets to midcourt with the ball, throws it up, and it goes in. We lose by one. I can't believe it. This time, unlike at St. Albans, my guys didn't do anything wrong. Kid just threw in a prayer. Awful feeling. But it happens to you once, maybe twice in a lifetime, right?

"The next year, we're in the play-offs again. Close game again. We're up one with a couple of seconds left, again. I'm thinking, 'Boy, this is a lot like last year's game.' Last few seconds they throw it inbounds, kid gets to midcourt and throws one up. You guessed it — it goes in *again!* This time I really can't believe it. How can that happen two years in a row the exact same way? That's the lesson, though: you never take anything for granted in basketball or any other sport. Anything you think can't possibly happen not only can happen but probably *will* happen."

Remarkably, when he talks about all the years as a player, as a coach, as a general manager, as a team president, those three losses at the prep level still stand out. Part of that is the one-and-out nature of high school and college play-offs. One loss ends your season. In the NBA, it takes more than one loss to send you home.

"There were some times, I remember, losing the first game at home in the [NBA] finals and that was tough because you were in a hole," he said. "But you had the chance to come back. I remember one year when I was the GM [Kareem]

Abdul-Jabbar beat us with a hook shot that practically came out of the corner in game six. That one hurt. But it didn't end the series.

"The ones in high school, especially those two half-court shots, they really hurt. Because you can't go in the locker room and say to your guys, 'Okay, they got lucky today. We'll get 'em tomorrow.' Because there is no tomorrow."

There was also no third season at Roosevelt for Red. It was 1943 and World War II was under way. Zang, having finished high school, enlisted in the marines. Hymie went into the army and began training to become a paratrooper. Red enlisted in the navy.

"Reinhart set that up for me," he said. "He had friends in the navy, so when they lined us up to choose which branch we were going into, he made sure the guy pointed at me and said, 'Navy.'"

At the time, it didn't seem like a big deal except that Reinhart had told him to do it. As it turned out, being in the navy in 1945 would point Red on a path that would end his career as a teacher and as a high school coach.

3

Join the Navy —
See the U.S.A.

"I EVER TELL YOU about how I got to know Joe DiMaggio? Actually, it was because I met [Phil] Rizzuto and [Yogi] Berra when I was in the navy. Boy, was that Rizzuto an athlete. Little guy. But he could do anything.

"After the war, when I was in New York or when the Yankees came to Washington, I'd go to dinner with Berra and Rizzuto. One time they brought DiMaggio. What an impressive guy he was. The great ones, you know, the really great ones never have to tell you how great they are or show off. Russell's always been that way. After DiMaggio retired, I'd see him in New York sometimes. The one thing I noticed that's the same with all athletes was how much he missed it. You could tell. As much as he accomplished, he would have liked to have been able to go back. That's the tough thing. No matter how great you are, you can't go back."

He smiled. "Unless, I guess, you're Michael Jordan."

❊   ❊   ❊

After basic training, Red was sent to the navy base in Norfolk, Virginia. He had been promoted to chief petty officer by then — promotions come quickly during wartime — and, thanks to his coaching background, he was put in charge of all recreational activities on the base. There were a lot of professional athletes in the service during the war, and Red became friends with a number of them, including the aforementioned Phil Rizzuto, the New York Yankees star shortstop. Rizzuto was at Norfolk only because the base commander had refused to allow him to go to physical training school. Red had been stationed at Great Lakes Naval Base initially, had gone to physical training school, and had been sent to Norfolk.

"What happened was, once you went to training school, you got promoted to chief," he said. "And you were always sent someplace else. The base commander wanted Rizzuto for the baseball team there, so he didn't let him go to training school. So he got stuck staying there and never got promoted from being a seaman. It really wasn't fair."

Fair or not, Red and Rizzuto struck up a friendship. They played ball together — basketball — and Red enjoyed his sense of humor and his competitiveness on the basketball court even though he was barely five-foot-seven. Later, Rizzuto introduced him to another young sailor, a kid from St. Louis named Lawrence Peter Berra, "Yogi" to his friends. At the time, Berra was a minor leaguer in the Yankee system. "Rizzuto tried to look out for him because they were both Italian," Red said.

Norfolk was filled with professional athletes and former college athletes. Bob Feerick and John Norlander, both college basketball stars, were there. So were baseball players Charlie Wagner and Jack White. Clyde McCullough, the Chicago Cubs catcher, was there too. The basketball games played on the base were fierce, of a high quality, and competitive.

Because he had been living in Washington, Red was familiar with the black barnstorming teams that had sprung up during the 1930s. Many of them came to Washington to play the DC-based Lichtman Bears (the owner's name was Lichtman). The Bears were a force in basketball, a team that almost never lost. They played most of their home games on Sunday afternoons in a place called Turners Arena, which was in Northwest Washington, at 14th and W Streets.

Sunday was usually an off day around the base. Red came up with the idea of putting together a group of the athletes and making the three-hour drive to Washington to challenge the Bears. He made a call to Mr. Lichtman, explained who he was and what kind of team he could bring, and was offered $300 to bring his group to Washington.

"I got five guys and me," he said. "Clyde McCullough was my chauffeur. I told the guys I was taking two shares of the three hundred bucks because I had set up the game and I was coaching the team in addition to playing. They said fine. We get up there and the place was packed. They were a phenomenon. They'd won like one hundred games in a row.

"This was back when a lot of games were played in three periods — fifteen minutes each. First thing I did was I went out and checked the baskets. One had a slightly looser rim, so I said we would shoot on it in the first and third periods. There were exactly six white faces in the building — us. As the game went on and it was close, you could feel the crowd pulling for us. We were the underdogs. No one expected us to beat them. But we won. They hadn't seen guys as good as Feerick and Norlander in a long time.

"Immediately they challenged us to a return game. I told them I couldn't guarantee when we could come back, but we would. We ended up going back up there twice more — beat 'em once, then they beat us. It was good basketball, a lot of fun. And it was the first time I'd actually coached adults. That was good experience for me."

Red never did get sent overseas. Hymie Perlo did. On June 16, 1944, ten days after D-day, he jumped into southern France during the Battle of Anzio. Of the 550 men who jumped that day, more than 300 died because of a miscalculation that caused them to jump into the Mediterranean Sea. Hymie was one of the lucky ones. He managed to land on the ground and was immediately shot in the leg. Hobbling and in search of help, he saw one of his squad members in a lake, also shot, unable to move. He dragged himself into the lake and carried the other paratrooper to safety.

"People talk about heroism in sports all the time," Red likes to say. "They ought to talk to Hymie. He can tell you what real heroism is about."

Hymie received the Silver Star for his heroism. But talking to him about it isn't easy. The man who has an opinion on everything from Shakespeare to King Solomon gets very quiet when the subject of his war experience comes up.

"Anyone who tells you that war is heroic has never been to war," he will say, the vigor that is so much a part of his character replaced by a voice so soft you have to lean forward to hear him. "War isn't heroic, it's misery, absolute misery. No one goes to war and comes back the same person, whether they're shot or not shot, whether they get a Silver Star for carrying some idiot out of a lake or not.

"I was lucky. I lived. I can't tell you the name of the guy in the lake because I don't remember it. Don't want to remember it. I did what I had to do, what I was supposed to do, what I'm sure the guy would have done for me. Nothing heroic there. The most heroic thing I did was live. I didn't jump into the Mediterranean Sea and I got out of there alive.

"I'm proud to have been in the U.S. Army. I'm proud of what we did over there. We did our job. We had to do our job to save lives. But I don't even like to think about what it was like, what I saw."

Hymie goes to lunch almost every Wednesday at the American Legion with veterans of World War II and other wars. They talk about many things: ball games and grandchildren and the weather. They do not talk about war or heroism. At least not when Hymie is in the room.

Zang ended up in the marines. He was sent to the Pacific, where he spent two months on a troop transport ship that got caught in a series of storms and actually went backward for several days because the seas were so fierce. His assignment was as an artillery spotter, landing in the first wave of marines to direct the artillery fire that would follow. He came home unscathed but, like Hymie and so many others, never had any real desire to talk about what those days were like.

Late in 1944 Red was transferred back to the Washington area, to Bethesda Naval Hospital, where he was a rehabilitation officer. There was a gym on the grounds, and Red played there frequently. One of the people who came to work out at Bethesda was Fred Davis, who was then a starting tackle for the Washington Redskins. The two often worked out together, which back then meant playing one-on-one basketball. In those days, professional athletes needed to supplement their income during the off-season. The Redskins, the Philadelphia Eagles, and the New York Giants had formed basketball teams, and they traveled around the East Coast playing one another. Sometimes they played in their home cities, other times they went to small towns where a basketball game among pro football players wasn't just a novelty but a chance to do something fun on a cold winter night.

The Redskins needed someone to coach their team in the winter of 1945, and, after learning about Red's background as a high school coach, Fred Davis asked him if he would be interested. Red was still planning to return to high school as a coach and a teacher when he got out of the service, but he figured it would be fun and he would make some extra money. He agreed. The greatest coach in basketball history began his professional career coaching football players at basketball.

When the Redskins were in Washington, they played in a place called Uline Arena, which was at 3rd and M Streets Northeast. Mike Uline, the owner, was in the ice business. "He had something like seventy different patents having to do with ice," Red said. "I understood, I think, all except sixty-nine of them. But he had built an arena right next to his ice plant and had put a minor league hockey team in there to play. On the off nights he looked for anyone who was willing to rent the building."

Uline was apparently curious enough about his basketball-playing football team tenant to wander into his arena on a few occasions to watch them play. The Redskins, then as now deities in Washington, actually drew pretty well. "The place seated about five thousand and we probably drew around three thousand a night," Red said. "That was pretty good. We charged something like five bucks, maybe three bucks farther from the court. We did okay."

Red coached the team for two winters. He was discharged from the navy early in 1946 and planned to return to teaching and coaching in high school that fall. But before the fall semester began, another opportunity presented itself.

With the war ending, Uline was one of eight men who got together and decided to form a professional basketball league. Again, for Uline, the basketball team was little more than a way to keep taking in revenue as often as possible. The brand-new Basketball Association of America would have teams in New

45

York, Boston, Toronto, Cleveland, Chicago, St. Louis, Philadelphia, Providence, Pittsburgh, Detroit, and Washington. The teams would be stocked with players coming out of college and the armed services. They would play a sixty-game regular-season schedule.

In the summer of 1946 Red went to see Mike Uline. "You need a coach," he told him. "I can coach and I know enough guys to get a team put together quickly that will be good right away."

Uline was impressed with Red's self-confidence. He had seen him coach the Redskins, so he knew that he could coach professional athletes. What's more, he didn't have a clue who he would hire if he didn't hire the confident twenty-eight-year-old just out of the navy who was offering his services. He agreed to pay him $5,000 and told him to go put together a team.

"I figured why not take a shot?" Red said. "I liked coaching, and I thought I might have a chance to do it well. I didn't know what would happen with the league, but I figured worst-case scenario it would be a learning experience."

What's more, the $5,000 Uline was offering was almost twice the $2,900 he would have made had he gone back to coaching and teaching that year.

Even so, most of Red's friends thought he was crazy. Professional basketball? What the hell was that? He had worked to get his master's degree in education so he could coach a professional basketball team? What was he going to do in two years when the league folded?

"I told him he was nuts," said Hymie, who was back from

Europe by then and enrolled at George Washington. "Here he had a chance to make a respectable career teaching and coaching high school, and he wanted to waste his time on something that wasn't going to get him anywhere. Of course he didn't listen to me. He didn't listen to anyone."

One person who didn't think Red was nuts was Zang. "He was going to be good at whatever he did," Zang said. "The funny thing about Red is, as confident as he always seemed, he never understood how smart he was. He talks about me having talent. His talent has always been with people, knowing people, understanding people. I knew he'd do a good job coaching. I just didn't know if the league would succeed or not. Of course nobody knew."

Red wasn't really concerned at that point about the future of the league. He was interested only in the present, which meant putting together a team. "I did it for about three hundred bucks in phone calls," he said. "I started by calling guys I knew from the navy like [Bob] Feerick and [John] Norlander. They told me about guys they had played with, and I called some guys I had played with and against in college. Feerick brought [Fat] Freddie Scolari with him. He had signed a baseball contract with St. Louis, but he had a vision problem in his left eye. He was afraid that as a right-handed hitter he might not pick up an inside pitch and could get hurt. So he decided to play basketball. The one guy I really wanted that I didn't think I could get was Bones McKinney. He was six-eight, could run, shoot. But someone told me he had already signed a contract with Chicago. I thought I'd lost him.

47

"I figured I'd call him anyway just to make sure. He said to me, 'I haven't actually signed with them yet, but I'm taking a train out there next week and I'm going to sign then.' I said, 'Train? You're taking a train from North Carolina?' He said he didn't like to fly. He said he was going to take a train to Washington, lay over there for a couple of hours, long enough to get something to eat or something, then take an overnight train to Chicago.

"I had an idea. I said, 'I'll meet you at Union Station and buy you dinner.' He agreed. I met him there, took him out for dinner, and I said, 'How much they gonna pay you?' He said six thousand seven hundred fifty. I told him I'd pay him six thousand seven hundred fifty and, being on the East Coast, he'd be closer to home and wouldn't have to fly nearly as much since most of the teams were in the East. He took the deal and never went to Chicago."

McKinney became one of the better players in the league, and he and Red struck up a lifelong friendship that would benefit both men after McKinney retired from playing and became the coach at Wake Forest.

In their first year, the Caps were living proof that Red had an eye for talent. They were 49–11, the best record in the league. At home they were 28–2 and played to sellout or near sellout crowds in Uline Arena. The home-court record was indeed a reflection of how good the team was, but it was also, according to Red, due to a unique home-court advantage.

Rats.

"You would not believe how many rats there were in Uline Arena," Red said. "I mean big ones. When the teams would walk out from the dressing room, if you stood in the runway leading to the court and looked to your right or left under the stands, you would see these big green eyes just staring at you from the dark. I mean hundreds of them. See, the arena was right next to Union Station, so it attracted a lot of them from over there. Plus, they'd smell the popcorn and all the food and come running. We were like a rat magnet over there. Our guys got used to it, but the visiting teams would say, 'What the hell is that?' And we'd tell them not to worry, usually they stayed under the stands all night, that no more than a dozen or so might get out during the game. There were guys who were really scared by the time they hit the court.

"Finally, we decided something had to be done. So we went out and bought the biggest, meanest cat we could find. Named it 'Old Bones' after McKinney, because it was long, quick, and tough. We'd come in for a game and there would be the cat all beat up from fighting with the rats. I mean, it was cut up. He got a lot of 'em, but he didn't get all of them."

Old Bones, as it turned out, wasn't the only one working to decrease the rat population. "One morning I came in early because we were going to practice in the arena. I'm walking in the door and I see these guys walking out carrying shotguns. I recognized them because they worked in the building. I said, 'What the hell is going on here?' So they told me that they all liked to come in early in the morning, turn the lights on, flush the rats out from under the stands, and shoot 'em for sport. Who knows how many they got? But even with all that, we still had all you could want under the stands every night we ever played in there."

Four of the eleven teams advanced to the play-offs that season, and the Caps had to play Chicago in the opening round in a best-of-three series. They were swept in two games, another of those long-ago defeats that still angers Red. That series also proved to be the beginning of a long, testy relationship between Red and many referees.

"There was a guy, I don't remember his name because I don't want to, who absolutely robbed us blind in the first game of that series," he said. "If we were called for thirty fouls, he called twenty-nine of them. Honest. I don't know what was going on but that SOB was out to nail us. Maybe he didn't like my style, who knows? I'll tell you one thing, though, he wasn't in the league the next year. He went to work in the Big Ten and they threw the bastard out too. Served him right."

Not that Red ever held a grudge.

Right from the beginning, Red was an innovator, with a remarkable eye for detail. During his first season, he came up with the idea of a "sixth man." Nowadays, basketball people take the sixth man for granted, an accepted part of the game to the point where the NBA gives out a sixth-man award each season. Very few teams start their five best players now, always holding someone back on the bench to give the team a burst of energy early in the game. Almost always, the sixth man is on the court in the endgame, and he is usually one of the team's three top scorers. On occasion, the sixth man has been the *leading* scorer.

It wasn't that way in the 1940s. Conventional wisdom held that you start your five best players and keep them in the game at all times unless fatigue or foul trouble forced you to go to your bench. Red had the notion that he could gain an edge by holding one of his five best out for the first six, eight, or ten minutes of each half. "When a game or a half starts, both teams get into a certain rhythm," he said. "After a little while, a little bit of fatigue sets in and everyone begins to lose just a little. My thought was, 'If I send one of my two or three best players into the game at that point and he's completely fresh, he's going to be able to take advantage of people. He'll probably make some plays right away because his legs are fresh. In turn, that gives my other guys a burst of energy and picks up the whole team.' "

Irv Torgoff was the sixth man in Washington. When Red first arrived in Boston, Frank Ramsey was his sixth man, followed by John Havlicek. Later, when Red was the general manager, Paul Silas and Kevin McHale served in the sixth-man role. All were all-stars. Ramsey, Havlicek, and McHale are in the Hall of Fame.

There were other, more subtle things Red did. "I always kept my biggest guy sitting right next to me," he said. "That way, whenever there was a scramble for a loose ball and I saw a potential jump ball coming, I'd send him right to the table to check in when the whistle blew so he could go in and jump."

The league finally figured that one out and changed the rule so that the two men who tied the ball up had to jump for it.

Years later, Red came up with another way to help his team with the jump ball. Call it the Abdul-Jabbar rule.

"When Kareem came into the league, there was no one who could beat him on a jump ball," he said. "In the eighties, if we wanted to win championships, we had to beat the Lakers. If you had a jump ball to start every quarter, the Lakers were going to get the ball every single time with Jabbar jumping center. So I suggested getting rid of the jump after the first quarter and alternate possessions to start the other quarters. I said to everyone, 'Look, the referees aren't very good at throwing the ball up straight' — which is true — 'so let's take the luck out of it and have them do it just once a night.' They went for it. So instead of the Lakers getting four guaranteed possessions at the start of quarters, they got two and we got two."

Off the court, Red came up with ways to make life easier too. In those days air travel was just becoming a part of American life and it wasn't all that comfortable (as if it is now), so teams traveled by train. Conventional wisdom held that sleeping in a lower berth was easier and more comfortable. Knowing that only half his players could have lower berths, Red one day announced to his team that he had measured the berths on several trains because someone had told him the upper berths were three inches longer than the lower berths. "Turns out they were right," he said. "I never knew that myself, but since it's true, I think it makes sense if we put the big guys up top to give them the extra legroom."

Everyone agreed.

Of course Red had never been told the upper berths were longer and had never measured anything. But this way there was no bickering on the trains over who would get the lower berths and who would get the upper.

The next two seasons with the Caps were similar to the first season. The team was very good in the regular season but unable to get over the hump in the play-offs. They did reach the finals in 1949 but lost to Cleveland. Even back then there was a difference between play-off basketball and regular-season basketball. Red had taught his team Reinhart's principles of the fast break, and during the regular season they were able to use them very effectively. But in the play-offs, the only way to run was to rebound, and the Caps never had a great rebounder. Teams slowed them to a walk-it-up pace and took away their strength.

By the end of the 1949 season, Red and Mike Uline were not getting along all that well. Uline wanted a championship. So did Red, but he didn't think Uline understood that it wasn't as easy as his team made it look during the regular season. "He was never a basketball guy," Red said. "He was a hockey guy. He didn't really understand basketball."

Frustrated, Red was tempted by an offer from Eddie Cameron, the athletic director at Duke. Cameron was looking for an assistant coach who wasn't actually an assistant coach to work with Gerry Gerard, his head coach. Red didn't have much interest in being an assistant coach, but the circumstances were unusual: Gerry Gerard had cancer. Neither he nor Cameron knew how much longer he was going to be able to coach. Both men wanted a coach on hand who would know the players and the school in case Gerard couldn't finish the season. Technically, Red would just be there as a consultant since there were no assistant coaches. He would be paid to teach PE classes and be available if needed to coach.

Red was uncertain. He was tempted because the school was beautiful, the money was better than he was currently making, and he thought he needed to get out of Washington. The flip side was that he felt a little ghoulish. "In a way, they were offering me a job where I was supposed to sit around and wait for Gerry to die. They had told me that once he stopped coaching they didn't expect him to come back. He said he didn't have a problem with that, he wanted someone there. But it still felt awkward to me."

In the end, he took the job. He had never coached in college before, and he thought his young family might enjoy life in the bucolic South. Red and Dorothy's first daughter, Nancy, had been born in 1946. Nancy Auerbach had a serious case of asthma, and Red, Dorothy, and Dorothy's father, a pediatrician, all figured a somewhat warmer climate would probably be good for the little girl's health. That also factored into the decision to accept the job at Duke.

As it turned out, Red was right about Duke — on both counts. He enjoyed the school and the players, but he was never able to feel comfortable with the situation. Since he wasn't technically an assistant coach, Red didn't feel right going to practice. "It was almost as if by being there I'd be sending a message to the players that eventually I was going to be the guy they answered to," he said. "Gerry wanted me to work with the players to try and help them, so I did that whenever they had time."

One of the players Red spent a lot of time with was Dick Groat, who would go on to be a first-team all-American and the first player in school history to have his number retired. "I can honestly say I learned more about basketball from Red in three months than from all the other coaches I ever played for or worked with at any level," Groat said more than fifty years later. "He made me aware of things about my game I hadn't ever thought about. When I played in the NBA, I could still hear his voice in my head at times telling me to do something. If he had stayed at Duke, he would have been a great college coach. I only wish I'd had a chance to actually play for him."

Instead, after graduating from Duke in 1952, he ended up playing against Red in the NBA. Groat, who later quit basketball and became an all-star in Major League Baseball with the Pittsburgh Pirates and St. Louis Cardinals, played for the Fort Wayne Zollner Pistons. By then, Red was coaching the Celtics. Having spent hours and hours working with Groat, he knew his game cold. "I told [Bill] Sharman that if he brings the ball down after catching a pass, back off him, he's going to drive. If he's got it up over his head, that means he's looking to shoot or pass and you come up on him. The key was keeping him out of the lane because he was so strong he made trouble for any team once he got the ball in there."

Groat didn't score a single point all night, the only time in his pro career that he was held scoreless. The Celtics won easily. As luck would have it, both teams ended up on the same overnight train that evening, each connecting to a different city for its next game.

"I was in an absolute state of shock about what had happened," Groat said. "I couldn't ever remember being held scoreless in my life. And I knew Red had done it to me. As soon as we all got settled on the train, I went and found the compartment he was in. I knocked on the door and I heard a voice say, 'Come on in, Dick. I've been waiting for you.'"

Groat walked in and pleaded with his old coach to tell him what he had done to him. Red explained how Groat was telegraphing his moves.

"See, that's where I made a mistake," Red said, years later. "I liked the kid too much. I knew he'd come and ask me what we did, and I told him. Next time we played against him he scored twenty-two. Never should have told him what he was doing."

As much as Red enjoyed working with Groat and other players, he simply couldn't handle the feeling that he was hanging around waiting for Gerry Gerard to die — or at least be sick enough that he couldn't coach any longer. Soon after the season began, he was contacted by Ben Kerner, who was then the owner of the Tri-Cities Blackhawks (in the region of Moline, Illinois; Rock Island, Illinois; and Davenport, Iowa). Kerner had fired his coach and was looking for someone to step in right away. He knew what kind of a job Red had done in Washington and knew that he wasn't actually coaching at that moment. Would he be interested?

Yes. "I think deep down I knew I would end up back in the NBA," he said. "I enjoyed coaching the Caps. Not winning the championship was frustrating, but I still enjoyed the guys and the challenges. Maybe I would have liked being a college coach under a different circumstance, but I'm not sure. I'm not sure I would have been willing to kiss people's rear ends the way you have to do in recruiting. Every college coach I've ever known has always told me how much he hates recruiting. There's no doubt in my mind that I would have really hated it."

And so Red's career as a college coach ended before it started. He arrived at Duke in September 1949 and was gone by New Year's. He left with mixed emotions but knew it was a move he had to make.

As it turned out, Gerry Gerard finished the 1950 season and then retired. He died that summer. "I really don't know what would have happened if I had stayed until the end of that season at Duke," he said. "But if I hadn't been back in the NBA during the second half of that season, who knows where I would have ended up. Of course that was a long tough winter. Ben Kerner and I were not exactly a match made in heaven."

The problem was simple: Red thought he knew more about basketball than Kerner and should have final say on any and all personnel matters. Kerner thought he was the owner and if he wanted to make a change he had the right to make a change.

Both were right. But Red wasn't going to accept the notion of an owner making changes on his roster without consulting him. If he was going to coach the team, he was going to coach the team he wanted to coach, not the one his owner wanted him to coach. It was inevitable that two stubborn, proud men would butt heads.

The beginning of the end for Red and Kerner came when Kerner decided that acquiring a six-foot-five forward named Gene Englund would bolster the team. He wanted to trade John Mahnken, the team's backup center, for Englund.

"I told him there was no way we should make that deal," Red said. "Neither of our centers was great, but together they were a decent combination. If we traded Mahnken, we would be in trouble in the play-offs when things got physical. I knew that. I explained that to Ben and he said, 'Okay, I won't do it.' We went on the road and I get a wire from him: 'Have acquired Gene Englund in return for John Mahnken.' I hit the ceiling. After that, I knew I was going to leave one way or the other."

When Walter Brown, the owner of the Celtics, called Kerner after the season to see if there was any chance he might be able to hire his coach away, he was surprised to learn that he could. Red had signed a two-year contract with Kerner when he had left Duke, but Kerner was more than happy to let him out of the second year of the deal.

And so, for the third time in less than a year, Red packed his bags. Before he did that, he and Dorothy sat down to talk. When Red had gone to Tri-Cities, Dorothy and Nancy had not followed. Durham had not worked well for Nancy, perhaps because the family lived in a house out in the country. Taking her to the Midwest smack in the middle of the winter had been out of the question, so mother and daughter had gone back to

Washington, a place where Dorothy was comfortable and where her father was right nearby if Nancy needed a doctor.

Now the question became what to do about Boston. Both Dorothy's father and the pediatrician who regularly cared for Nancy did not think that a Boston winter was a great idea for a little girl with serious asthma. Red and Dorothy decided that she and Nancy would stay in Washington. Red would rent an apartment in Boston and get home whenever a break in the schedule allowed him to. The season was much shorter then — the finals were usually over in early April — so it wasn't as daunting a prospect as it might be today. Even so, the decision was very difficult. Red believes that, in the end, it was the right choice.

"For one thing, it was clearly better for Nancy," he said. "It was also easier on Dorothy. She felt more comfortable with her dad close by, and she didn't have to deal with all the pressures of coaching she would have felt in Boston. She always took anything written about me that wasn't nice very personally. It bothered her. Being in Boston, she would have been exposed to a lot more of it than she was in Washington.

"The other thing was me. I was never easy to be around during the season. I was tired, uptight, nervous all the time. That's one of the reasons why I had to quit coaching at a young age. It was just wearing me out. I'm not so sure how well it would have gone for us if my family had to put up with me on a day-to-day basis during the season. It wasn't always easy, but in the long run, it was the right move."

And so, during the summer of 1950, Red moved Dorothy and Nancy into a house on Legation Street in Northwest Washington. When training camp began, he headed to Boston, where he lived in a suite at the Lenox Hotel during his first few seasons with the Celtics. "I paid one hundred dollars a month the first couple of years," he said. "Then a new manager came in and doubled it to two hundred. No problem, I paid it. Then the next year he doubled it *again* to four hundred.

"That was enough for me. I walked over to the Prudential Building that day and rented an apartment. When the owner of the Lenox found out I was moving because the guy had upped my rent, he was furious. He offered to take me back for one hundred dollars a month. I said, 'Don't bother. I already signed the paperwork.' "

Red grinned his wicked grin. "I think that manager got fired soon after."

4

Welcome to Boston

"DID I EVER TELL you how I ended up with Cousy? I didn't really want him. In fact, I didn't want him at all. He was a megastar in New England because he'd been a star at Holy Cross, and college ball was much bigger than pro ball back then. Everyone in the media was saying I had to take him in the draft. My response was simple: I'm here to build a team. I've got no interest in local yokels."

Red had been hired by Walter Brown to take over a truly bad team. The Celtics had finished the 1949–50 season with a record of 22–46 under coach Alvin "Doggie" Julian, meaning they had the first pick in the draft. And so, soon after arriving in Boston, Red found himself under tremendous pressure to use the first pick in the draft to take local hero Bob Cousy.

"I had seen Cousy play," Red said. "He was very flashy. He wasn't the first guy to dribble behind his back, a guy named

Bob Davies was, but he was the guy who made it popular. The local press was all over me to take Cousy. I wasn't interested in making the press happy — I had a ball club to build. You don't build a club with guards, you build it with big men. So, when it was my turn to pick, I took Charlie Share out of Bowling Green. He was six-eight, big, strong guy. Later, I traded him for Bob Brannum, Bill Sharman, and Bob Harris. That turned out to be a pretty good deal. But they were all over me for not taking Cousy. Here I was, the new guy in town, and I'm turning my back on the local hero."

Red wasn't exactly intimidated. In fact, shortly after the draft, the Chicago franchise, which had drafted Cousy, folded. Three players were made available in a dispersal draft to the three worst teams in the league. That included the Celtics. The league decided that the only fair way to decide where the players went was to put the three names into a hat and let the teams draw.

"If I had a choice, my third choice would be Cousy," Red promptly announced. "The other two guys [Max Zaslofsky and Andy Phillip] are proven pros. Phillip has long arms and is a great defender. Zaslofsky can really score. Cousy's just a rookie."

Red didn't get his way. The Celtics picked Cousy out of the hat, and Red was stuck with the rookie local yokel who was too flashy, just a guard, and not someone you could build around. All that said, his opinion of Cousy changed soon after he met him.

"I was surprised because, watching him play, I expected him to be loud, a cocky kind of guy," Red said. "He wasn't. He was quiet, modest, a lot different than the way he played. Plus, when we started practicing I could see that the flashy plays he made had a purpose. He didn't throw fancy passes just to throw fancy passes, he threw them because that was the best way to get the ball where it needed to go. Still, I called him in early on to talk to him. I wanted him to understand why I'd said I wanted Zaslofsky or Phillip. He understood. Then I said to him, 'I've now had a chance to watch you play up close a little. You're ahead of your time with the way you pass the ball. But I want you to understand one thing. You can throw passes to people any way you want to. You can throw them between your legs, behind your back, sidearm, underhanded, or backward. I don't care. But I'm telling you one thing: no matter how you throw a pass, someone better catch it. If it goes off a guy's hands, it's your fault. If it hits a guy in the chest and he drops it, it's your fault. If you turn the ball over, you won't play.'

"I wasn't trying to be tough on him, but I've always believed that ninety-five percent of turnovers are caused by the passer. I wanted him to understand that. He was amazing, though, the way he adjusted his game when he had to. Once, he had a problem with his shoulder, so he figured out how to throw a long pass sidearm. He said, 'You okay with that, Arnold?' [Cousy is one of a handful of people who has ever called Red anything other than Red.] I said, 'I'm okay with it as long as the ball gets where it's supposed to go.'"

Having made his point about not drafting Cousy — or anyone — simply because the local media wanted it done, Red set out to knock down the myth of collegiate dominance. "You have to remember the times were different then," he said. "People really didn't get the pro game or understand the pro game at that point. They actually thought that a very good college team might beat a pro team. Well, Holy Cross was a national power back then. So I came up with the idea that we'd go up to Worcester and play them during preseason. Most of the time back then pro teams would barnstorm together in preseason, play each other in these small towns.

"My idea was we'd go in and play local teams — college teams, rec teams, whomever they could find to play us. People really and truly thought they could beat us, in part because when pro teams in the past had played those games, they'd keep them close to keep the crowd interested and so as not to embarrass the local guys.

"I didn't want to do that. I thought we had to sell the game, market the game, make people understand just how good these guys were. They really didn't get it. When we arranged to scrimmage up at Holy Cross, people were excited for two reasons: Cousy was coming back and they thought Holy Cross would beat us. So we went in there and beat 'em by fifty. Most nights, I'd tell the guys to win by thirty, no more than forty. I wanted to beat Holy Cross by fifty. People noticed."

He laughed. "Of course I'm sure some people thought if Cooz had played for Holy Cross, they'd have beaten us. I'll tell you one guy who knew better than that for sure — Cooz."

Red had never had a losing season in Washington. He had coached at Tri-Cities for less than a full season, going 28–29. That would turn out to be the only losing record he would have in twenty-four seasons of coaching (four in high school, three in Washington, one in Tri-Cities, and sixteen in Boston). And yet, when he first arrived in Boston at the age of thirty-two, he felt as if he might be down to his last chance as a coach at the professional level.

"I'd won games in Washington, but not a championship. I had to leave because Ben Kerner and I couldn't agree on personnel in Tri-Cities. The Celtics were not exactly a model franchise when I got there. They'd been losers and they didn't have any money at all. My thought was, 'We better get good in a hurry or there might not be a team to coach for very long.' From day one there, I felt like everything was on the line with every decision I made."

What made Boston work for Red from the beginning was the owner, Walter Brown. Since Brown's death in 1964, the Celtics have been owned by a myriad of people — including, briefly, a bankruptcy court — and Red's relationships with those owners have ranged from very good to god-awful. The worst was probably John Y. Brown, whose relationship with Red was so bad that Red in essence fired him as owner of the team.

"That was when Sonny Werblin was running Madison Square Garden," he said. "It was the late seventies, and John Y. Brown and I just didn't get along. He was paranoid about everything — loved attention, hated the media. You can't have it both ways. At that point, Sonny calls me up and wants to talk to me about taking over all basketball at the Garden — the Knicks, college basketball, the whole thing. I go down and meet with him and he makes me a hell of an offer. Lot of money, apartment, car and driver, everything you could want.

"If things had been better in Boston I probably wouldn't have taken the offer all that seriously, nice as it was. But the way things were, I felt I had to consider it. I mean, my heart is in Boston, but I did grow up in New York."

Red returned to Boston and met with Brown. "I didn't want him to think I was blackmailing him or using Sonny's offer as a threat," he said. "So I just said this: 'You and I don't work well together. It's not comfortable for me, I don't think it's comfortable for you. So here's what I'm going to do. In two weeks, if you haven't sold your half of the team to [co-owner] Harry Mangurian Jr., I'm going to resign. Now, it's your team and you may not give a damn if I resign. Heck, you may be happy if I resign. But that's what I'm going to do.'"

Whether Brown had tired of ownership or simply didn't want to be known as the man responsible for letting Red Auerbach leave the Celtics, he sold his half of the team. On the fourteenth day.

"Waited until the last possible moment," Red said. "But he did it."

Red's relationship with Walter Brown was 180 degrees the opposite of that. Right from the beginning the two men liked and respected each other. "Walter Brown was a gentleman in the old-fashioned sense of the word," Red said. "He always tipped his hat to ladies, held the door for people, whether it was the queen of England or the janitor in the building where our offices were. He was polite, never talked down to people.

And he was generous. In fact, if he had a weakness as an owner it was that he was too generous."

The most important thing Brown did as an owner was let Red run the team. Red wouldn't have had it any other way and Brown, after four years of bad basketball (the Celtics' best record pre-Red was 20–28), was willing to let the new guy sink or swim on his own since his first two coaches had been abject failures.

Money was always an issue with the Celtics, even after they became one of basketball's dominant teams. Walter Brown was not a wealthy man. He didn't have the resources that some of the other league owners had, and the Celtics didn't have the means to make outside money the way some teams did. One reason for this was that they were a tenant in the Boston Garden. The Bruins hockey team owned the building, which meant the Celtics played when the Bruins didn't want to play. It also meant that outside revenues from concessions, parking, and souvenirs went to the Bruins. During Red's first season with the Celtics, Brown had to convince Lou Pieri, who had owned the now-defunct Providence team, to buy into the club for $50,000 or the team might not have survived the season.

"We had to sell the game and we had to sell ourselves," Red remembered. "I wasn't just the coach and general manager, I was the marketing guy too. We were constantly trying to come up with ideas to get more fans to come. Even after we started winning we didn't sell out during the regular season because the fans figured we were going to win anyway and the play-offs were what mattered. So we had to come up with different ways to get them to come."

Remarkably, during Red's entire seventeen-year run as coach, including the last ten when the team won nine championships, the Celtics averaged more than ten thousand fans per game in the regular season just once: in 1957, the first championship season. The year before Red arrived, the average attendance — to watch a bad team — was 4,252 per game. In Red's first season, with a much-improved team, attendance grew to 6,184 per game. After that it hovered between 5,500 and 7,500 the next five seasons. The year after the first championship it dropped back below 10,000 to 8,308, and that's about where it stayed for the rest of Red's coaching career. It wasn't until Larry Bird arrived in 1979 to revive what was then a sagging team that the Celtics began selling out on a regular basis.

Because drawing fans was always a struggle, the Celtics were one of the first teams to have giveaways — basketballs, mugs, baseball bats.

Baseball bats?

"Guy came to me and said he had three thousand Louisville Sluggers," Red said. "He said he would sell them to me for a dollar apiece. I figured it was a good deal, so I did it. Of course today, you couldn't possibly do something like that. One bad call and the court would be full of baseball bats.

"The dumbest thing I probably did was beer steins. They were really nice, the players autographs were stenciled into them. We start the game and I'm thinking to myself, 'What have I done? One guy gets pissed off and we're going to have shattered glass all over the place.' Amazingly enough it never happened. It was a different time."

Whenever Red was offered a product as a potential give-away — there were no corporate sponsors in those days, so he bought everything — he had to calculate if the cost would be made up in ticket sales. He also had to be certain that every-thing he bought ended up in the hands of the fans.

"One of the things we always liked to give away for obvious reasons was basketballs," he said. "One year, we get five thou-sand basketballs. I'm standing at the gate to count the house and see how many of the balls we give out. Think about that — thirty minutes before tip-off, I'm tracking basketballs at the front gate. Anyway, someone comes to me and says, 'Coach, we've given out forty-five hundred, and there are none left.' I couldn't figure out what happened. Next time we did basketballs I had someone keep an eye on them. Turned out the security people were stealing them. So we had to have the basketballs *guarded* by our own people to make sure the security people didn't steal them."

One year, Red came up with the idea of playing Sunday af-ternoon games in the Boston Arena, an older five-thousand-seat building located a short drive from the Garden. "The idea was to sell every ticket in the building for a dollar," he said. "First come, first serve, no reserved seats. It would give people who might not be able to afford an expensive ticket a chance to see the game up close if they were willing to wait in line for a little while.

"I'm walking into the arena a couple of hours before the

game and the first two guys in line are two bellhops from across the street at the Ritz-Carlton Hotel. I'm thinking, 'This is perfect. These are the kind of guys we want to get the best seats, front row, center court.' Just before the game starts, I look up and I see the owner of the Ritz and his son walking in. They take the two front row seats the bellhops are in. I find out later, the guy had the bellhops wait in line to hold the seats for him and his son. They didn't even get to go upstairs and watch. They had to go back and finish their work shifts."

While he was trying to sell tickets any way he could, Red was building a pretty good team. In spite of Red's objections, Cousy arrived that first season along with Ed Macauley. Sharman and Brannum came a year after that. Then, in 1953, Red made a move that proved to be one of the most important of his career. That season, Kentucky's program had been shut down in the wake of a point-fixing scandal. Adolph Rupp told Red that Frank Ramsey and Cliff Hagan, his two best players, were planning to come back for a fifth season even though both were eligible to graduate in the spring.

At that time the NBA rules said you couldn't draft a player until his college eligibility had been completed. During the league meetings that winter, Red made a proposal: why not change the rules to allow players to be drafted four years after they graduated from high school? "It's the same as the NFL," Red reasoned. "Why not just do it the way they do it?"

No one could see any harm in changing the rules. Why not go along with football? So the proposal was quickly passed.

"What I always did when I had something I wanted to get

through for a specific reason was I waited until the end of the day to bring it up," Red said. "Guys were tired, they wanted to go out and get dinner. I'd bring something up kind of casually and usually there wouldn't be much conversation about it. They'd just go ahead and pass it. That's what happened with this."

A few months later, when the draft rolled around, Red stood up and announced that his first draft pick was Frank Ramsey. "People jumped up and said, 'What are you talking about? You can't take him. He's going back to Kentucky,'" Red said. "I said, 'Read the rule. We passed it a couple months ago.'"

In the third round, Red drafted Hagan. Now people were really upset. "Ned Irish [who was president of the New York Knicks] stood up and said, 'Hey, fellas, we goofed. Red's right. The rules say he can do this.'"

Neither player would play for the Celtics that year. But Ramsey would join the team a year later and be a key player for ten years, taking over the critical sixth-man role that Red had first created in Washington. Hagan had to serve two years in the military after graduation since he had joined the ROTC during the Korean War. He ended up playing on the Andrews Air Force Base basketball team — coached by John Toomay (whom Red had once cut), a man who went on to become a three-star general — and finally reached the NBA in 1956. He would go on to have a Hall of Fame career — but not with the Celtics. And yet, his role in making the Celtics the greatest dynasty in the history of basketball is undeniable.

✦   ✦   ✦

"I took my lumps those first few years. People forget that. They think we came out of the chute winning championships and just kept on winning. I wish that were true. But it wasn't the case."

Red never had a losing season with the Celtics. In his first season, the team, after being twenty-four games under .500 the year before, was 39–30. They became consistent winners, making the play-offs every year, usually finishing with one of the best records in the league. But just as in Washington, Red found himself unable to get over the play-off hump. He had a team built on speed and quickness. He had great guards in Cousy and Sharman and a slew of good forwards, especially after Ramsey and Tom Heinsohn joined Macauley up front. But he didn't have a great center, a rebounder who could start the fast break with consistency in postseason play.

"In the play-offs, winning usually comes down to one simple thing," Red said. "You have to have people who can get you the ball. Those first six years we didn't have the guy who could get us the ball."

It was during those early Celtic years that Red first began smoking his famous victory cigar. He had been a cigar smoker since his navy days but never smoked during games. It was his concern with bench decorum at the end of a one-sided game that got him started on the cigars.

"It has always bothered me to see coaches who are up twenty or thirty points jumping up and down and screaming with two minutes or a minute to go," he said. "I see coaches do it today and it drives me nuts. It's such a 'Look at me' thing. My attitude was, when we had a game in hand, I'd get the subs in, sit down on the bench, and relax. Let people know I wasn't trying to embarrass the other team, just get the game over and done with.

"But I'd kind of sit there and not know exactly what to do. Cross my legs? Maybe that's *too* casual. Sit back? I didn't know. Then I noticed that Joe Lapchick [then the coach of the Knicks] always smoked on the bench. Back in those days you could do that. So I decided if we had a game comfortably in hand, I'd smoke too. I'd light a cigar and just sit back. That ended up becoming the signal to people that we'd won the game, so guys started calling it my victory cigar.

"Then it became a big thing. People waiting for me to light the cigar. I never did it on the road — *never.* That would have been rubbing it in. Of course one night we went into Cincinnati and I found out they'd given out five thousand cigars and told the fans when the Royals won the game they should all light up. I said to the guys in the locker room before the game, 'If you don't win this one, I'll kill you.'"

The Celtics, of course, won. Red resisted the urge to break his rule about lighting up on the road.

"The cigar didn't really become a big thing until we started winning championships," he said. "People in Boston noticed before then, but it became a big thing around the league after we started winning."

The phone call that turned the Celtics from pretenders to contenders came shortly after New Year's in 1956. Red's old college coach Bill Reinhart had just taken his team to the

West Coast to play in a tournament. One of the teams in the event had been the University of San Francisco, the defending national champion. The Dons, who were in the midst of a fifty-five-game winning streak, were led by a six-foot-nine center named Bill Russell and a superb point guard named K. C. Jones.

In those days no one had scouts. Red was the coach, general manager, chief scout, and marketing guru. He attended as many college games as he could and watched what little there was on TV. There was no such thing as getting film of a player either. So for the most part he relied on friends to tell him about players he might not have had a chance to see. He was also one of the first pro coaches to call college coaches and ask them for their assessment of players — those they had coached and those they had coached against.

As soon as he returned from California, Reinhart called Red. "I've seen the guy," he said. "I've seen the guy who can make you into a championship team. You have to get this guy."

Red trusted Reinhart implicitly. Reinhart described his defensive dominance, his ability to get rebounds and trigger the fast break. "How is he on offense?" Red asked.

"Not much," Reinhart said. "He's not a very good shooter at all. But it doesn't matter. One way or the other, you have to get this guy."

Red kept tabs on Russell for the rest of that season. He was certainly impressed with the fact that his team never lost; San Francisco went on to a second straight NCAA title. Reinhart was right: he didn't score much. Winning in college was different from winning in the pros. Still, he needed a center, and he needed a rebounder. He decided to trust his old coach's instincts and go after him.

Of course that was easier said than done. The Celtics were scheduled to draft seventh that season. There was no way Russell would still be around at that point. At the end of the season, Ed Macauley had approached Red and asked him if it might be possible to make some kind of trade that would allow him to return to St. Louis, which was his hometown. He had a child who had been ill, and being away for that much time in the winter was just too tough. Red could certainly relate to a dad dealing with a sick child and the notion of missing them during the season. He had promised Macauley he would make some kind of deal to get him back to St. Louis.

So he called his old boss Ben Kerner, who by then owned the team in St. Louis. He offered Macauley and a swap of first-round draft picks — Kerner's number two slot for Red's number seven slot. According to Red, Kerner said, "Deal."

There was still, however, the issue of Rochester, which had the first pick. That was when Red came up with the idea of having Walter Brown call Rochester owner Les Harrison and offer up the Ice-Capades as compensation for not taking Russell with the first pick. Harrison accepted and everything seemed set. Then came another phone call from Kerner.

"I need more to make this deal," he said.

"More than Macauley, who is an all-star and my number one?"

"Yes."

"But, Ben, we had a deal."

"Deal's off unless you add another player."

"Who do you want?"

"Cliff Hagan."

Red almost gagged. He had been waiting three years for Hagan and had figured he would slide into Macauley's spot on the front line after the trade. Now Kerner wanted both of them.

"I had to decide if I was going to put all my eggs in one basket, because that's what I was doing," he said. "I already had people telling me I was crazy to take Russell, that he couldn't shoot or score. But I believed two things: One, I believed Reinhart knew what he was talking about. Two, I believed we needed to change. We were a good team, but we weren't a championship team. I had to let Macauley go to St. Louis regardless because I'd made him a promise that I'd do it. Hagan was talented, but with him we were going to be the same kind of team. With Russell, we were going to be different. I decided to take the chance and make us a different team — for better or worse."

He called Kerner back and told him he would give up Hagan too. Then came sweating out the days until the draft, hoping Harrison wouldn't change his mind and decide that Russell was a better first pick than the Ice-Capades. On draft day, the Royals selected Sihugo Green, a talented shooting guard from Duquesne, with the first pick. Auerbach immediately grabbed Russell. The deed was done.

The next step was to see what Russell looked like once he put on a Celtics uniform. That wouldn't happen right away. He had been selected to play in the 1956 Olympic Games in Melbourne, which would not be held until November. That meant Russell would not be able to join the Celtics until after the first two months of the season and would miss all of training camp. That really didn't bother Red. This was a long-term project, not a short-term one.

In September, Russell came east with the Olympic team to play an exhibition game at the University of Maryland. Since training camp hadn't started yet, Red was still in Washington. He called Walter Brown and suggested he fly down so the two of them could go see their new star together.

The evening did not go as Red had planned.

"Russell was awful," he said. "I mean truly awful. He couldn't do anything right. I sat there watching and I literally felt sick. I thought, 'Oh my God, what have I done? This is the guy I traded Macauley and Hagan for?' It was just terrible."

Red had made arrangements for him and Brown to take Russell to dinner after the game. "First words out of his mouth were, 'I'm sorry,' " Red remembered. "He said, 'It was just one of those nights. I was nervous and I couldn't get myself out of the doldrums. It won't happen again.' "

Words like that can be empty, but there was something in the way Bill Russell delivered them that comforted Red. "I believed him," he said. "Don't ask me why, I just did. Maybe it was because I knew Reinhart couldn't possibly be that wrong.

But I believed him when he said it. And he more than lived up to it."

Much has been made of Red's relationship with Russell. Some have said he was the one player Red bent for, had a double standard for. Red says it's not true. "I never let him do anything I wouldn't let another guy do," he said. "I remember once, we're in New York and he comes over after a game and says, 'Can we talk?' I said sure. He says he doesn't want to fly back with the team in the morning, that he never sleeps well after the game and he wants to drive back to Boston that night. I knew what was going on — he had a date. But I said, 'Okay, go ahead.'

"The next time we're in New York he comes up after the game and says, 'Can we talk?' I said, 'Absolutely not. Once, yes. But not twice.' Any other guy on the team had asked me the same thing I'd have said yes — once."

Red had one ironclad rule when it came to team rules: he didn't have any rules. "If you make rules, set curfews, things like that, then you put yourself in a position where one guy screwing up can hurt the whole team," he said. "I've never understood coaches who suspend players for being late for a team meal or practice. You do something like that, you hurt all the other guys too, not just the guy who screwed up. I might make them run or keep them late or just yell at them — depending on how serious it was. But I never had an ironclad rule on anything because I wanted flexibility. If I had ironclad rules, then I had to enforce them equally. That's not always the best thing for the team."

Actually Red did have one other ironclad rule: no one was allowed to eat pancakes on game day. Red thought they would sit in your stomach and slow you down on the court. One night, the team had flown into Rochester after a game earlier that evening. They checked into the hotel at about 1:00 a.m. with a game to be played much later that night. There was an IHOP next to the hotel, and Russell and Sam Jones, hungry after the game and the flight, went over there to eat.

Both ordered a stack of pancakes. Seconds after the pancakes arrived, Red walked in. Russell was about to take his first bite; Jones had already taken one. To this day, Jones and Red argue about what happened next.

"That bite just cost you five dollars," Red says he said. "And either one of you takes another bite, it's five dollars a bite."

Jones swears the threatened fine was $10.

"So we both said to him, 'What are you talking about?' " Jones said. "This isn't game day. We just played."

"And I said, 'It's one a.m. We're playing at eight o'clock *tonight*,' " Red always says, choking back laughter. "I said, 'I've got one goddamn rule and you two can't even follow it.' "

Russell and Jones didn't eat another bite. They sent the pancakes back and ordered eggs.

Did Red ever collect the $5 or $10?

"Nah, I let it go."

"Like hell he did. He collected. And it was ten dollars."

Almost fifty years later, Jones still gets a bit shrill remembering the pancake rule. "Tommy Heinsohn used to sit in the locker room and smoke before games, at halftime of games, after games," he said. "No rules about that. But pancakes, that was a rule."

"If Heinsohn wanted to kill himself that was okay with me," Red said. "As long as it didn't make him run any slower."

Of course nowadays many coaches insist that their players eat pancakes and pasta — also considered too heavy to eat before games for many years — as their pregame meal to load up on fast-burning carbohydrates. "So it turns out my theory was wrong," Red said. "But back then, who knew?"

Red's approach to rules may have been best summed up by an incident that took place in the 1980s, when K. C. Jones was coaching the team. Kevin McHale got stuck in traffic one day and missed a plane flight leaving Boston. He had to catch a later flight and meet the team. Jones asked Red how much he should fine McHale for his transgression.

"Let me ask you a question," Red said. "Has he ever done it before?"

"No."

"Is he ever late for practice?"

"No."

"Is there anyone on the team that works harder than he does?"

"No."

"Then why the hell are you going to fine him? Just tell him to make sure it doesn't happen again and let that be the end of it."

One person who copied Red's approach to rules was Bob Knight. During the mid-1960s, when Knight was the coach at Army, Red would often spend afternoons during his annual sojourn to Kutsher's (the Catskills resort that was a longtime haven for basketball players and coaches) visiting with Clair Bee, who by then had retired from college coaching and was working at the New York Military Academy, which was just a few miles up Route 9W from West Point. Bee and Red and Joe Lapchick and Frank McGuire would gather to talk basketball, and the eager young coach from West Point occasionally sat in and soaked it all in. One thing Knight picked up was Red's and Lapchick's philosophy on rules — which were identical. Throughout his time at Indiana, Knight had one rule and one rule only: don't do anything that embarrasses the team. Players were expected to understand what that meant.

Of course, on those occasions when players did screw up, Red could make them wish he did believe in fines. In 1967, Russell's first year as player-coach, Boston was hit by a blizzard. Russell couldn't get his car out of his driveway, and Red had to coach the team that night. Russell arrived in the final minutes with the game comfortably in hand.

"I gave him hell," Red said. "He said it took forever to get out of his driveway, that you couldn't drive more than ten miles an hour, that the traffic was awful. I said, 'All of that came as a surprise to you? The rest of us got here. We all figured it would take longer, so we left earlier. You didn't *plan* correctly.'

"I didn't yell at him to embarrass him," Red said. "I yelled at him because I figured we'd have another blizzard — if not that winter, the next. I was thinking about the next time."

All of that came much later. Sixteen games into the 1956–57 season, Russell finally joined the team in mid-December. The

Celtics were already in first place. But Russell's presence transformed them from a solid team to a great one. He averaged a respectable 14.7 points per game but that wasn't what was important. His rookie year, he averaged more than nineteen rebounds a game and, according to Red, completely changed the game with his defense and shot-blocking ability. No one kept stats on blocked shots back then, but everyone agrees that Russell revolutionized the game with the *way* he blocked shots — redirecting them, often to a teammate to start a fast break, rather than swatting them out-of-bounds.

That spring, the Celtics marched through the Eastern Division finals, sweeping Syracuse in three games. In the finals, they had to play St. Louis, led by Macauley, Hagan, and Bob Pettit. The series went the full seven games, the Celtics finally pulling out the finale, 125–123 in double overtime. Red was completely exhausted and drained when it was over.

But, after seven seasons in Boston; eleven in the pro ranks; and fourteen in coaching, he finally had his championship. Stick-to-itiveness, as Dorothy called it, had paid off. The goal had finally been reached.

5

Glory Days

"LET ME TELL YOU something about Rupp. All I ever hear from people is that he was a racist. You know what? He did hate black guys — who couldn't play! He also hated white guys who couldn't play, blue guys who couldn't play, and green guys who couldn't play. He hated Jews who couldn't play, Catholics who couldn't play, and Muslims who couldn't play. That was it. All these people who never met the guy said he was a racist. I *knew* the guy. I traveled with him, I spent time with him. I never saw any sign from him or heard anything from him that indicated to me that he was a racist or a bigot in any way.

"Now cheap, that was another story. He was the single cheapest person I've ever met in my life."

Red became friends with Adolph Rupp, the legendary coach at Kentucky, while scouting some of his players. It wasn't often that he got the chance to go watch college teams, but whenever Kentucky came to New York to play in Madison Square Garden, Red would go see them if his schedule allowed. In those days, Rupp's program was one of the dominant programs in the game, if not *the* dominant program. Kentucky won the national championship in 1948, 1949, and 1951. Then in 1952–53 the NCAA shut it down as part of its investigation into the point-shaving scandals of the early 1950s that infected — and destroyed — a number of prominent programs, most notably the one at CCNY, the school Red couldn't get into as a high school senior.

It was the shutdown of the Kentucky program in 1952–53 that led to Red getting the draft rules changed so he could pick Frank Ramsey and Cliff Hagan. Those were the days when Red often socialized with Rupp, sometimes in New York when he went to see his team play and occasionally in Kentucky during the off-season.

"Once, I'm in New York and I go to lunch with Rupp. We go to the old Gayety Deli, which was a few blocks from the old Garden. I think we each had a couple of hot dogs. The bill came to something like three bucks. I paid it and then left a fifty-cent tip. That was pretty standard in those days.

"Rupp looks at me and says, 'Fifty cents! That's way too much.' Before I can argue with him, he picks up one of the quarters — and puts it in *his* pocket. Never said a word. I was so stunned I let it go. I kept thinking he was joking and was going to give it back to me.

"He never got around to it."

Rupp and Red, along with Bob Cousy, actually traveled overseas together in 1955 to do a series of clinics in Germany. "One of the guys we used in the clinics was an air force guy named Sidney Cohen," Red said. "He was a good player. Without saying anything to me, Rupp recruited him — convinced him to go to Kentucky. Now, if he were anti-Semitic, why would he recruit Sidney Cohen?"

One of the other air force officers the two coaches used in the clinics was a lieutenant named Dean Smith. "I think Rupp tried to recruit him too," Red said. "Then he found out he had already graduated from Kansas." Forty-one years later, Smith would break Rupp's record for college coaching victories.

Smith ended up starting his coaching career at the brand-new United States Air Force Academy as an assistant coach. He was also the golf coach his first year there. "I knew I was in trouble," he joked later, "when I realized the first day of practice that I was the best player there."

The Air Force Academy golf team was 1–4, the worst record any Dean Smith–coached team would ever record.

Smith, who is now seventy-three and has a memory comparable to Red's, still remembers those clinics vividly. "Red used Sid [Cohen] and me as the main demonstrators at the clinics, along with Cousy, of course," he said. "The thing I was struck by was his relationship with Cousy. There was such a clear camaraderie, a mutual respect, but there was no question about who was in charge. I always remembered that fact later when I became a coach that there was a way to have a friendship with your players while still maintaining their respect. I saw that with Red and Cousy."

A few years later, when Smith was working for Frank McGuire as an assistant coach at North Carolina, he was allowed to sit in on the sessions at the New York Military Academy with Red, McGuire, and Clair Bee. "My only regret about that," he said, "is that I didn't write more things down when they were all talking."

On that same trip, Red, Cousy, and Rupp went out to eat and sightsee on a regular basis. "Everywhere we'd go, when it came time to pay Rupp would pull out a one-hundred-dollar bill," Red said. "He'd say, 'Gee, I guess they can't make change.' Finally, we were going into Les Folies Bergere and I said, 'Adolph, you're breaking that one-hundred-dollar bill or we're not going in there.' He'd probably been carrying the thing around since 1950."

While Rupp may have signed Sidney Cohen in 1956, he did not sign a black player until 1969. "He got a bad rap for that," Red said. "I know he tried to recruit black players before that. Wes Unseld for one, but he went to Louisville. Hey, I'm not claiming the guy was a saint, I just know the only thing he cared about was winning."

Red also defended another legendary racist, longtime Washington Redskins owner George Preston Marshall. "He came to games at Uline Arena all the time when I coached the Caps," he said. "He would never take a free ticket. He said, 'You guys need the income, I don't want a freebie.' In 1949, when I told him I was going to leave the Caps, he offered to help me get the Dartmouth job."

When Red told this story one day at lunch, a number of his friends who had been around when Marshall was still alive insisted that Marshall was a racist — pointing out, among other things, that the Redskins were the last NFL team to integrate.

"He was a good guy," Red insisted.

"Let me ask you a question," said Zang, who usually spoke up only when his BS meter was pushed past the limit. "Is there anyone in the world who sucks up to you who you don't think is a good guy?"

Red paused to consider the question. "And how," he finally asked, "does that make me different than anyone else?"

Having finally won a championship, Red set out to win again. After the title in 1957, the Celtics had the last pick in the first round of the draft. Red really had no idea who to take with the pick. He made calls to all his ex-players and coaching friends around the country to see if they had any recommendations. Bones McKinney was coaching at Wake Forest.

"There's a guy down here who plays for North Carolina A&T," McKinney said. "He may be the best pure college shooter I've ever seen."

"What's his name?" Red asked.

"Sam Jones."

Sight unseen, having not heard his name until just prior to the draft, Red used his first-round pick to take Sam Jones. As with Reinhart's recommendation of Russell, he had faith in McKinney's judgment. McKinney knew what he was talking about: Jones became one of the great shooters in NBA history, famed for banking the ball from either side of the basket, notably over the frustrated, outstretched arms of Wilt Chamberlain. He would play twelve years with the Celtics and win ten championships.

Red never forgets a slight or a favor. A couple years after Jones had become a Celtic, Red was watching a summer playground game in Northwest DC. In those days, before the outbreak of summer basketball camps, city playgrounds were full of players throughout the summer months. A number of playgrounds became meccas for good players, places they would go knowing the competition was at its best there.

One of those playgrounds was off Connecticut Avenue, near what is now the National Zoo. Often, when he had free time, Red would hang out at the playground just to watch ball. He knew who many of the players were and, more often than not, who they played for — regardless of what level. One afternoon, Red spotted a player he hadn't seen, a big rawboned kid who was dominating the inside. When he came off the court, Red decided he wanted to know who the kid was and where he went to school.

He was shocked to learn that the kid was a high school senior who wasn't being recruited by any big-time college. He took down his name and phone number and placed a call to McKinney at Wake Forest.

"I got a kid for you," he told his old friend.

Just as Auerbach had faith in McKinney, McKinney had faith in Auerbach. He called Ronnie Watts and, having never seen him play, offered him a scholarship. Watts went on to become the third leading scorer in Wake Forest history and later played with the Celtics. He became truly famous many years later when he and Russell made a commercial together for a telephone company in which they discussed how they maintained their friendship across the country by phone.

The Celtics did not defend their title in 1958, losing to the St. Louis Hawks of Bob Pettit, Ed Macauley, and Cliff Hagan. Even so, it was a good year for Sam Jones. He had a solid rookie season, and his son, Aubre, was born. By the time his dad retired in 1969, eleven-year-old Aubre Jones was pretty certain of two things: the Celtics always won the championship and the *only* person in the world who was worthy of the title "Coach" was the man with the cigars.

"There were two years during my dad's career when the Celtics didn't win," Aubre said. "The first was in fifty-eight, a couple months after I was born. Don't remember much about that one. The second was sixty-seven, when the 76ers won with Wilt. I remember it being a shock that they didn't win. I also remember being kind of happy because Wilt finally won a title."

Aubre Jones's hero as a kid was Wilt Chamberlain. "My dad was my dad," he said. "I loved all the guys on the Celtics. But Wilt was my hero. I can remember when I was little, we'd stand outside the locker room and wait for my dad after games. The visitors' locker room was down the hall and Wilt would come walking by. He and Dad were friendly most of the time, so he knew who I was. He would reach down with one hand and just pick me up and carry me down the hall like I was some kind of little doll. I mean, try to imagine being six, seven years old and here's Wilt carrying you down the hall like that."

Aubre Jones was so loyal to Wilt that he asked his dad at one point if it would be possible for the Celtics to let Wilt win a championship. Sam Jones mentioned to a local reporter that his own son was actually rooting for Wilt to beat the Celtics, and Aubre ended up being the subject of a story with a headline that said something like, SON OF A CELTIC HOPES WILT WINS A TITLE SOON.

"It was old hat for the Celtics to win," Aubre said. "I figured they could let Wilt win once. Needless to say Coach Auerbach gave me a hard time about that.

"You know, the funny thing is, he always had this reputation as being such a tough guy, but I think all the Celtic kids would tell you he was anything but that. We'd always go up to his office before games and he'd have candy or soda up there for us. Maybe there were times when he was tough on my dad, but I never heard about it. I mean, when you win the championship every year, there's probably not going to be a lot of unrest."

Sam Jones retired in 1969 and moved to Washington to become coach and athletic director at Federal City College (now the University of the District of Columbia). Aubre finished high school there and went to the University of Massachusetts.

A couple times a year he and a few buddies would make the trip from Amherst to Boston for a Celtics game. Aubre always went by to see his dad's old coach, who by then was the general manager.

"Funny thing is, none of my buddies thought it was a big deal that I knew Coach," he said. "They always wanted to know about my dad and about Russell."

In 1989 Aubre landed at George Washington as director of recreation. By then, Red was seventy-one and semiretired. Most mornings he would come to GW and play racquetball with John Kuester, who was then the basketball coach. Aubre had a chance to get reacquainted with Red then. "I never knew he lived in Washington all those years until I came back here to work," he said. "I was a kid, what did I know? To me, Coach *was* Boston. I never dreamed that he didn't live there all the time."

When Kuester was fired after the 1990 season, Red needed a new racquetball partner. Aubre volunteered. "Let me tell you, he was still very competitive," Aubre said. "He liked to say he was the best over-seventy racquetball player in the country and I'm not sure he wasn't. The first time I saw what people now think of as the Tiger Woods fist shake was when Coach would hit a good shot. Tiger has nothing on him when it comes to that."

Not long after they became racquetball partners, Red invited Aubre to lunch. "He just said, 'Hey, come to lunch.' I had no idea who was going to be there, but I wasn't saying no to Coach. I started going almost every week after we played. The only time I would miss was if there were a staff meeting, and after a while I started telling people not to schedule staff meetings on Tuesdays because if they did, I wouldn't be there.

"Zang always used to give me a hard time because I never talked. Why was I going to talk with Red there and Morgan there and some of those older guys Red brought? I was surrounded by greatness. I just wanted to listen. Even to Hymie."

When Hymie was still working at the Cap Center he would set Aubre up with tickets to see the Washington Capitols, since Aubre was both a basketball and a hockey fan. "He'd get me the tickets whenever I asked," Aubre said. "He'd get great seats. And then he'd give me the third degree about being a freeloader."

Having drafted K. C. Jones in 1956 and Sam Jones the next year, Red now had a young, fast backcourt to go with Cousy and Sharman — his aging, but still very effective, backcourt. "My goal was to get one player every year who would make the team better," he said. "Or one guy who was going to be able to step in when another guy retired. The only guy who was completely irreplaceable was Russell."

Red knew right from the beginning that Russell wasn't like anyone he had ever coached before, on or off the court. During his rookie season, Russell invited Red to his house for dinner. Red had a strict policy against going to players' houses for dinner. "I just wasn't comfortable with the idea that I'd go to a guy's house and play with his kids and the day might come when I had to trade him or cut him," he said. "Or I might have to yell at him or make him run or bench him. I just didn't think it was the right thing to do."

When Russell asked him to dinner, Red said yes.

"Russ was always conscious of the fact that he was a black man in Boston," he said. "I know that wasn't always easy for him. He was still dealing with a lot that first year and I didn't want him to think even for a second that I would hesitate to come to his house for any reason. So I went. I thought it was important."

Not long after their dinner, Red sat Russell down and told him his policy on dinner at players' houses. Then he told him why he had gone to his house. Russell understood. He never invited Red to dinner again while he was still playing.

There is little doubting the affection between Russell and Red and the fact that it goes well beyond the championships they won together. Each was — and is — one of the few people who could truly give the other a hard time and live to tell about it. One year, after the Celtics had won another title, the team gathered in a downtown hotel to prepare for the victory parade. Outside, it was pouring rain.

"I'm not going out in that rain and ride in an open car just to wave at people," Russell said.

"I wouldn't even think of asking you to do it," Red said. "But let me ask you one question: you still own that rubber plantation in Liberia?"

Russell did own a rubber plantation in Liberia for several years. Yes, he said, he still owned it.

"What makes rubber grow?" Red asked.

"Rain."

"So you should be thankful for rain wherever it might be. Without it, you can't make rubber."

Russell cracked up. "All right, I'll ride in your stupid parade," he said.

Red saw a side of Russell few people got to see. Russell was famous for not signing autographs. One day in New York, Red and Russell were standing outside their hotel waiting for Red's car to be brought around. A man walked out the door of the hotel and did a double take when he saw the two of them standing there alone.

"Unbelievable," the man said. "Red Auerbach and Bill Russell. I can't tell you how much I respect both of you and the Celtics. Is there any way at all I could get your autographs?"

Red signed. So did Russell.

A minute later, a second man came out. Same thing. "What an honor," he said, shaking both their hands. "Is it at all possible . . ." They both signed again.

Soon after, a third man rounded the corner (Red was now wondering where the damn car was). He too recognized the coach and the player. "Hey," he said, walking up with paper and pen in hand, "I need your autographs. Just sign right here."

Red signed. Russell looked down at the man and said, "Sorry, don't sign autographs."

Russell's feelings about Red may have been best expressed in an on-court incident years ago when Red's constant needling finally got to Chamberlain, who stormed toward Red.

Before he could get there, Russell jumped in between them. Chamberlain was, arguably, the strongest man to ever play the game. Only Shaquille O'Neal might match him for size and strength. He was seven-foot-two and weighed at least 300 pounds, just about all of it solid muscle. Russell was no dwarf, but at six-nine, 220 pounds he was no match for Chamberlain.

"You want him," Russell said to the charging Chamberlain, "you have to come through me."

Shocked, Chamberlain stopped and pointed at his arm. "You see that arm?" he roared. "You know what I can do to you with it?"

"Don't care," Russell said. "You don't get him without getting me first."

Maybe Chamberlain was shocked that someone actually stood up to him, but he turned and walked away.

Red liked Chamberlain and had coached him during the summer at Kutsher's resort. Soon after he became the Celtics coach, Red had been introduced to the camp by his father, who went there for vacation. Hyman Auerbach proudly told Mr. Kutsher about his son the basketball coach and Kutsher suggested that if Red wanted to get his family out of the oppressive Washington heat, he could come to Kutsher's — for free. All he asked in return was that Red do a little coaching in the semiformal summer league at the resort.

Even though Dorothy was never crazy about the place, Red eventually agreed to the deal, in part because he liked spending time in the cool mountains of upstate New York; in part because the girls (Randy had come along four years after Nancy) liked it; and in part because it gave him a chance to spend a few weeks around basketball people each summer.

During the 1960s, when Kutsher's was at its zenith as a basketball haven, Chamberlain was one of many NBA players who came to the camp to play. On occasion, he played for Red's team. "I remember one game, we weren't playing well the first half," he said. "We go into this cabin near the court at halftime and Chamberlain goes into the back room and lies down on the bed. I scream at him, 'Get out here right now!' I don't think anyone had ever talked to him that way. He got up, but you could see he was shocked. I remember thinking, 'If I coached him instead of Russell, it probably wouldn't work.' Russell understood the notion of being coached, that someone had to be the boss, that I didn't tell him to do things just to prove I'm in charge. I don't think Wilt could be that way."

As much as Red liked Wilt, he liked torturing him even more. "Wilt always wanted to know everything that was going on during a game," he said. "So I would call time-out and I'd call the referee over to ask a question or discuss something. Anything. Under the rules, if I called a ref over during a time-out, the other coach had to be there too. So the coach would come over and I'd be talking and I'd look up and see Wilt standing behind us, listening. I'd say to the ref, 'What's he doing here? No players should be hanging around listening to this.' The ref would tell Wilt he had to leave and it drove him nuts.

"That one time when he tried to get to me, I was telling Russell, 'Let him go, let him go. He hits me once and I'll own that mansion of his. Either that or I'll be dead."

Chamberlain always liked to introduce himself to people as "the world's strongest man." He would say that while crushing you with his handshake, smiling the whole time. In the late 1960s, he came up with the idea that, since he was the world's strongest man, he could take on heavyweight champion Muhammad Ali in a boxing ring. Howard Cosell even had Ali and Chamberlain on one of his ABC TV shows to discuss the possibility of the fight.

That summer, Ali, who also spent time at Kutsher's, cornered Red at breakfast one morning. "I am sick and tired of Chamberlain running his mouth," he said, the irony of that comment not lost on Red. "He keeps saying he could take me. Here's what I want you to tell him: get in the ring with me and I'll give you the whole damn purse. I just want to fight him, show him and people that boxing isn't just about size and strength. Most ridiculous thing I ever heard. You tell him — the whole purse is his if he gets in the ring with me."

Red passed the message on to Chamberlain. The fight never took place. "Ali would have killed him," Red said, "unless he happened to wander into the way of one punch."

Russell and Chamberlain often socialized, frequently having dinner the night before games. Because of their summer ties and because teams played one another so often in those days — eleven times during the regular season if you were in the same division, plus the play-offs — Red and Chamberlain were also friendly. But when Alex Hannum became the coach of the Philadelphia 76ers, that changed abruptly.

"We're playing them, and before the game I see Wilt. I walk over, stick out my hand, and say, 'Hey, Wilt, how's it going?'" Red remembered. "He ignores my hand and says, 'Fuck you,' and walks away. Did the same thing to Russell. We couldn't figure out what was going on. I find out later that Hannum had told him that Russell and I were friendly to him just to soften him up and that if they were going to beat us, he had to stop being friendly and act like a prick. So Wilt tried it. We kept on beating them anyway, so after a while he just gave it up."

Red forgave Wilt but never Hannum, whom he didn't like much to begin with. Hannum was one of basketball's most successful coaches — this side of Red. He coached the Hawks to an NBA title in 1958; won another title with the 76ers in 1967; and later won a title in the ABA, coaching the Oakland Oaks. Ask Red to list the NBA's best coaches and he will go on at length without mentioning Hannum's name. Phil Jackson, whom he has feuded with at times in the media, comes up right away. Not Hannum.

"Guy wasn't any good," he says dismissively.

End of discussion.

As it turned out 1958 was the last time Red coached a team that did not finish the season by winning the NBA championship. The Celtics won eight straight titles beginning in 1959. At the end of the 1965 season, having won seven straight and eight out of nine, Red announced that he would coach one more season and then step down to become a full-time general manager.

"You got one more shot at me," he told the rest of the NBA and the world.

His reason for giving up coaching at the age of forty-eight — these days guys who are forty-eight are often referred to as upcoming young coaches — was simple: exhaustion. Dealing with the pressure of being everyone's target year after year, of having to scout and be general manager and keep replenishing the team's talent pool, had worn him out.

The first generation of Auerbach players — Cousy, Sharman, Ramsey, Heinsohn — had retired. The Jones boys — as Red called K. C. and Sam then and now — Don Nelson, Satch Sanders, and John Havlicek had taken over for them.

Havlicek was the last great piece of the second generation of Auerbach Hall of Famers to arrive in Boston. He had been a part of the Fred Taylor–coached Ohio State dynasty, playing on three straight Final Four teams from 1960 through 1962. Red had seen him play often and, with Ramsey's career winding down, was convinced Havlicek would be the ideal person to take over Ramsey's sixth-man role.

There was one other player Red was tempted to take with his number one pick that year: Bradley's Chet Walker. "I wasn't one hundred percent sure Havlicek would still be there when we picked," he said. "I needed to figure out an alternative just in case. Walker was that alternative." Red was impressed enough with him that he gave some thought to taking him even if Havlicek was available. As he often did, Red called Walker's college coach, Chuck Orsborn, to find out more about the player's personality.

"I remember he said to me, 'Don't take him. He's gutless,'" Red said. "I was surprised by that. For one, when I'd seen him play, I hadn't seen evidence of that. For another, it surprised me that a guy's coach would say something like that about him."

Red was leaning to Havlicek anyway and ended up taking him. Walker went to Syracuse and later Philadelphia and became a star both there and then in Chicago. He was one of the toughest, most hard-nosed players in the history of the league, about as far from being gutless as you can possibly be. "To this day I'm baffled by that conversation," Red said. "Maybe he didn't get along with Chet. I've got no idea. But that may have been the worst scouting report I've ever gotten. Of course Havlicek didn't turn out to be bad."

Before Havlicek showed up to play for the Celtics, though, he went to camp with the Cleveland Browns. He was six-foot-five and ran like a deer. The Browns thought he might make a good wide receiver. They gave him a car as a signing bonus — a big deal in those days — and brought him to camp. Then they cut him.

"What a mistake," Red said. "They already had some receivers, but there's no doubt in my mind John could have been a great football player. If I'd had him and I had a bunch of receivers, I'd have moved him to defensive back. But I'm not complaining."

Havlicek was cut just prior to the start of Red's summer camp. He had started the camp in 1960, one of the very first basketball-only camps for kids. Often Red brought Celtic rookies to camp to work with the kids and play pickup games at night. It gave them a chance to get acquainted and gave him an early look at new players. "The first time Havlicek stepped on the court, I remember saying, 'Oh my God, have we got something here,'" Red said. "You could just see he was something special right from the start."

Havlicek brought youth and enthusiasm to a team that was starting to get older. The Celtics kept on winning with him coming off the bench. But by 1965, after the seventh title in a row, Red knew he had to make a change — the Celtics needed a new coach. Russell was entering his tenth season. Red knew the team would have to be remade again when he retired, and he was certain he wasn't up to the task of doing that and coaching in a league where all the teams now had full-time general managers and full-time scouts.

"I had to stop coaching," he said. "If I hadn't, I would have killed myself. I was completely worn out. I've looked at pictures of myself from back then and I look older then than I do now. It was just too much, especially with spending all that time away from home during the season. This way, I'd be at home more, I wouldn't have to deal with the rigors of the road and running practice all the time, and I could just focus on trying to keep getting good players."

One other thing factored into his decision: the death of Walter Brown. Red was devastated when Brown died during the 1964–65 season. By then he and Brown had become far more than owner and coach — they had become close friends.

"Walter had one weakness as an owner," Red said. "He was too damn nice to people. Once a year, at least, he would call me and tell me he had invited the son of some guy to camp for a tryout. Or he wanted to give some guy a job when we didn't have any jobs and he didn't have any money. Walter was never wealthy, he made just enough to keep the business going. If we hadn't had a good season my first year coaching and drawn a few more people, he would have had to fold the team. We were always on the brink of financial disaster even when we were winning championships."

One of the few real fights Red and Brown ever had concerned money. One day, in the middle of all the championships being won, Brown walked down the hall to Red's office and demanded to know why Red had to keep eleven players on the roster. "You never play more than eight," he said. "Why do I have to pay for eleven?"

Red, who can see a media conspiracy in a kid delivering papers on a bicycle, didn't even answer the question. "Who got to you?" he demanded. "Cliff Keene [a columnist Red had a running feud with dating back to his refusal to draft Cousy]? One of those other guys in the media? Who was it?"

"It wasn't anybody," Brown huffed. "It was me. I just think we're wasting money paying eleven guys. Don't tell me I can't think for myself."

He stalked out. Soon after, he came back, clearly chastened. "Let's go to lunch," he said.

"NO!" Red said. "I'm not hungry."

Brown went to lunch alone. He never brought up cutting

back to eight players again. Red took him to lunch the next day and all was well.

"He wasn't being cheap," Red said later. "Meeting the payroll was never easy. Of course, every summer when I went back to Washington, Ramsey and Heinsohn would wait until I was out of town and then try to negotiate with Walter because they knew he was a softy. I finally had to tell Walter he wasn't allowed to negotiate contracts anymore without me in the room. He was paying guys much more than we could afford."

Red's negotiations with Brown were about as simple as any in the history of sports. Red never had a contract when he worked for Brown. "I always believed that if a guy wanted to get rid of you, he should just be able to get rid of you," he said. "I didn't want to work for someone who didn't want me anyway. And if I didn't like what was going on, I wanted to be able to walk out if I felt like it."

So, at the end of each season, before he went back to Washington, Red would tell Brown that they needed to talk about the following season before he went home.

"Let's go to the bathroom," Brown would say, apparently not wanting anyone else in the office to know such high-level negotiating was taking place.

They would walk into the bathroom.

"So," Red would say, "do you want me back next season?"

"We just won another championship, Red. Of course I want you back next season."

"Okay, since we won I think I should have a ten-percent raise."

"Sounds fine."

They would shake hands after washing and drying them. Then Red would go home for the summer.

Brown's generosity, especially when it came to other teams in the league, often made Red crazy. "To his credit, Walter always wanted what was best for the league," he said. "I was worried about what was best for the Celtics. Sometimes he went too far. One year, the Knicks were lousy. They'd been lousy for a while. So he goes to the other owners and suggests the Knicks get an extra pick in the first round because it's important for the league that New York have a good team.

"I said, 'Walter, I understand the sentiment, but for crying out loud, there's going to come a day when we're going to need help. You think anyone in the league is going to try to help us?' He didn't want to hear it. They ended up giving the Knicks and San Francisco [last in the West that year] extra picks so it wouldn't look like they were just doing it for the Knicks."

Brown's death shook Red. After the Celtics had won the title again that season, he publicly dedicated the victory to Brown and made the announcement that he would coach just one more season. The person who was most upset with the decision was Russell. He tried to talk Red out of it. Then he called Dorothy Auerbach and tried to talk her into talking Red out of it.

"He got nowhere with that," Red said. "She was glad I was doing it. She thought it was the right thing and, believe it or not, she liked the idea of having me at home more often. She told him there was no way she was going to talk me out of it and she would be very upset with him if he did."

At that point, Russell and Red sat down to discuss the post-Red future. Red remembers Russell telling him he didn't want to play for any other coach but he wasn't ready to retire. "If you really are going to quit, let me coach the team," Russell said.

In those days, player-coaches were not unheard of. Just a couple years earlier, Dave DeBusschere had been player-coach of the Detroit Pistons at the age of twenty-four. "I'll make you a deal," Red said. "I'll make you coach if you promise to keep it a secret until the end of the season."

Russell agreed.

It never occurred to Red at that moment that he was about to make Russell the first African-American to coach a team in a major professional sports league. He had already made the Celtics the first team in any sport to start African-Americans at every position and hadn't given that a second thought. To him, the notion of Russell as coach made perfect sense: he was smart, tough, and a natural leader. The other players looked up to him. Later, when much was made of the breakthrough, Red shrugged it off.

"Why make a big deal out of it?" he said. "I didn't do it because I was trying to make some kind of statement, I did it because it was the best thing for the team. In fact, if I *had* made a big deal out of it, Russell probably wouldn't have wanted to do it. The thought never crossed my mind, to tell you the truth."

As always, though, Red found a way to make the announcement work in his favor. That spring, for the fourth time in five years, the Los Angeles Lakers were the Celtics' opponent in the finals. The Celtics had beaten them in 1962, 1963, and

1965. In '62 the series had gone seven games and the Celtics had won game seven in overtime. Fred Schaus, the Lakers coach, couldn't stand Red and often said so publicly long after both men had quit coaching. He kept insisting that Red wasn't a great coach, merely a lucky one.

Red knew how Schaus felt about him. The two men had clashed on more than one occasion. In game one of the '66 finals, the Lakers came into the Boston Garden and won in overtime. It was a huge victory for them. After the game, Red met with the media, standing, as he always did, just outside the Celtics' tiny locker room. Back then no one had heard the now-dreaded term "interview room."

Red addressed the game briefly, gave the Lakers credit for making big plays down the stretch, and then said, "Oh, by the way, fellas, we're having a press conference tomorrow to announce who is going to succeed me as coach. If you're interested, it's going to be Russell."

Red still giggles retelling the story. "It was as if the game had never happened," he said. "All of a sudden all that mattered was that Russell was going to coach. Would he keep playing? When had this been decided? Schaus went nuts. Here he comes into Boston, gets this monumental win, and there might have been four lines in the paper about it the next day."

The Celtics won game two by twenty and three straight before the Lakers and Schaus rallied to take the series to a seventh game. Naturally, the outcome was no different from the past: the Celtics won — in overtime — 95–93, and Red walked away from coaching with an eighth straight title, nine in ten years. By that time, the Celtics were established in the sports pantheon as one of the great dynasties ever — in the same sentence with the New York Yankees, the Montreal Canadiens, and Notre Dame football.

Bob Campbell was nine years old when Red retired from coaching. He was the son of a fire chief, the youngest of Tom Campbell's four sons. His earliest memories are of watching Boston's teams — the Red Sox, Patriots, Bruins, and Celtics — and understanding that when they won, all was well with the world.

"They didn't do a lot of winning when I was young," he said. "The Red Sox were terrible, the Bruins were awful because [Bobby] Orr hadn't gotten there yet, and the Patriots won a division title [1963] but that was in the old AFL and it was almost like it didn't count. I remember my big brothers telling me all the time, 'Always remember to thank God for the Celtics.' "

When he was eight, young Bob made his first trip to the Boston Garden. "The thing I remember is the banners," he said. "I looked up in the rafters and there they were, all the championship banners. I never forgot what it felt like to look up and see all the banners."

Bob became a regular at Celtic games once he was old enough to ride the T from Dorchester to the Garden with his buddies. "There was a back door we'd go to," he said. "We'd give the usher five bucks and he'd let us in. Back then, there were always empty seats, so it wasn't that hard to find a pretty good place to watch the game from."

One night, soon after Red had stopped coaching, Bob and a friend summoned their courage, sneaked downstairs into the seats behind the bench, and approached the great man for an autograph. "He signed," Campbell said. "He wasn't outgoing or anything, but he was very gracious. What kills me is I don't know what I did with the autograph."

One of Bob's most vivid memories is of sitting in the kitchen with his entire family in 1965 listening to Johnny Most scream, "Havlicek stole the ball!" in the seventh game of the Eastern Conference finals, one of the most memorable moments in Celtics history. "I just remember all of us jumping up and going crazy when that happened," he said. "In my house, Red was always spoken about in reverent tones. He was just The Man in Boston. Whenever we went to games and the Celtics were up late, you always started looking for the cigar. That was always one of the highlights. So many of my best memories as a kid are connected to the Celtics."

Campbell ended up playing baseball in high school, where one of his teammates was Ron Perry Jr., who went on to star in basketball at Holy Cross and later was taken in the third round of the 1980 NBA draft by Red, although he never played for the Celtics. While he was in college at Bridgewater State, Campbell did some rent-a-cop police work on Cape Cod with his brother Jack, who was working on the police force at the time. Until then, he had planned to major in physical education and coach at the high school level — the exact same plan Red had in college forty years earlier.

But police work, even of the rent-a-cop variety, intrigued him. He liked the notion that he was helping people in trouble and thought that doing that sort of work on a higher level was worth a shot. When he graduated he knew he couldn't get on the Boston police force because just about every opening that came up was filled by someone who had been in the military. He and several friends applied for jobs on the police force in Nashua, New Hampshire, and got hired.

That was in 1979. The next year, when Ronald Reagan came to New Hampshire campaigning for president, Campbell was assigned to work with the Secret Service on Reagan's protective detail. "They were impressive," he remembered. "Good guys, very smart, knew what they were doing. I thought they were the real deal."

That thought remained with him when he moved closer to home in Lexington, Massachusetts. In 1983, with the help of a friend who had gone to work for the organization, he got an interview with the Secret Service. That led to taking a required test. "Forty percent of it was math," he said. "I'm no good at math. I was convinced I'd flunked. I was completely depressed. I thought this was my one chance and I'd blown it."

Three days after taking the test, he got a call: he hadn't blown it, he had passed. By the end of that year he was working out of the New York office, where he spent a lot of his time on details assigned to foreign dignitaries at the UN. In 1992 he was sent to Washington to be part of the vice president's detail. Soon after he arrived there, Bill Clinton and Al Gore defeated

George Bush and Dan Quayle. Campbell spent the time during the transition shuttling between the Gores and the Quayles. "Let's just say it was an interesting time," he said. "They were *not* alike in personality."

Eventually he moved to the liaison division, where he met Pete Dowling. They became friends, and when Dowling was promoted to special agent in charge of the Washington field office, he brought Campbell there. One afternoon, Dowling walked into Campbell's office and said, "Hey, guess who I just went to lunch with?" Campbell was pretty convinced that whatever name Dowling threw out wasn't going to impress him that much — until Dowling said, "Red Auerbach."

"No way," Campbell answered, not only impressed but stunned.

Dowling explained to him that he had met Red through a mutual friend, Don Casey, and had been able to arrange lunch for Red and Casey at the White House staff mess. In return, Red had invited him to lunch with a group of his friends at a restaurant called the China Doll. Knowing Campbell's Boston background, Dowling thought he would get a kick out of the story.

He did. But when Dowling told him a few weeks later that he had now become a regular at the China Doll lunches, Campbell began campaigning: "Get me invited, just once," he pleaded. Dowling, who still felt like the outsider in the group at the time, told him he would try to pick the right moment to ask Red, but his impression was that it was a pretty closed group.

"The irony," Dowling said later, "is that I grew up a Knicks fan. I never hated the Celtics, I respected them too much to hate them, but I rooted for the Knicks. Here's Bobby, bleeding Celtics green, and I'm the one going to lunch."

Not long after that, Dowling saw an opportunity to get Campbell and Red together. Red had called him to say that President Clinton had invited him to the 1999 Saint Patrick's Day dinner at the White House. "What the hell is that about?" he asked Dowling.

Dowling explained it was a big event with perhaps five hundred people invited. Red wasn't sure that either he or Dorothy wanted to go through the hassle of waiting in line to get in. "I figured I could go pick them up, drive them onto the grounds, and make it easier for them," Dowling said. "Then I realized I had to coach one of my kids in a basketball game that night. I needed someone else to do it: who better than Bob Campbell, Mr. Boston Celtic?"

Campbell was, needless to say, thrilled. "When I called him to set things up, I was shaking like a leaf," he said. "But when I got there, Mrs. Auerbach was so gracious. It helped me relax."

Campbell had to spend a few minutes chatting with Dorothy because when he walked in, Red was on the phone trying to get a tryout in Europe for a player from George Washington named Shante Rogers. The last thing Campbell heard Red say on the phone was, "If you don't think the kid can play just because he's little [five-foot-three], then the hell with you."

Campbell drove the Auerbachs to the White House and got them inside the door and into the security line. One of his colleagues was standing there checking off names. "I said to the guy, 'Auerbach, Mr. and Mrs.,'" Campbell said. "He said, 'Yeah, sure,' then he looked up and saw Red. Our guys don't show people very much emotion, but when he saw Red he said, 'Hey, it's Red Auerbach. *The* Red Auerbach.' I said, 'Yeah, I know.'"

Campbell walked the Auerbachs into the party. It was a political crowd and Red was a lot more comfortable talking to Campbell about the old days with the Celtics — "He liked it that I remembered guys like Willie Naulls, not just the stars" — but as 9:00 approached, Campbell started getting nervous. He was doing some work on the counterfeiting squad and had to leave for a potential bust. He spotted Ray Flynn, the former mayor of Boston, who had played basketball at Providence.

"Coach," he said, "do you know Ray Flynn?"

"Know him?" Red said. "Hell, I cut him."

Campbell worked the Auerbachs over to Flynn. Seeing Red, Flynn threw his arms around him, took him by the hand, and began introducing him around the room. Campbell's work was done. When he said his good-byes to the Auerbachs a few minutes later, Red said, "Hey, next Tuesday, come to China Doll for lunch. Pete knows the details."

Campbell's feet barely touched the ground as he left the White House that night.

The man he had thanked God for as a kid had invited him to lunch.

6

Travels Near and Far

"I EVER TELL YOU about how I got Heinsohn arrested by the secret police in Poland? He was scared to death. Cousy had already told every person we met on the street that Heinsohn was German, and the Poles hate the Germans, so Heinsohn was convinced they had come to get him. I'm not much on practical jokes, but that was one that was worth it. Heinsohn deserved it."

With all the emphasis these days on international basketball and the influx of foreign players into both the college and the pro game, most people forget that the first basketball person to spend considerable time overseas was Red.

As far back as the fifties, at the behest of the State Department, Red traveled overseas to do clinics and, on occasion, to coach teams that played exhibition games against national teams and European pro teams when the European leagues began to flourish.

"In the fifties when we went in there we did very basic stuff," he said. "The thing I noticed right away, even back then, was that they were very well coached on fundamentals." He laughed. "They all said they read my book." (Red wrote a classic instructional book in 1952 called *Basketball for the Player, the Fan, and the Coach* that initially sold for twenty-five cents and was eventually translated into twelve different languages. "Made out like a bandit," he said. "I got a penny for every book sold.")

"I would bring Cousy or Heinsohn and sometimes a referee with me. We would work with the coaches and the players too. I always enjoyed it because they were all so eager to learn."

By the 1960s, basketball was getting serious around the world — especially behind the Iron Curtain. In 1964 Red got a call from Nick Robis, an old friend who had gone to Harvard with Bobby Kennedy and was working at the State Department. A tour had been proposed for an NBA team to Poland, Romania, Egypt, and Yugoslavia. Poland and Yugoslavia were especially significant since American athletes had traveled very rarely behind the Iron Curtain, especially on goodwill tours.

"You think you can put together some kind of team to go over there?" Robis asked.

"Yeah, I think I can do it," Red answered.

He then put together a team of Bill Russell, Bob Cousy, Tom Heinsohn, K. C. Jones, Oscar Robertson, Bob Pettit, Tom Gola, and Jerry Lucas — almost all of them many-time all-stars, all future Hall of Famers.

These days, with players from all over the world playing in the United States, it is difficult to imagine what a major undertaking a trip like this was. Before the team left the country, they were all brought to Washington for a briefing at the State Department with Secretary of State Dean Rusk on what to expect and how to act, especially in Poland, Romania, and Yugoslavia, where it was very possible they would encounter a good deal of anti-American sentiment. After that, Red and the players were taken to the White House, where they were given a tour and met with President Johnson in the Oval Office.

Red has, at one time or another, met every president since Truman (he is good friends with a number of the Kennedys). But he has never reached the point where talking to a president or being in the Oval Office is passé. He thanked Johnson, who was in the middle of an election campaign, for taking the time to see the team and told him they would do their best to represent the country well.

"Remember one thing," the president said. "No matter how hard it is, try to always remain patient."

"Mr. President," Red said, "patience is one of my great strengths."

The four Celtics on the team got a good laugh out of that line.

Red has always been an adventurer. To this day, he enjoys going places he's never been and doing things he's never done before. He was determined that the trip be more than just games and hotels for everyone involved. So he arranged to have guides and tours in all the cities on the trip.

"First day in Poland, I had it set up for a bus to pick us up at the hotel at ten o'clock. Everyone is there at ten on the dot — except for Russell. By the time we chase him down, we're running twenty minutes late. I know what's going on. He's making sure everyone knows he's the star in the group even though they're all stars. After I got through yelling at Russell, I turned to Sam Jones and said, 'Tomorrow, guaranteed, Oscar's going to be twenty minutes late.' Next day comes, bus is there at ten. Everyone's there — except Oscar. Exactly twenty minutes after ten, he shows up.

"That afternoon, before practice, I called them all together and I said, 'Look, fellas, we've got a long trip ahead of us. We're going to a lot of places. I want it to be fun. But I'm going to tell you right now, today was the last time one of our buses is going to leave late. You're late, you're responsible for getting where we're going — whether it's a gym, a restaurant, or the airport. You miss a plane, that's your problem, not mine.' That was the last time anyone was late."

The week in Poland went well. The team staged clinics, played a couple games against Polish teams — Red would allow the lead to get to about forty, then tell the players to gear back so as not to completely humiliate the opponent while still letting them know there was a wide gap between the Americans and the rest of the world — and did a lot of sightseeing.

Naturally, Tom Heinsohn was in the middle of various jokes and high jinks, forcing everyone to be on the alert at all times. Near the end of the week, Red decided it was time to turn the tables.

One afternoon, shortly before the team was to go out to dinner, there was a knock on the door of the room Heinsohn was
sharing with Jerry Lucas. Standing in the doorway were two
hard-looking men wearing trench coats, snap-brim hats, and
menacing looks.

"HEINSOHN?" they demanded.

"Yes?" Heinsohn answered.

"You come with us," they said. "Right now."

"Where?" Heinsohn said.

"Just come."

One walked around behind him, the other turned to lead
the way.

"Jerry," Heinsohn said, now clearly frightened, "find Red.
Tell him what's going on."

Lucas promised to find Red. Heinsohn was taken downstairs
and placed in the small hotel bar, just off the lobby. A car would
come, he was told, and take them all to "headquarters."

Heinsohn sat in the bar for a while, chain-smoking. A few
anxious moments later, Red walked in, a somber look on his
face. "They're really mad at you, Tommy," he said.

"For what?" Heinsohn said. "What in the world have I
done?"

At that point Red couldn't go any further. Heinsohn was
starting to look ashen. He called the two "agents" in and introduced them. They were both coaches with the Polish National
Team.

Years later, when Heinsohn would retell the story, he
claimed he hadn't really been fooled, that he had suspected a

prank all along. Not so, according to Red. "Just to be sure I wasn't imagining things, I asked Lucas about it when I saw him at a game about a year ago," he said. "I said, 'Am I crazy or was Tommy terrified?' He looked at me and said, 'He was completely terrified.' I said, 'Good. I got him at least one time.'"

They went from Poland to Romania, where they conducted several more clinics and played a couple more games. No one was arrested. From there it was on to Egypt, where basketball was almost a brand-new sport. As in Poland and Romania, arrangements had been made for the group to visit the American embassy. Soon after they arrived, Heinsohn began chatting up the young liaison who had greeted them.

"Do . . . you . . . like . . . working . . . here?" he asked, banking on the old American theory that anyone can understand English as long as it is spoken . . . very . . . slowly.

"I like it here very much," the young woman replied in perfect English.

"Wow," Heinsohn said. "Your . . . English . . . is . . . very . . . good."

"It . . . should . . . be," she answered. "I'm . . . from . . . Toledo."

Heinsohn was having a tough trip.

The last stop was Yugoslavia. From the minute the plane landed in Belgrade, almost nothing went right. To begin with, when they arrived at the airport at 1:00 in the morning, there wasn't anyone there to meet them. No one from the embassy, no one from the Yugoslav basketball federation, no one. Red finally reached someone at the hotel where they had been told they were staying, and somehow a bus was rounded up to come and pick them up.

It was after 2:00 when they arrived at the hotel. "It was a dump," Red said. "I mean, a dump — the kind of place at home where you paid by the hour. I was furious. I demanded to see someone from the basketball federation. They said there was no one to call at that hour. We had no choice. So we checked in. The guys headed to their rooms while I'm still in the lobby demanding to know how I get in touch with someone in the morning to get all this straightened out. The phone at the front desk rings. It's Russell, for me, calling from his room. He says, 'Can you come up here for a minute?'

"I said, 'Bill, it's two o'clock in the morning. I'm really tired, I'm really pissed off, I'm in no mood for any kind of jokes.'"

Russell insisted this was no joke. Finally, Red went up to the room.

"I walked in and almost fell down laughing," he said. "Bill was standing in front of the door holding his arms out to the side. Only he couldn't hold them all the way out without touching the walls. There was one cot in the room that might — MIGHT — sleep one person. He was rooming with Pettit."

Red stormed down to the front desk and demanded single rooms for everyone in the party. If he didn't get them, he said, he would start waking up everyone and anyone he could find all over town. Single rooms were found. The next day, when the head of the basketball federation finally showed up, Red demanded a new hotel. Very sorry, he was told, no other hotel is available. This is the best we can do.

119

Red was tempted to say no hotel, no games. But he remembered the State Department briefing and President Johnson's warning about being patient. So he asked for a schedule, which he had not yet been given, for the team. There were games every night. That was fine.

"Don't you want us to do any clinics while we're here?" Red asked the federation head.

"We don't need your clinics," he was told. "In the last World Championships, our team finished ahead of the American team."

Red didn't know whether to laugh or cry. The United States had been represented in the World Championships the year before by a group of college players, not even particularly distinguished college players since the event was not considered very important back then. "How do I explain that to this guy?" he said. "How do I tell him those were kids, these are pros, the best players in the world?"

There was really only one way to explain. But before the team could prove their superiority, there was one more glitch. When the Americans walked into the outdoor arena where the game was to be held that night, Red noticed there was no American flag. He immediately went to the American representative from the embassy and demanded to know where the American flag was.

"Oh, there's no way they'll display an American flag here," he was told.

"Well, you tell 'em, 'No flag, no game,'" Red said. "Maybe they can insult *me*, but they aren't going to insult the country we represent. Looks to me like they sold a lot of tickets and I don't think this crowd will be too happy if there's no game. If they think I'm kidding, tell them to try me and see what happens."

A flag was found. The game was played. And the Americans made it clear that there's a difference between college kids and pros. Knowing that the Yugoslav team probably thought it was every bit as good as the Americans, Red gave very explicit pregame instructions: "No letting up," he said. "Beat them as badly as you can." Then, turning to Russell, he pointed at the star of the Yugoslav team, a six-eight redhead named Belov. "He scores *once* and I'll have your head," he said. "I mean it, *once.*"

When the game began, the Yugoslavs went straight to Belov as soon as they got the ball. He made a spin move on Russell, turned, and Russell blocked the shot, starting a fast break the other way. Five times, the Yugoslavs got the ball; five times, Russell blocked a shot. The sixth time down, Belov caught the ball thirty feet from the basket and, with Russell racing at him, heaved a shot that hit the side of the backboard and bounced away as the crowd hooted. A few seconds later, with the Americans already up twenty, the Yugoslav coach called time.

"Russell," Red screamed, "I'm gonna kill you! You let the guy hit the backboard!"

The next time Belov caught the ball, he tried to go up-and-under Russell, who slammed the ball back at him so hard it hit him in the head and bounced away. Completely exasperated, Belov grabbed the ball, kicked it into the stands, and was promptly ejected.

"Russell runs by the bench, looks at me, and winks," Red remembered.

The Americans won by fifty-five. Red spent most of the second half eating ice cream on the bench, legs crossed just to make it absolutely clear that this game was too easy to even merit his attention. That night, at a postgame banquet, the head of the Yugoslav federation asked Red if perhaps the Americans might do a clinic the next day.

Red's first response was direct: "Tell him," he said to the interpreter, "I got two words for him: no way."

"I am always willing to forgive," Red likes to say, "but I never — *ever* — forget."

The next night the Americans won by sixty.

"One thing that people today don't understand is how long it took for people — here and overseas — to understand just how good the pros were, what incredible athletes they were," Red said. "In the fifties, when we would barnstorm in the exhibition season, there were teams we played who had a couple guys who had been local hotshots and they actually walked on the court thinking they had a chance to beat us. We used to go around during the season holding clinics in parking lots, places like that, because we had to bring the game to people who didn't think of it as a big-time sport.

"What helped a lot, believe it or not, were the athletes in other professional sports — baseball, football. A lot of times, they were the ones who would say to guys in the media, 'Hey, you're missing the boat. You don't understand what unbelievable athletes the basketball players are.' It had to be repeated over and over before it began to sink in."

The superiority of the Americans sunk in by the time they left Yugoslavia. Red flew home and briefed the State Department: Poland had been a success; so had Egypt — except for the American ambassador, who was too busy to greet the team (Red later saw him with his feet on his desk, reading a newspaper). Yugoslavia had not gone so well, he reported.

A few years later, Dirlo Treddinick, a friend of Red's who was a vice president at Tufts University, asked Red if he would come and speak at the prestigious Fletcher School of Law and Diplomacy at Tufts. Red gave a rousing speech on the rigors of travel and how to deal with people in foreign countries, and mentioned that the single worst act of diplomacy he had ever witnessed had occurred in Egypt when the American ambassador didn't even have the common courtesy to come out and greet the American basketball team during its trip there.

Red was surprised when he heard nothing from Treddinick about how the speech had gone. Finally, Red called him.

"It was a good speech," Treddinick said, "but I don't think you'll ever be invited back again."

"Really? Why not?"

"The head of the school was the ambassador to Egypt in 1964 when you were over there."

In 1960 Red got into the summer camp business. By then, he was an icon in Boston, and the idea of a summer camp strictly for basketball made sense. It was another way to promote the sport and was also good business, since any kid with any interest in playing basketball was bound to be attracted to a camp with Red's name on it.

The camp was an immediate success and still flourishes today, held every summer at Brandeis University. Through the years, Red says the only problems he has ever had have been with ex-players who send their kids to the camp, then insist on stalking their every move throughout the week.

"I almost had to throw [Tom] Heinsohn and [Bob] Brannum out," he said. "Johnny Most [the longtime Celtics radio voice] was just as bad. They would stand there and scream at their kids, scream at the coaches, scream at the referees. I finally had to tell 'em: 'If you can't behave, I'm gonna have to throw your kids out of here.' And the kids were all good kids. The fathers were the ones who were a pain. I mean, you see that all the time, but you'd think guys like that would know better. Wrong."

A year after he had started his camp, Red got a call from Morgan Wootten, then a young high school coach at DeMatha High School in Hyattsville, Maryland — a DC suburb. Red had met Wootten several years earlier when he was an assistant coach under Joe Gallagher at St. John's High School. They had been introduced by Bob Dwyer, the coach at Archbishop Carroll, which was then the powerhouse high school program in the DC area.

Soon after getting the DeMatha job, Wootten needed a speaker for his first postseason banquet. Almost on a whim, he called Red and asked if there were any chance he'd do it. Red almost never says no to another coach. He went and spoke and Wootten never forgot the favor. Now, in 1961, Wootten was calling to ask another favor: He and Gallagher wanted to start a summer camp of their own, but they had no idea how to go about doing it. Would Red sit down and explain the nuts and bolts to them?

Of course.

"Red spent a couple of days with us," Wootten said. "He laid the whole thing out. How many counselors you needed to campers; how you did it as a day camp; how you did it as an overnight camp; everything. Then he volunteered to come up and speak the first year, which was absolutely critical to our success."

Forty-three years later, the camp is one of the largest and most successful in the country and has provided Wootten and Gallagher with income well beyond what either was making as a high school basketball coach. It also helped spark one of Red's closest friendships. Since he lived right near St. John's High School, where the camp was held the first few years, he often went over to watch camp or to play tennis. When there was downtime, he and Wootten spent long hours talking basketball.

"His mind has always amazed me," Wootten said. "He just sees things, picks up things the rest of us don't."

Most would say the same about Wootten. He was the son of a retired naval officer, who landed in Hyattsville, Maryland, after leaving the service. After graduating from Montgomery Blair High School in 1950, he enrolled at Montgomery College. While he was there, an opening for a baseball coach came up at St. Joseph's Orphanage. Morgan, looking for some extra money and coaching experience, got the job and proceeded to go 0–16 in his first season. Even so, the orphanage kept him on to coach football and basketball the next fall, and he had a lot more luck, going undefeated twice in football and reaching the semifinals of the local CYO Championships in basketball.

By then Wootten was enrolled at the University of Maryland, and Gallagher hired him as an assistant and to coach the JV team. The year he graduated from Maryland, he was offered the DeMatha job. Following Gallagher's advice, he turned it down. "Joe thought it would be too much my first year out of college to be a full-time teacher and full-time head coach," he said. "Turned out to be great advice."

A year later, the job opened again. This time he took it: head basketball and football coach, athletic director, and history teacher — five periods a day — all for $3,800 a year. He quickly began building one of the great high school programs in the country. In 1965, Lew Alcindor's senior year at Power Memorial High School, DeMatha played Power in Cole Field House at the University of Maryland. In what is still considered the most famous high school game ever played, DeMatha upset Power, ending the school's seventy-one-game winning streak in front of a sellout crowd of 14,500 — the first time the building had ever been completely sold out. Wootten prepared his team for the seven-foot-two Alcindor by having his second teamers hold tennis rackets over their heads during practice so the starters could try to shoot over them.

In the mid-1960s, Washington's best-known summer basketball league, the Jellef League, was finally integrated after
years of whites playing whites and blacks playing blacks. Wootten had always had an integrated team, so the change allowed
DeMatha, which was by then a national power, to participate in
the league. On the final night of the summer season, DeMatha
played the Interhigh All-Stars in a game that was hugely anticipated in DC — the Catholic powerhouse against the best of
the public schools. The Jellef playground was so packed that
night that Wootten had to put several of his friends — including Red — on his bench because there was no place else for
them to sit.

"It was a great game," Wootten remembered. "I thought my
team played as well as it possibly could. It went back and forth
all night, and they finally made a play at the end and beat us by
one in triple overtime. It was one of those games where you
couldn't feel bad about losing because it was such a good game
and my kids had played so hard and so well. I left there feeling
high about the whole thing.

"The next day, as normal, Red came over to St. John's to play
tennis. He said hello, we chatted for a few minutes, and he
never said a word about the game. Finally, I couldn't resist. I
said, 'Red, what'd you think of that game last night?' He
paused and looked at me and finally said, 'I felt bad for you.' I
said something about it being a tough loss and all, and he shook
his head and said, 'No, that's not it. I think it's a shame that you
cost your team that game.'

"I was stunned. I think I said something like, 'Huh?'

"He said, 'You lost the feel of the game. In the time-outs, you were talking about offense. Your team's offense was fine. You weren't having any trouble scoring. You were having trouble on defense and on the boards. You never once got on them about blocking out better, and they were doing a lousy job of blocking out. If you're going to be a coach, you can't lose the feel of the game.'

"It was hard to hear him say that. And I wonder if I hadn't asked about the game if he would have brought it up. But I never forgot it. In fact, that may have been the most important thing anyone ever said to me in my entire coaching career. I always tried to be very aware of having a feel for what was going on in front of me on the court every night I coached."

Wootten did a pretty good job of it. When he retired in the fall of 2002 he had won 1,274 games, more than any high school coach in history, and had lost only 192 times. His DeMatha teams won at least twenty games an amazing forty-four straight years and he never *once* had a three-game losing streak. In the first season of his retirement, DeMatha went through a nine-game losing streak. When someone asked Morgan at lunch one day what his longest losing streak had been, he paused. The questioner pressed, "Was it three, four?"

Morgan looked as if someone had just given him an electric shock. "Three?" he repeated incredulously. "Oh my gosh no, we never lost three in a row."

Morgan really does say "oh my gosh." Red's response to a similar question would not have included the word "gosh."

The two men are the perfect odd couple. Red is loud, opinionated, and often profane. Morgan is quiet and unassuming, always asking others their opinion on things. He never uses profanity, even during a game or during practice. His players always knew not to use profanity around him. Red can use most profanities as verbs, adjectives, adverbs, and nouns. Say hello to Red and he will tell you what he thinks about anything and everything from the state of the economy to international basketball to women in locker rooms. Morgan must be pushed and prodded before one can elicit an opinion from him on anything as controversial as the weather.

Several years ago, Morgan suspended his best player, Keith Bogans, after Bogans got into a fight in practice. Red, who has always believed that you should never discipline a player in a way that hurts the rest of the team, was aghast. That week when Morgan walked into lunch, Red jumped on him before he had a chance to sit down.

"What are you, nuts — suspending Bogans?" he said.

"Red, I had no choice," Morgan began. "He knows that fighting is against our rules and he got into a fight. If I let him off the hook, people think I'm doing it because he's a star —"

"The hell with people. Find another way to discipline him. Don't suspend him."

"Well, what in the world should I do?"

"Fine him!" Red roared.

Morgan laughed. "Not a bad idea at that," he said.

Red starts 90 percent of his sentences with, "Let me tell you what I think . . ." Morgan starts most of his with, "What do you think . . ." And yet they could not be closer, trusting one another implicitly, each respecting the other totally and completely.

"Most coaches don't want to do something unless they think of it," Red said, talking about Morgan. "Morgan has never had that kind of ego. He sees something good, someone gives him an idea, if it makes sense to him, he uses it. He never needs credit, never needs to prove he's the smartest guy in the room. He was one of the first high school coaches I met who thought about basketball and tried to learn basketball twelve months a year. It wasn't just a job with him. He always wanted to learn and get better. He never let his ego get in the way of what he was doing. There aren't a lot of guys as successful as him that you can say that about."

To this day, Red and Morgan can sit and discuss basketball for hours. They will talk about the game technically and they will talk about personalities. More often than not, Morgan asks questions and Red supplies answers.

"He talks about feeling the game," Morgan said. "What I've always been amazed by is his feel for people. Back in the old camp days, Bill Bradley would come in to work out. He was an intern in Washington during his summers at Princeton. Even back then he was about as impressive as any young man I've ever met. I can remember all of us sitting around one night talking about him. Someone said, 'Now there's someone who will be president someday.'

"Red pulled the cigar out of his mouth and shook his head. 'Nope, he won't be president,' he said. 'He's too damn honest. He'll be a senator or a Supreme Court justice.' "

In the summer of 1996, Morgan almost died. He needed a lifesaving liver transplant. He came back to coaching in large part because he was determined to use his fame to raise money for transplant and liver disease research. He set up the De-Matha Classic and spent a lot of time and energy making it a success by bringing in top high school teams from around the country. He also began discussing his retirement with the powers that be at DeMatha. In an ideal world, he would coach for another two or three years and then turn the job over to his son, Joe, who was working for him as an assistant coach.

The DeMatha people hedged. Then, in 1998, they told him directly that they would not consider Joe for the position when he retired. Morgan was hurt. He thought that after all he had accomplished DeMatha should be willing to give Joe a chance to succeed him. "Believe me, if I didn't think Joe was up to the job, I never would have brought it up," he said. "That wouldn't have helped Joe and it wouldn't have helped the school."

That spring, he was exhausted, not sure if he wanted to coach any longer. He was sixty-eight. The Classic was up and running and would continue even if he stepped down. Joe wasn't going to succeed him and had, in fact, become the head coach at O'Connell, another school in the Catholic League, meaning Morgan had to coach *against* him, something he truly dreaded.

One day at lunch, Morgan turned to Red and, in a rare serious moment, said, "Red, do you think I should retire?"

"Absolutely not," Red answered.

"Why not?" Morgan asked.

"Because you feel lousy right now, right?" Red said. "You're tired, you're pissed off at DeMatha, and you aren't happy with the season you just had. So you're thinking you'll get away from it all by retiring. That's completely wrong. That's not when you retire. If you do that, your last memories are bad ones. With the career you've had, that's not the way to go out.

"Plus, remember one thing. The day you retire you become an old man. Whether you feel that way or not, that's the way people look at you."

Morgan decided to keep coaching. "I was ready to quit," he said. "Red talked me out of it that day. And, as usual, he was right. We had two great seasons, won two more city championships, and when I decided it was time, that trying to rebuild one more time just wasn't for me, I felt great about walking away. I couldn't help but remember the look I saw on Dean Smith's face [a longtime friend of both Red and Morgan's] after his team lost to Arizona in the Final Four in 1997. There's one of the great coaches ever and his last memory is a really disappointing loss. Red went out a winner and I was able to do it too — only because I listened to him."

Red also turned out to be right when he told Morgan that his son, Joe, had been fortunate that DeMatha refused Morgan's request to allow him to succeed his father. "You don't want that for him," Red said. "The last thing he needs in his first job is to be compared to you all the time. Let him go someplace else and make his own mark."

Joe did just that, getting the job at Bishop Denis J. O'Connell High School five years ago. The tough part was when the two Woottens had to face each other. "He sits there on the bench with that angelic look on his face," Joe said, laughing. "And the thing people don't know is he'll do anything — I mean *anything* — to beat you." Joe did finally beat his dad in his third season at O'Connell, but DeMatha still walked away with one last city title — Morgan's fourteenth — at season's end.

For Morgan, the best news about being retired was being able to make it to the China Doll on Tuesdays on a much more consistent basis. "I can remember when my girls were teenagers, my wife trying to tell them that the best part of the prom is buying the dress, getting excited about who you're going with, and all the preparation and anticipation," Morgan said one day, sipping a cup of tea as Red hustled out the door to get to Woodmont and the card game. "Most of life is like that. The anticipation is actually better than the reality.

"Not with lunch on Tuesday. I'm always excited about going, but the event is always better than the anticipation. Almost without exception, when I walk out of here I'm fired up, filled with energy. Whenever I'm on my way down here I always find myself thinking, 'I wonder what Red thinks about such and such,' whatever it is that's in the news that day."

He smiled. "And the one thing I know for sure is that when I get here, I'll find out *exactly* what he thinks."

7

Building and Rebuilding

"I EVER TELL YOU how I got thrown out of the all-star game in 1967? Ejected. First quarter no less. I'm not even a coach anymore and I get thrown out of the all-star game. How many guys can make that claim?"

Only Red.

Even though he had retired from coaching, Red was asked to coach the East in the 1967 all-star game in San Francisco. Back then, the coach of the team that had won the conference title the previous season was the all-star coach, and the Celtics, under Red, had won the East in 1966 en route to their eighth straight title. Red wanted to win the game in part because he had won the last four all-star games he had coached in and also because the game represented one last chance to torture Fred Schaus, who was, of course, coaching the West.

"I got on one of the guys in the first quarter because they were letting too much go and I was afraid someone was going to get hurt," he said. "All of a sudden, one guy, I don't even remember who it was, turns around and hits me with a technical. I said, 'What are you, nuts? This is the all-star game. You don't give people technical fouls.' He says, 'Oh yeah? You just got another. You're outta here.' At first I didn't think he was serious. But he was. I didn't make it through the first quarter."

That wasn't the only coaching Red did that year. Russell was player-coach of the Celtics, but whenever Red was up in Boston, two or three times a month, Russell asked him if he would run practice just to take a look and see what he liked and didn't like. Red, who was weaning himself from all the feelings that come with being in the locker room and on the bench on game night, was happy to put on a whistle again, even if it didn't involve any games. "Actually it was better that way," he said. "I never lost."

Only he did lose — when the Celtics lost. Being the general manager didn't make losing any easier. In some ways it was tougher because he couldn't help when things went wrong during a game. All he could do was sit and watch. The Celtics were 60–21 that season, a great year by almost any standard. But this was the season when Wilt Chamberlain finally got the Celtics yoke off his back. His Philadelphia 76ers won a league record sixty-eight games, took the Celtics out in five in the Eastern Conference finals, and went on to win the NBA title.

At least Aubre Jones was happy. Red wasn't. Neither was Russell. The following season, with Chamberlain looking for a second straight title, the 76ers led the Celtics three games to one in the conference finals. This time, though, the Celtics came back. They won the last three games of that series and went on to beat (who else?) the Lakers in the finals. A year later, the team looked old during most of the regular season, winning only forty-eight games to finish fourth in the East. But somehow Bill Russell, Sam Jones, Satch Sanders, Don Nelson, and John Havlicek found the magic one more time, beating three straight teams with better records during the regular season — Philadelphia, New York, and (of course) Los Angeles to win an eleventh title in thirteen seasons.

The seventh game in Los Angeles, which the Celtics hung on to win 108–106, was one of Red's bigger thrills. He was doing the color on the radio with Johnny Most that night, and prior to the game he happened to see a memo that was supposed to be seen only by Laker employees. It gave the exact time during the postgame awards ceremony when Lakers owner Jack Kent Cooke wanted the five thousand balloons that had been hung in the rafters to be dropped.

As the game ended, Red couldn't resist: "Boy, this is really too bad," he said. "I wonder what Jack is going to do with all those balloons up there."

That turned out to be the last hurrah for Russell and Sam Jones. Both retired that summer, Russell shocking most basketball fans by making his announcement in a story in *Sports Illustrated*. Red wasn't surprised. "They could both still play," he said. "But they were like me, burned out. The thing that comes with winning all the time is tremendous pressure because anytime you lose, the other guy throws himself a big party. The coaching wore Russell out too. I wasn't happy when they left, but I certainly understood."

For the first time since he had arrived in Boston to take over an awful team, Red had to rebuild. He hired Heinsohn to coach the team, knowing that without Russell and Sam Jones and with up-and-coming young teams in New York and Baltimore, he was probably in for a rocky year or two. He was right: the next two years were rocky — the Celtics won thirty-four games the next season, missing the play-offs for the first time since 1950, the season prior to Red's hiring. They then improved to 44–38 a year later but missed the play-offs again.

But Red was rebuilding, using his one-player-a-year theory. In 1968 he had taken Don Chaney, a six-foot-five guard who was a hard-nosed defender, in the first round of the draft. A year later he took another guard, Jo Jo White, from Kansas. Then in 1970, drafting fourth — which was higher than any year since he had traded up to get Russell in 1956 — Red took a chance on a six-foot-nine center from Florida State who most scouts thought was too small to be effective in the NBA. His name was Dave Cowens.

"I drafted him for two reasons," Red said later. "He could run like the wind, which reminded me of Russell, and he had a killer attitude. He'd run through a wall to win. I figured there was no way you could go wrong taking someone like that."

He went very right. The Celtics won fifty-six games in Cowens's second season and sixty-eight the following season. In both seasons they lost the Eastern Conference finals to the

Knicks, who were at their zenith with Willis Reed, Walt Frazier, Dave DeBusschere, and Bill Bradley as their anchors. Another Red — Holzman — was their coach. Like his Celtics counterpart, he was a New Yorker. Unlike Auerbach, he had gotten into CCNY.

"He was a damn good coach. I had great respect for him," Red said. "But the media fell completely in love with that team because it was from New York. Don't get me wrong, they were great. But can you imagine what it would have been like if we had been in New York when we won all those titles? The Knicks won twice and I swear their twelfth guy wrote a book about it. That's the way it's always been. When the Knicks are good, people write poems about them. They're like the Red Sox and the Cubs in baseball. All those writers in New York are in love with them."

The Knicks have always been a little bit of a sore point with Red, even though the Celtics have dominated them for most of the last half century — those two play-off series in the seventies aside. Red was always convinced that the league — even his beloved owner Walter Brown — bent over backward to help the Knicks. Even though Red and current NBA commissioner David Stern are good friends, Red insists that Stern is a Knicks fan.

"Sometimes I bring it up just to upset him," he says with a smile. "But it's also true."

"It's *not* true," Stern insists. "I *was* a Knicks fan years ago. Now I'm just a basketball fan."

Spoken like a true commissioner.

Red has always gotten along with the commissioners of the league, from Maurice Podoloff to Walter Kennedy to Larry O'Brien to David Stern. Not that he hasn't battled with them.

"Kennedy used to fine me all the time," he said. "He'd fine me for yelling at referees for getting ejected or for getting into it with fans. You name it. I never paid a fine. He would announce he had fined me and I would tell him I wasn't paying. Then we'd move on."

Once, O'Brien fined Red for putting a reporter he was feuding with, Steve Hershey, then of the *Washington Star*, in a seat in the rafters of the Boston Garden, rather than downstairs with the other writers. The NBA Writers Association complained to O'Brien, who fined Red and told him Hershey would be restored to his regular seat the next time he was in Boston.

"Over my dead body," Red said. "Fine me all you want. But in my building, he sits where I put him."

Red still laughs about that story. "I got the article out and I read it to O'Brien," he said. "I told him that what really got me mad was that my wife read it and it really upset her. Hell, I wasn't even coaching anymore and the guy went after me. After I finished, Larry said to me, 'Red, if you ever quote me on this, I'll kill you. But I agree with you.'"

Red has great respect for the work Stern did restoring the league to prominence in the 1980s. "The most important thing he did was getting the union to accept the salary cap," he said. "Larry Fleischer [then the head of the union] deserves credit too for understanding that it was needed and not standing in the way of getting it done. But David did a great marketing job. The only thing he's done that I disagree with is going along with the idea of putting the NBA players in the Olympics. I understand what he was doing and it probably helped build the game globally, which I know was important to him. But now it's gone too far. We've become the ugly Americans with the way our players have behaved overseas, with the way they've acted so spoiled, with that whole Jordan flag thing [Michael Jordan wrapped himself in an American flag during the 1992 medal ceremony to cover up a Reebok logo. Reebok was the official sponsor of USA basketball; Nike has been the official sponsor of Jordan's life since 1984].

"Now we've had the embarrassment of finishing sixth in the World Championships with pros, but not our best players. Next year [2004] Larry Brown has his work cut out for him in the Olympics. Not only had he better win, but the players had better behave themselves."

Red would have liked to be involved in coaching an Olympic team once the pros were included in 1992. "Not as the head coach, I was too old for that," he said. "But as a consultant of some kind. I do know a lot about the game internationally — I was the first guy to spend a lot of time overseas. If the coach didn't want to listen to me, he wouldn't have to listen to me. But it would have been nice to have been asked. When I was still coaching I couldn't do it. When I was younger and a general manager I could have done it, but back then it was college kids, and I understood them wanting a college coach. Now it's different."

Red never spoke to Stern or anyone in the NBA about his desire to be involved with an Olympic team. "That's not my way," he said. "I don't like to ask people for things. Maybe in this case I should have said something because it probably didn't occur to David that I'd be interested."

The Cowens-led, rebuilt Celtics won Boston's twelfth NBA title in 1974 and another one in 1976. By then, Red's fame had spread in different ways: he was doing a segment called *Red on Roundball* for CBS at halftime of NBA telecasts, and he had become part of the famous Miller Lite "less filling, tastes great" commercials. Naturally he smoked his cigar throughout the commercials.

The biggest issue in his life continued to be Celtics ownership. After Walter Brown's death, the Celtics went through a series of owners, none of whom were close to being Brown as far as Red was concerned.

"I still remember when we had the first expansion draft [1966, when the Chicago Bulls became the league's tenth team]. Marvin Kratter owned the team. He called me and wanted me to come to New York for a meeting with the team's board of directors. I went. It was in the Pan Am Building — he was chairman of National Equities Company. So I go down there. Kratter starts talking about who we should leave unprotected in the expansion draft. He says, 'I think we should put Satch Sanders and K. C. Jones in there.' I'm just sitting there listening to this. He goes around the room and asks for opinions. What does he expect them to say? They all say, 'Oh yes, Mr. Kratter, you're right about that.' Finally, I get up and say,

'I'm outta here.' I walk out. Kratter follows me into the hall and he says, 'Red, what's wrong?' I say, 'What makes you think you know anything about basketball? You know about business. You pay me to know basketball. We can't afford to lose K. C. or Satch. But if you want to make those decisions, fine. You make them, but get somebody else to run the team. Either I run the team or you run it. Can't be both of us.'

"To his credit, he got it. He told me to calm down, come back in, and tell everyone what I wanted to do and then we'd do it."

Kratter wasn't even close to being Red's worst owner. His relationship with John Y. Brown almost caused him to leave the Celtics for the Knicks. Prior to that, though, was the ownership of Woody Erdman, another New York businessman. "Now he was the absolute worst," Red said. "A bunch of his other investments went bad and he was stealing money from the team. He insisted that all the gate receipts be sent directly to him in New York. He said he would pay all the bills from there. He didn't want our accounting office involved at all.

"Except he never paid the bills. Things got so bad people wouldn't do any business with us unless it was COD. One time I had to write a check from my own account for three thousand dollars because the phone company was about to turn all our phones off. Another time we were about to get on a plane to charter someplace and the charter company said we had to pay eight thousand up front because the last time they had billed Erdman they had never been paid. I had to write another check or we wouldn't have been able to get to the game. He finally sold the team and there were a whole bunch of lawsuits because people were suing to get the money he owed them."

Red has always considered himself a pretty good businessman — in and out of basketball. In the 1960s, he was part owner of a Chinese restaurant in Boston called Anita Chou's. The restaurant lasted five years. The food was great — according to Red — but problems ensued when Ms. Chou fell in with a man who apparently ran off with a good deal of the profits. Red had seen the same thing happen to Russell when he owned a restaurant, so he got out while the getting was good.

"It was too bad it didn't work out better," he said. "I liked having a place to go after games. Normally, I had always just gotten takeout and gone home or to my hotel room. When I owned the place, I'd take people there after games and eat. It just didn't work out."

The Celtics hit hard times again after their championship in 1976. Cowens, who had always taken a pounding playing center at a shade under six-foot-nine, began to wear down. In 1977 he played only fifty games, and even though he didn't miss many games the next two seasons, he wasn't the same player. All his numbers eventually dropped off, and he retired after the 1980 season at the age of thirty-one, having played ten very hard years in the NBA.

With the team struggling, Red was forced to make some difficult decisions. Heinsohn was let go as coach midway through the 1977–78 season with the Celtics on their way to a 32–50 record. "Tommy was his own worst enemy," Red said. "He was very smart and tough, but he would never listen to anyone. He was just too stubborn. And he drove himself in a way that wasn't healthy."

What finally forced Red to make a change he really didn't want to make was his belief that Heinsohn had lost control of the team, specifically the team's two starting forwards, Curtis Rowe and Sidney Wicks. They were gifted players who had been together on three NCAA championship teams at UCLA. But it became clear to Red that neither cared very much about the team or about what Heinsohn was trying to get them or the rest of the players to do.

"I couldn't figure out what it was with those guys, so I finally asked Tommy if it would be okay if I ran practice for a couple of days," he said. "I had never done that before, except when Russell asked me to do it when he was playing and coaching, and I've never done it since. But I just thought maybe I could get an idea of what was going on and give him some help. First day, I blow the whistle to get everyone together, and ten guys hustle over. Two guys barely move — Wicks and Rowe. In fact, Rowe is just sitting on a basketball. I say, 'Hey, guys, get over here right now.' They come — but slowly. I tell them, 'When I say right now, I mean *right now.*' The rest of practice they're okay. No problems. Tommy comes back a couple days later and I tell him I think Wicks and Rowe will respond if you get on them when need be. He agrees. About a week later I go to practice and Wicks and Rowe are up to their old tricks. Tommy's not doing a thing to stop them. That's when I decided

I had to make the change. Tommy was worn out. He just didn't want to fight the battles anymore. I understood."

Satch Sanders was brought in to coach after Heinsohn, and that was a mistake. He was the polar opposite of Heinsohn (not to mention Red) in temperament, and Red knew it before he gave him the job. Sanders had coached at Harvard after retiring as a player, and Red had gone to see a game one night in which the Crimson had blown a big lead and lost at the buzzer. Red thought the team had gotten cocky and then didn't know what to do when the game got close.

"I'd have been all over them after a game like that," he said.

He went into the locker room with his former player, waiting for the explosion. It never came. "Tough one, guys," Sanders said. "Let's be in here for practice at four o'clock tomorrow."

When they were alone later, Red lit into Sanders. "You can't let 'em off the hook like that," he said. "There was no excuse for losing that game. You gotta get on 'em after a game like that."

Still, Red thought Sanders could be a good coach in the NBA. He was smart, the players certainly respected him, and perhaps, coaching pros instead of scholars, he would be tougher. Red had always had a soft spot for Sanders because he had been a grinder throughout his thirteen-year Celtics career. He played tough defense, rebounded, and was willing to do whatever Red asked of him to help the team win.

Red had drafted Sanders out of New York University in 1960, and he showed up at camp wearing glasses and a thick knee brace on each leg. "You can't wear glasses during a game,"

Red told him. "It makes you look timid. If you need contacts, we'll get 'em for you, but no glasses."

Sanders understood. "Now what's the matter with your knees?" Red asked. Nothing, Sanders said, he just felt more secure wearing them.

"I don't think I can play without them, Coach," he said.

Red said nothing. Before the first exhibition game of the season, he ordered Jim Loscutoff to hide the knee braces. Sanders had no choice but to play without them. He did fine and never used them again. Hiring Sanders was important to Red because he always wanted to hire as many members of the Celtics family as he could. One of the underlying and often missed factors in Red's success was the intense loyalty he had to his players and, as a result, their loyalty to him. Loscutoff was an example. Early in the 1957–58 season, Loscutoff tore up a knee, requiring major surgery that ended his season. In those days knee surgery was a very big deal, career threatening, sometimes career ending.

When Loscutoff showed up at training camp the next year, Red could see he was favoring the knee. "I had asked the doctors if he was okay," he said. "They said the knee was probably stronger after the surgery and the rehab than his other knee. But he was scared. I could see that.

"I finally sat him down and I said, 'Jim, this isn't working. I know your knee is okay, the doctors know your knee is okay, but you don't. The only way you're going to make it back is if you put yourself completely in my hands and do everything I tell you from now until the season begins.' "

Loscutoff agreed. For the rest of the exhibition season, he and Red left two hours before the team to travel to wherever the game was that night. The two of them worked in the gym alone before anyone else had arrived, Red putting Loscutoff through loose-ball drills, diving drills, stop-and-go drills — every one of them designed to force him to put pressure on his knee. "If he didn't do it the way I wanted, I threw balls at him," Red said. "One day, the rest of the team came in while we were working. I was just throwing balls out and making him chase them down and dive on them. The guys stood there yelling, 'Fetch, doggie, fetch!' Jim never flinched. And he made it back."

Specifically, he made it back to play six more years on six championship teams.

The way the old Celtics feel about their old coach may best be described by an incident involving Bob Brannum, who played on Red's first teams in the early and mid-1950s. Brannum went on to become the basketball coach at Brandeis and, like all the old Celtics, knew he was always welcome in Red's office before and after home games when Red was the general manager.

"I always kept a refrigerator in my office for the guys," Red said. "I'd have sodas and beer in there all the time. One night Brannum's in there and he's drinking a beer. I walk in and he puts the beer behind his back. Then he starts laughing. 'Look at me,' he said. 'I'm fifty-five years old and I still don't want you to see me drinking a beer.'"

Red really wanted Sanders to succeed as coach. But he was in a tough position from day one: John Havlicek was in his final season, Cowens was slowing down, and the team was a mess in the backcourt. Jo Jo White was also getting older. Forwards Wicks and Rowe were both talented but selfish. Red did swing a trade that brought Don Chaney back to the team from the Lakers along with Kermit Washington, a hard-nosed, unselfish rebounder whom the Lakers were looking to get rid of in the wake of the infamous incident in which he had punched Rudy Tomjanovich so hard he'd nearly killed him. Chaney and Washington helped, but not enough.

That summer came the franchise swap that made John Y. Brown the new owner of the Celtics and meant that Washington ended up in San Diego with ex-Celtics owner Irv Levin. Early in the 1978–79 season, Sanders was fired. "He never really had a chance," Red said. "We weren't very good. In fact we were bad. We were old and slow. But I knew it wasn't going to work when we blew a game one night that reminded me of the game at Harvard. I walked into the locker room and waited.

"Satch just said, 'Tough one, guys. See you at practice tomorrow.' I knew he just wasn't cut out for this at that moment, especially when we were rebuilding."

Cowens became player-coach after Sanders, and the team struggled to a 29–53 record. Cowens told Red he didn't want to do both jobs anymore at the end of that season. Red was forced to make a difficult decision. For the first time since he had come to Boston in 1950, someone from outside the Celtics family was hired to coach the team. The new coach was Bill Fitch, a veteran coach whose experience with the expansion

Cleveland Cavaliers in the 1970s seemed to fit the situation the Celtics were in.

But Red had made a move prior to hiring Fitch that would make his job much easier than anyone had anticipated.

Everyone who scouted college basketball in the late 1970s knew that Indiana State's Larry Bird was a gifted player. At six-foot-nine, he had great shooting range, was an excellent passer, and had a wonderful feel for the game. In 1978, as a fourth-year junior, he was clearly one of the two or three best players in the country. Bird was planning to return to Indiana State for his fifth year. He had started his college career at Indiana University (he never played a game there) and then transferred to Indiana State, meaning he had to sit out a transfer season.

Everyone knew Bird was going back to Indiana State for the 1978–79 season. Red had the sixth pick in the draft in 1978 after the Celtics' 32–50 disaster. Teams coming off bad years need immediate help if it is available. When the Celtics' turn to pick came up, they announced they were taking a player who wouldn't even put on a Celtics uniform the next season: Bird.

"Anyone tells you they knew Bird would be as good as he turned out — including me — is a liar," Red said. "I thought he was good, very good. He also played a position where we needed help, a lot of help. But did I know he had one of the great work ethics ever? No. Did I know he had a genius IQ for the game? No. Smart, yes. Genius, no.

"But I took him because I knew he would go one or two in the draft the next season, and I wasn't planning on having the worst record in the league. I knew this was my shot at him and I was thinking long term. We weren't going to win anything the next season. But he was someone who I thought could help us win again in the future."

The trick for Red was signing Bird before the 1979 draft. If he didn't sign him, Bird would go back into the draft and would no doubt be the number two pick — behind Magic Johnson. Bird had led Indiana State to the national championship game, where his team had lost to Johnson and Michigan State in what is arguably the most famous college basketball game ever played. To this day it is simply referred to as "Magic versus Larry," as if their teams were just along for the ride.

Shortly before the draft, Bird and his agent, Bob Woolf, came to Red's office. Red knew he was going to have to pay Bird a lot of money because he had the option to return to the draft. "I offered him five hundred thousand a year," he said. "That was more than any rookie had ever been paid in the history of the league. We all agreed on the money.

"Then Bob pulls out a list of 'extras' that he said had to be part of the deal."

Among the "extras" were airfare for Bird's mother whenever she wanted to fly in from Indiana to see Larry play; tuition for Bird if he ever decided to go back to Indiana State to graduate; a car; an interest-free loan (if needed) on a house; and a bonus if Bird made the all-rookie team. When Red saw the final demand, he blew up.

"You think I'm gonna pay a guy the highest rookie salary in the history of the game and not *expect* him to make the all-rookie team?" he roared at Woolf. Then, more quietly, he turned to Bird and said, "Look, Larry, this is how I do business. I pay you what I think you're worth. I don't play games. I didn't come in here and offer you half of what I can pay you and then bargain. I offered you what I think you're worth — which is a hell of a lot. But I am not in the automobile business; I am not a banker; I'm not paying for you to go to college; and I'm not going to sit here and haggle with you over three hundred dollars in airfare for your mom to come see you play. At this salary you can afford pretty much anything you want. You play as well as I think you can play, and you'll make more. But this stuff isn't happening."

Bird, according to Red, looked at Woolf and nodded. The negotiations were over. Bird signed and went on to be one of the great players in the history of the league. His impact was remarkable. In his rookie season the Celtics went from 29–53 to 61–21. They lost in the Eastern Conference finals to the 76ers but clearly they were back. Then Cowens decided to retire, leaving Red with virtually no inside game to augment Bird.

That led to his greatest heist since the Russell / Ice-Capades deal.

Red had traded an aging Bob McAdoo to the Detroit Pistons and had gotten the Pistons' number one draft pick in the 1980 draft and M. L. Carr in return. The man Red made the trade with was Dick Vitale, who was coach and general manager of the Pistons at the time. Years later, after Vitale had become a wildly successful TV analyst and star, he told Red that if it wasn't for him, he wouldn't have become so rich and famous. "If I hadn't traded you the number one pick and Carr for McAdoo, I probably wouldn't have gotten fired," Vitale told Red. "I'd still be a mediocre coach somewhere if you hadn't fleeced me on that deal." In 1980 the Pistons, who would finish the season 16–66, were well on their way to the worst record in the Eastern Conference, meaning they would flip a coin with the worst team from the West for the number one pick in that spring's draft.

Red knew exactly who he wanted if he had the number one pick: Ralph Sampson. At the time, Sampson was a seven-foot-four freshman at the University of Virginia who appeared to be the game's next great big man. Even at his height, Sampson could handle the ball like a guard, had a soft shooting touch, and ran the floor, if not like Russell or Cowens, then remarkably well for a man his size. Even with Sampson on the team, Virginia struggled during the regular season and ended up in the NIT after failing to make the NCAA Tournament. Sampson finally got rolling in the NIT and the Cavaliers won the tournament, beating a good Minnesota team in the final in Madison Square Garden. Red was at that game and came away talking like a lovesick teenager about Sampson's potential. He was convinced he could get Sampson to leave Virginia after his freshman year for the chance to become a Celtic — and play next to Bird.

Virginia coach Terry Holland was pretty certain that Sampson, who had arrived on campus weighing a spindly 188 pounds
and had only reached 205 by the end of his freshman season,
wasn't ready to leave UVA and probably didn't want to leave at
that stage. Plus, he wasn't completely convinced that Red really wanted him, in spite of his public pronouncements.

"I remembered hearing a story about Red walking out in the
middle of a game Dave Cowens played at Florida State in
order to throw people off the scent that he wanted Cowens,"
Holland said. "So I wondered if he was talking Ralph up to
throw people off of what he was really up to."

Before taking the Virginia job in 1974, Holland had met Red
on several occasions years earlier when he had played and
coached under Lefty Driesell at Davidson. "I felt I knew him
well enough to at least give him a call, so I did," he said. "He
told me he was absolutely serious about wanting Ralph. I said if
he would guarantee that he would take Ralph with the pick and
pay him the kind of money a number one pick was making, I
would talk to Ralph about at least meeting with him and hearing what he had to say. He said he would pay him the same
kind of money he had paid Bird the year before. I thought that
was fair, so I told Ralph and his parents that I thought they
should meet with him because this was Red Auerbach we were
talking about."

Red flew to Charlottesville and met Holland. From there,
they drove one hour east to Harrisonburg, Sampson's hometown (but only after Red had asked Holland to recommend a

Chinese restaurant so he could eat before the visit). In addition to Red and Holland and Sampson and his mother and father, a professor from Virginia's law school was at the house.

"I knew, five minutes in, I had no chance," Red said. "Every time I tried to say something, the lawyer broke in and started giving the Sampsons five reasons why what I was saying made no sense.

"My pitch was simple and direct: this was a chance that wouldn't come again. We were a good team, a team that was going to contend for championships as soon as Ralph arrived. If he stayed in school, the chances were good he'd end up with a bad team where he had to be the Man from day one. We already had Bird, that would take pressure off. Plus, if he got hurt while he was still in college, all the money he was counting on was out the window. They were all very polite. I knew there was no chance before I walked out the door. But I gave it my best shot."

"I think Ralph was very impressed with Red," Holland said, years later. "He listened and what Red said made a lot of sense. But I also think he wanted more time to be in college and to grow, physically and emotionally." That sense proved true. Sampson ended up spending four years at UVA and, unlike most superstar athletes, graduated on time.

Not long after Red had learned that Sampson was staying at Virginia, Red got a call from someone at the University of Virginia School of Law. The law professor who had spent the evening in Harrisonburg contradicting Red had been very impressed with his presentation. Would he like to come down and address the law school's graduating class?

Red laughed. "I got four words for you," he said. "Not on your life."

Remember Red's motto: Forgive, but don't forget.

Sampson wasn't coming out. Red won the coin flip for the number one pick. He really liked Kevin McHale, the center at the University of Minnesota. But he was hearing rumblings that Golden State general manager Al Attles wanted to draft Joe Barry Carroll, the seven-foot center who had led Purdue to the Final Four that year. Red was convinced that McHale was a better player than Carroll, if only because he played much harder, but he wondered if Attles might be so desperate to get Carroll that he could make a deal that would allow him to get both McHale and another player.

The Warriors had a young center named Robert Parish who was still developing. Parish would in theory become expendable if the Warriors drafted Carroll to play the center position. So Red made a proposal: I'll give you the number one pick so you can take Carroll, and in return you give me your pick — the number three pick in the draft — and Parish, whom you aren't really going to need or want once you get Carroll.

Attles took the bait. He got Carroll, who went on to a mediocre NBA career, and Red ended up with two players who are now in the Hall of Fame. Parish played for the Celtics for fourteen years; McHale for thirteen. Thus, with two moves Red had returned the Celtics to power after back-to-back seasons in which they had won a total of sixty-one games. In 1981, with Bird and Parish starting up front and with McHale taking over the crucial sixth-man role, the Celtics won their fourteenth championship. Between 1981 and 1987 they won three titles and reached the finals on two other occasions. Their battles in the East with the Philadelphia 76ers and their classic confrontations with the Kareem Abdul-Jabbar and Magic Johnson–led Lakers in the West were what brought the NBA back to life.

Magic versus Larry took on a life of its own. Red had built and rebuilt. In 1986, when the team went 67–15 and won its sixteenth NBA title, he was in the process of rebuilding once again. Only it didn't happen because events that even Red couldn't control interceded.

8

Dark Days

THERE ARE TWO people Red has known whom he has no stories about. Never once will he begin a sentence with, "Did I ever tell you about Len Bias?" or with, "Did I ever tell you about Reggie Lewis?"

Both names bring a cloud to his face, a look of sadness. They are, without question, the two most tragic figures in the history of the Celtics.

In October of 1984, beginning the season as the defending league champions, the Celtics traded Gerald Henderson, a solid veteran point guard, to the Seattle Supersonics for their first round pick in the 1986 draft. This was classic Red, always looking a step ahead. He knew the Celtics were going to continue to be good for a while with the nucleus of Bird-McHale-Parish, and a year earlier he had added Dennis Johnson, an outstanding guard who had won a title in 1979 in Seattle. With Danny Ainge coming into his own, Red saw a chance to trade a twenty-nine-year-old player to a weak team for a number one pick.

Seattle came through for Red, going 31–51 and earning a place in the NBA draft lottery, then in its second year. To make things even better, the Sonics moved up to the number two slot in the lottery. Red was ecstatic. He knew the Cleveland Cavaliers, with the number one pick, were going to draft North Carolina center Brad Daugherty. That meant the Celtics could take Maryland's Len Bias.

Red probably knew Bias as well as he had ever known a college player. Lefty Driesell, Bias's coach at Maryland, was a good friend, and Red often went to practice at Maryland, in part because Driesell always had players with NBA potential and in part to see Lefty.

"Before they changed the rules I'd occasionally help Lefty when he was recruiting a player," he said. "I'd talk to him, maybe take him to dinner. I did it because Lefty thought it helped him with a kid but also because I would tell Lefty what I thought of the kid, if I thought he'd be someone he wanted in his program.

"I remember once he asked me to talk to a kid at practice. I talked to him for a while and there was no doubt in my mind the kid had his hand out. I told Lefty, 'Don't bother with that kid. He's going to ask you for money.' Lefty said there was no way, the kid had an uncle who was a doctor and he didn't need money. Sure enough, a few weeks later he calls and tells me the kid asked for money. He ended up going to one of those schools where everybody got paid."

When Red saw Bias, he was convinced he was looking at one of the great players he had ever seen. Bias was six-foot-eight, with guard quickness and a feathery jump shot. He could shoot off the dribble and jump so high it was almost impossible to block his shot. What's more, he had a great work ethic. Each year he was at Maryland, he got better.

"When I saw that Seattle was in the lottery, I fantasized that maybe they'd move up to where we could get Bias," Red said. "But that's all it was, a fantasy. Then they get the number two pick and I'm thinking, 'Oh my God, Bias and Bird together, we're going to be unbelievable.'"

Red had spent considerable time talking to Bias, in part because he wanted to be prepared in case he had a chance to draft him, but also because he liked the kid. "He was as nice as any kid you've ever met," Red said. "He was polite, he was a hard worker — I genuinely liked him. I probably would have drafted him if I didn't like him because he was so talented, but being the kind of kid that he was made it a no-brainer." On the night of the draft, Bias, who had told Red that it had been his dream as a kid to play for the Celtics, was in Boston, modeling his new Celtics uniform after the pick was formally announced. He flew home after the draft and, as everyone now knows, joined some friends to celebrate.

Shortly after 4:00 that morning, Red's phone rang. It was Driesell, sounding sick. "Something's happened," he told Red. "Leonard was at a party and he collapsed. He's at the hospital."

Red was, of course, stunned. What in the world would make a twenty-two-year-old kid in perfect shape collapse? Maybe, he thought — hoped — he'd just had too much to drink. But something in Driesell's voice told him it wasn't that simple. It wasn't long after the initial phone call that Driesell called back. His voice was a whisper. "He's gone," he said.

"It was one of those deals where you understand what has happened but you just can't believe it," Red said. "I mean I'd been with the kid a few hours earlier and he couldn't have been healthier or happier. I couldn't imagine what had happened."

He found out soon enough. Bias had overdosed on cocaine. To this day Red believes that Bias was either very inexperienced with the drug or had never used it before. "We tested him a week before the draft and he was clean as a whistle," he said. "The Knicks and Golden State had tested him too. Nothing. There was no indication from anyone I had talked to that he was involved with this sort of stuff at all. If that's true, if it was a onetime deal because he had realized his dream and wanted to do something like that with his friends, then it's even more tragic — if that's possible."

Stories that surfaced later indicated that Bias's drug use was not a onetime or a first-time thing. Red really doesn't like to talk about those stories. He only knows that Bias was someone he genuinely liked and he never saw any evidence that he was a drug user.

"I think it's very hard for people to understand what losing Bias did to our franchise. We were riding high. We'd just won another title and he was going to be the next generation, the way we'd always done it, bring in great young players to take the place of other great players as they got older. You aren't talking about an injury, you're talking about losing a guy who would have been an all-star for ten years — at least — and losing him in the worst possible way.

"But it wasn't just that. There was a pall cast. It was almost like a foreboding of doom. You know the old saying about bad things happening in threes? This was certainly one. We had always been the franchise where people were successful during basketball and after basketball. This wasn't supposed to happen to a Celtic."

The team was still very good the next couple years, even without Bias. The following year in the draft, another very good player Red was familiar with dropped into the Celtics' laps. Reggie Lewis was a talented guard from Northeastern University, someone Red had seen play during trips to Boston and during the summer when he was in Boston for his camp. Most basketball people had projected Lewis to be one of the first ten players taken in the 1987 draft, but he had played poorly in the predraft camp in Chicago and his stock had dropped.

"People didn't know he was sick that week," Red said. "He shouldn't even have played. But he didn't want the scouts to think he was chickening out, so he went and played anyway. A mistake for him, a break for us. You see, that's one of my big complaints with scouting today. These guys go to games all season, they go watch these guys practice, they talk to their coaches. Then they watch them play for two days in Chicago or for one day in a workout and they change their minds about them. If a guy is good in *games,* he's a good player. If a guy works hard in practice, that means he's going to work hard in practice. You never know if a guy is that good or that bad off a day or two in a camp. Suppose he's sick like Reggie? He'll look bad. Suppose the guy *guarding* him is sick, then he may look a lot better than he is. I really don't understand a lot of the scouting that goes on today."

When the Celtics' turn to pick in that draft came up at number twenty-two, Lewis still hadn't been chosen. Red took him immediately. "One of the easiest picks I ever made," he said. "We couldn't believe he was still there."

Red was almost seventy years old when the '87 draft was held, and times and the Celtics had changed. For years, Red had been the entire coaching staff and the entire front-office staff. The Celtics didn't have an assistant coach until 1972. But it was all different by the 1980s — and is, of course, entirely different now, when some teams have so many assistant coaches that a few of them have to sit *behind* the bench. Red had actually ceded the title of general manager to Jan Volk in 1984, allowing Volk to manage the day-to-day operations of the team. There were, by this time, scouts and assistant coaches who, along with the head coach, weighed in on who they thought could play and who they thought couldn't play. Red always listened, but he made his position clear about who had the final word.

"I would always say, 'Gentlemen, this is not a democracy. It is a dictatorship,'" he said. "That didn't mean you couldn't disagree with me — you could. But you were going to have to show me exactly why someone you liked was better than the person I liked."

Did it ever happen?

"Not very often."

If ever.

There was no doubting the soundness of the Lewis pick. He didn't play very much as a rookie, but when Bird went down with what would prove to be congenital back problems the following season, he stepped into the lineup and averaged 18.5 points per game. Even when Bird returned the next season, Lewis remained a vital cog. Bird's back (bad thing number two, according to Red) never allowed him to be the player he had been before the initial injury. He came back to play well, but by 1992 just getting onto the court had become a struggle for him. He retired at the end of that season. Lewis was chosen to succeed him as captain, an extraordinary honor given the names of the men who had preceded him: Bob Cousy, Bill Russell, John Havlicek, Dave Cowens, and Bird.

"It was natural for him to become captain," Red said. "He was outgoing, a natural leader, the kind of guy everyone liked and everyone looked to for leadership. I thought he would be our captain for the next ten years."

With Bird gone and McHale and Parish slowing down, the Celtics were a very different team in 1992–93, but still a solid one. They were 48–34 and went into their first-round play-off series against the Charlotte Hornets with the home-court advantage and as the favorites to advance.

In game one, Lewis was superb. Early in the second quarter, he had already scored seventeen points and the Celtics had burst to a big lead. But as he ran down the court on a fast break, Lewis suddenly stumbled for no apparent reason and collapsed in a heap. He had had a heart attack. The Celtics hung on to win that game but without Lewis lost the next three. The initial reports on Lewis were devastating: he had a congenital problem with his heart and would not be able to play basketball again.

Clearly, bad thing number three had happened. Only it got worse. "When I heard the initial medical report, I figured that was it, he just couldn't play again," Red said. "You can't take a chance with something like that. It's not like he broke an ankle or even had knee surgery. We're talking about heart disease."

But Lewis wasn't ready to stop being a basketball player. He found a doctor who told him it was okay for him to play again, that he would not be risking his life if he continued playing basketball, that his heart was healthy enough for him to play. A joyous press conference was held with the doctor, Gilbert Mudge, saying he saw no reason for Reggie not to play and with Lewis saying he planned to be on the court in his Celtics uniform opening night.

Red was skeptical. "I just didn't understand it," he said. "I was hoping he hadn't found a doctor who told him what he wanted to hear. I thought we would have to wait and see. But it made me nervous.

"I understand what the kid was feeling. He's a basketball player. The idea that you're twenty-seven years old and being told you can never play again is something that has to sound unacceptable to someone like that. All ballplayers are the same, especially when they're young; they think they're invulnerable."

Lewis was anything but. On July 27, a little less than three months after his collapse, he was playing pickup ball when he collapsed again. This time the heart attack was massive. He died that day.

In some ways, even though there had been warning that he had a health problem, his death shocked Boston and the Celtics even more than the death of Bias. Lewis was one of the family, he had played for six distinguished seasons with the team. He had been the team's *captain.* The Celtics were already heading in the wrong direction: McHale had retired at the end of the season; Parish was clearly near the end; Bird was already gone. And now this, the clear leader of the next generation, dead at the age of twenty-seven.

Even though he was spending less time in Boston and letting others make most of the decisions, Red was crushed. He was crushed for Lewis and his family but also crushed for his family — the Celtics. As with Bias, there were later allegations of drug use and there were also lawsuits, which just made the situation muddier and uglier. More than ten years later, it is still a subject Red doesn't like to linger on.

"There's no question about one thing," he said. "What happened to us the next few years started with Bias, got worse when Bird got hurt, and went over the top when Reggie died. Those are body blows to an organization. Bird was bad because it was an injury to one of the great players. Bias and Reggie were worse because two young men died and their families suffered a lot more than we did."

He paused and looked at his cigar for a moment. "One thing that makes me mad about all of it is the way the NBA handled it, especially Reggie. We had suffered, in both cases, the kind of loss you can't possibly anticipate and that is clearly, absolutely permanent. Never did anyone in the league think to offer us any kind of relief or help. In fact, in Reggie's case, they made us carry his salary against our cap even though he was dead.

"I still remember back in the sixties, when Walter Brown came up with the idea to try to help the Knicks with the extra draft choice and I said to him, 'Walter, there's going to come a day when the Celtics are going to need help from the league and I promise you we won't get it.' He didn't believe me. But that's exactly what happened. The Knicks were incompetent and the league went to help them. We were struck by tragedy and they never lifted a finger to help. I think a lot of people enjoyed seeing the Celtics finally suffer after all our years at the top. That still makes me angry.

"A couple of years after Reggie died, they changed the rule to say if you lost a player for an entire season you could replace him and spend a certain amount of money under the cap. They never talked about grandfathering us in at that point and we were still struggling big-time. Never. For that, I'll never forgive them."

※   ※   ※

Lewis's death marked the beginning of the worst period in the history of the Celtics. Not since the first four seasons that they existed had the team played as badly for such a long period of time. There were eight straight losing seasons, including a 15–67 year. The team made the play-offs once with a 35–47 record, then lost quickly in the first round — and never won more than thirty-six games in a season.

Red still held the title of team president at the time of Lewis's death, but he was well into his seventies by then and, even though those running the team still consulted with him on occasion, was only peripherally involved. That didn't mean he was any less emotionally involved. All the losing devastated him. Watching games on television was painful because he knew the team simply didn't have enough good players to seriously compete against the powers in the league.

Red's dictatorship had ended — with his approval — in 1990 with the hiring of Dave Gavitt, the former commissioner of the Big East and a man generally regarded as one of basketball's brightest minds, as executive vice president. Volk, the general manager, reported to him. Technically Gavitt reported to Red, but the understanding was that Gavitt was brought in to run the team.

One of Gavitt's first assignments was to hire a new coach. Jimmy Rodgers had been fired that spring after back-to-back first-round play-off eliminations. Gavitt, who had spent his entire professional career around the college game, wanted to bring in a great college coach: Duke's Mike Krzyzewski. Red thought it was a great idea.

"There are some college coaches, many in fact, who cannot adapt to the pro game," he said. "Their whole thing is their system. They bring in players and say, 'You will play *this* way,' even if their skills aren't right for playing that way. One thing I always noticed with Krzyzewski was that he changed the way he ran his offense every year based on the players he had. That's the kind of flexibility you need in the pros."

A meeting was set up. Krzyzewski would fly to Washington from Durham, Gavitt from Boston. They would meet quietly and discuss the job. "The only thing I had told Dave and Red was that I wanted to keep the thing quiet until it got serious, if it got serious," Krzyzewski said. "So I fly into the airport and Red meets me there. We walk to the curb and he's got this convertible parked out there with a license plate that says CELTIC on it. Every cop in the place knows him and they're saying as we get in the car, 'So, Red, you gonna hire Coach K?'

"That got us off to a good quiet start. Then we got to Blackie's Restaurant. Every single person in the place knows Red. I don't mean some of the people, I don't mean most of the people, I mean every single one."

"Nah, not true," Red said later. "A lot of people didn't know me."

"Maybe one," Krzyzewski said.

"The next three hours were as much fun as I can ever remember having in my life. You have to remember when I'm growing up in Chicago, we don't have an NBA team. I *loved* the Celtics, not just because they won but because of the way they played. You could tell, even just as a kid, that every guy on that team just wanted to win. There was no showboating, no pouting about getting the ball. Russell was their best player and he almost never touched the ball on offense. How many teams in history have been able to do *that?*

"I grew up thinking Red Auerbach was the greatest coach ever. Still think it. So here I am now sitting with him talking about coaching the Celtics. And he's telling me all these stories, smoking the cigar of course, and I'm wishing I could take a snapshot of this and put it up on my wall for people to see.

"It was an afternoon I'll never forget — even if it wasn't exactly quiet."

In the end, as much as the idea of coaching the Celtics and working for Red appealed to Krzyzewski and his boyhood basketball fantasies, he stayed at Duke. He had not yet won a national championship and felt as if he had unfinished business in that area. Plus, he has always believed that a college coach has more influence on the lives of his players than a pro coach, and that is important to him — as he proved again in the summer of 2004, turning down an $8-million-a-year offer from the Lakers.

"If it had been anyone other than the Celtics and Red, at that point in my career, I wouldn't even have gone up for the meeting," he said. "But because it was the Celtics and Red and Dave, whom I respect too, I had to listen. I even had to think about it. Red's a pretty convincing guy."

Although he was disappointed, Red understood Krzyzewski's decision. "Some guys should be in the college game," he said. "He's one of those guys."

The attempt to hire Krzyzewski was one of Red's last acts as a true final decision maker for the Celtics. He was seventy-three at the time and had willingly ceded his power to Gavitt, whom he liked and respected. As time went by, his life was more and more focused in Washington. Most mornings, he would go to his office in Northwest Washington, a few blocks from where he lived, and return phone calls and answer mail. From there he would go to lunch and then out to Woodmont for his daily card game.

By now Nancy had married, had a daughter, and in 1996 would become a grandmother — making Red a great-grandfather. Randy, Red's younger daughter, had moved to Hollywood to work in the movie business. She spent eighteen years working for Mel Brooks, another Brooklynite of Red's generation, before leaving to start her own production company.

"I remember once we were in LA on a trip and I took Bird in to meet Mel Brooks," Red said. "Mel loves basketball and he was all excited to meet Bird. He's performing, doing routines for him. Now Larry, getting him to smile is like getting the *Mona Lisa* to laugh. But Brooks was so funny he was holding his sides he was laughing so hard. I never saw him laugh that hard before or since."

Red had also reconnected with George Washington. When Stephen Trachtenberg became the school president in 1988, he and Bob Chernak, a university vice president, agreed that getting Red more involved with the school should be a priority. It wasn't as if he had been estranged — in fact he had always been quite loyal. But he wasn't actively involved.

The two men made it clear that they wanted Red to feel welcome, to feel he was a part of the place. This meant a lot to Red. "They were the ones who gave me my chance," he said. "Bill Reinhart promised me a scholarship and a chance, and he lived up to everything he promised. They were the ones that got me started."

In 1993 a plaque in Red's honor was unveiled outside the Smith Center, the building where the school plays its home basketball games. A banner was also unveiled inside the building. Trachtenberg and Chernak made occasional appearances at the lunch once it was expanded to include the GW group. Red was, unofficially, a close adviser to Mike Jarvis when he was GW's coach. This made perfect sense. Jarvis was a Boston guy, born and bred, had coached at Cambridge Rindge & Latin High School and then at Boston University before coming to GW.

"I would take him out to lunch [Chinese of course] and we would just talk," Red said. "I always felt that he wanted to know what I thought about things. That didn't mean he did everything I told him to, but there were times when I sensed he had taken my advice or when he told me that he had."

When Jarvis left to take the job at St. John's in 1998, he was replaced by Tom Penders, a very experienced coach who had been at Tufts, Columbia, Fordham, Rhode Island, and Texas before coming to GW. Penders occasionally came to lunch and was always deferential to Red, but he didn't seek him out the way Jarvis had. Red understood.

"He's been doing it a long time," he said. "He has his ideas about how to do things and I understand that. If he wants to talk, he knows I'm there and I'll help him any way I can. But I'm not gonna walk into his office and say, 'Here's what I think you should do.' I do that, I'm just another pain-in-the-ass alum."

Coincidence or not, Penders did not succeed at GW. He recruited too many kids who were academic risks and too many kids who got into trouble off the court. In April 2001 he was forced to resign. He was replaced by Karl Hobbs, a young coach who had been an assistant under Jim Calhoun at Connecticut for eight years. Knowing that Hobbs might be shy about asking Red for advice, Jack Kvancz, the athletic director who had hired him, made certain the two of them got together. Red had, of course, been paying close attention to Hobbs and his team since he almost never misses a home game.

"You have to understand where you are in your career," he told Hobbs over lunch (still Chinese, of course) one day. "You are not Jim Calhoun. You don't have his résumé yet. That means you can't jump up and down or get on the referees the way he does. You have to earn their respect and the respect of everyone else by winning and by behaving in a certain way. You'll do it, but remember, you haven't done it yet."

Hobbs tried. His instincts are to be extremely animated during a game. He was a tiny (five-foot-eight) hyperaggressive point guard as a player and that aggressiveness often comes out during games. There are moments when the GW person doing the most running and jumping while time is in is the young coach on the sidelines. During one game last season, as Hobbs jumped up and down in agony over his team's failures, Red

Red's college team. Red is in the back row, third from the left, next to coach Bill Reinhart. (COURTESY OF RED AUERBACH)

Zang the marine and Red the sailor. (COURTESY OF RED AUERBACH)

The Washington Caps, circa 1947. Front row, l to r: Sonny Hertzberg, Marty Passaglia, Bob Feerick, Irv Torgoff, Dick O'Keefe, Fred Scolari. Back row, l to r: Red, Doc Lantz, John Norlander, John Mahnken, Bones McKinney, Paul Rothgeb. "About three hundred bucks worth of phone calls to put the team together." (COURTESY OF RED AUERBACH)

Red's first NBA championship team, the 1956–57 Celtics. Front row, l to r: Lou Tsioropoulos, Andy Phillip, Frank Ramsey, Red, Bob Cousy, Bill Sharman, Jim Loscutoff. Back row, l to r: Walter A. Brown, Dick Hemric, Jack Nichols, Bill Russell, Arnie Risen, Tommy Heinsohn, Harvey Cohn, Lou Pieri. (COURTESY OF RED AUERBACH)

Red and Bill Russell go after Sid Borgia during a game against the Cincinnati Royals in 1960. Borgia was one of the refs that Red *liked*. (AP WIREPHOTO)

Red with his favorite owner, Walter Brown, shortly before Brown's death in 1964. (COURTESY OF RED AUERBACH)

Red with Bob Cousy in 1963 — the local yokel he didn't really want. (COURTESY OF RED AUERBACH)

Red and Bill Russell in 1967, the year Red made Russell the first African-American to coach a major professional team. (DANNY GOSHTIGIAN / *BOSTON GLOBE*)

Red and Dorothy in 1985. (JIM WILSON)

The China Doll gang, June 2004: Seated from l: Arnold Heft, Pete Dowling, Reid Collins, Stanley Copeland, George Solomon, Rob Ades, John Feinstein, Red, Lefty Driesell, Hymie Perlo, Joe McKeown, Herman Greenberg. Standing from l: Jack Kvancz, Bob Campbell, Murray Lieberman, Chris Wallace, Stanley Walker, Aubre Jones. (PHIL HOFMANN)

Red with three things he loves: a Celtics cap, a cigar, and a convertible.
(JOEL RICHARDSON / *WASHINGTON POST*)

Red at his eightieth . . . (COURTESY OF RED AUERBACH)

Red's eightieth birthday party in 1997. Cigars for all the Celtics.
(Courtesy of Red Auerbach)

Red with his favorite Knicks fan, NBA commissioner David Stern.
(Steve Lipofsky)

Red and Don Casey flank President Bill Clinton in the Oval Office on the day Red took over the White House in 1995. (OFFICIAL WHITE HOUSE PHOTO)

Red and Red in Faneuil Hall. (COURTESY OF RED AUERBACH)

Bill Russell prepares to lift the number 2 into the rafters (Walter Brown, *not* Cardinal Cushing, was number 1) in Red's honor. John Havlicek, whose number 17 is on the banner, stands behind Russell's shoulder. (STEVE LIPOFSKY)

turned to a couple of people sitting with him and said, "Is coaching really *that* hard?"

No one at GW listens to Red more than Kvancz. Again, there is a connection. Kvancz grew up in Bridgeport, Connecticut, the son of a fanatic Celtics fan. He was a good high school basketball player, good enough that Bob Cousy, then coaching at Boston College, came to his house to recruit him.

"Now, you have to picture this visit," Kvancz said. "Cooz coming to the house is no different to my father than God himself coming — unless maybe Red had come. And he brings with him this great-looking young priest from BC who my mother is immediately in love with. I was being recruited by some pretty good schools. Duke was interested, Holy Cross, South Carolina. After the home visit, though, it was over. Between Cooz and the priest, I had absolutely no choice but to go to BC."

While he was at BC, Kvancz got a chance to meet Red and the Celtics because they would often come to practice at the school. Even back then, Kvancz could tell that Red was not someone to be messed with. "I can tell you for a fact that the guy you see now has mellowed a *lot*," he said. "I mean he was a tough SOB. He knew exactly what he wanted and he knew when he wanted it, and if it didn't get done, you better watch out. Every once in a while, though, Cooz would get him to talk to our team and it was absolutely great. The guy knew exactly what to say to college kids to get us fired up to play. Of course if he had been reading from the *Farmers' Almanac* I would have thought it was brilliant."

While he was in college, Kvancz was able to get into Celtics games for a dollar with a student discount. "We played a lot of games in the Garden back then," he said. "Plus, all the ushers knew Cooz anyway. The only problem was, we'd walk in, grab great seats, and when the people came who had actually paid for them, we had to move upstairs. Still, it was the greatest deal in the world."

Kvancz was a good college player, averaging fifteen points a game in 1968, his senior season. He played semipro ball in the Eastern League for several years — for the late, lamented Hamden Bics (sponsored by the pen company) — driving to games on weekends for $200 a night while he was teaching and coaching at Masik High School. "My boldest move was to try to get Mike Gminski [later a star at Duke and a fourteen-year NBA player] onto the varsity when he was in the seventh grade. Didn't work. They said he couldn't do it. He was already six-eight at the time."

Kvancz went from Masik to Brown as an assistant coach, then moved to Washington in the late 1970s as the head coach at Catholic. He was hired for the specific purpose of taking the school from Division 2 to Division 1, with the promise of a new gym to bolster the program. "Every year I recruited by telling guys they would play in the new gym before they graduated," he said. "Of course it never happened."

Even though Catholic had some success in Division 1 — including a remarkable triple-overtime upset of a final-eight-bound St. Joseph's team in 1980 — a new president arrived and decided to go in the opposite direction, taking Catholic to

Division 3. A new gym did eventually get built, but it was much smaller than what Kvancz had envisioned, since it was for a Division 3 program. By that time he was long gone, having taken the job as athletic director at George Mason, a commuter school in Northern Virginia. Mason *did* get the new gym it had been promised — it didn't hurt that it was a state school and the building was built with state funds — and the program flourished, reaching the NCAA Tournament in 1989 for the first time in school history. In 1994 the George Washington job opened and Kvancz was hired.

"I had seen Red at games after I came to the Washington area," he said. "Whenever I was at GW I'd see him, but he was at other games too. He remembered me because I'd played for Cooz and because he remembers everyone he's ever met. But it was after I got to GW that we really became close."

By the time Kvancz got to GW, Red was regularly playing racquetball with Aubre Jones several days a week. "He would finish playing, come into my office, light a cigar, and we'd just sit and talk for a while," Kvancz said. "It helped that I knew all the names of all the Celtics and that I was familiar with a lot of the stories because Cooz would tell them to us. One day the lights went out in practice and he just sat there for two hours telling us old Celtic stories. So I knew a lot. That made him comfortable.

"One morning we're sitting there and he says to me, 'Come on, we're going.' I asked where and he looked at me like I was nuts and said, 'China Doll. Lunch.' I thought maybe my watch was broken because it was ten-thirty. But you don't argue with

Red. I got in the car and went with him and I've been going ever since. I'm the same as everyone else in the group: if something comes up that forces me to miss, I'm really annoyed. It is one of the few things I do in my life where I know — *know* — I'm going to walk out of the place in a better mood than when I walked in. That's just the way it is."

Red may not be aggressive about telling Kvancz's coaches what to do, but he isn't the least bit shy about telling Kvancz what to do, regardless of the subject.

"My first year as AD, he comes over to me at our first home game. He says to me, 'You got a problem here.' Now, we have a good team. We've just gone to the NCAA Tournament for the second straight year. So I can't imagine what he's talking about. I say, 'Problem, Coach? What's the problem?'

"He says, 'Your hot dogs aren't any good.' I think maybe he's joking. He's not joking. The hot dogs aren't any good. Red loves to eat a hot dog during a game. But he wants to eat a *good* hot dog. So I come up with this idea. I get five different kinds of hot dogs and I bring him into the student union for a taste test. We made a big deal of it, had people there to watch, the whole thing.

"He comes in, tastes all the hot dogs, and picks the one he likes. So we make a deal with that hot dog company to provide our hot dogs. First game with the new hot dogs, he comes over to me again. 'You still got a problem with the hot dogs,' he says. I ask what the problem could be — *he* picked the hot dogs. 'They're not hot,' he says. 'A hot dog has to be *hot* to be any good.' I say to him, 'Coach, we don't have the equipment to cook the hot dogs in the building. They have to be cooked someplace else, then wrapped up and brought in. We can't really get them any hotter than they are.'

"He looks right at me and says, 'Sterno. Get that Sterno thing. It keeps food hot.' Now, what am I going to do, invest in Sterno for the whole building? I can't afford that. So I come up with an idea. I get Sterno put into the AD's Club and tell Red to get his hot dogs in there. That way they'll be hot. *Finally* he's happy with that."

The AD's Club is a room in the Smith Center reserved for the school's boosters. A pregame reception is held there, complete with food and drinks (and Sterno), and desserts are served at halftime. Red is, as you might expect, the star of the AD's Club whenever he comes in. But at one point he told Kvancz he wasn't going to come anymore.

"*What?*" Kvancz said. "I got the Sterno for the hot dogs —"

"Yeah, that's great," Red said. "But you walk in there and everyone stands around eating and drinking. I can't do that. I'm too damn old."

So Kvancz came up with another idea. In the middle of the AD's Club there is a round table. Before every game there is a sign that says, RESERVED FOR RED AUERBACH. Red will come in with whomever has joined him at the game that night — frequently members of the Tuesday lunch group — and hold court at that table until just before game time.

Has anyone ever complained about the one reserved table in the room?

"Are you kidding?" Kvancz said, laughing. "Every once in a

while, when Red doesn't come to a game, I tell people to go ahead and sit there. They won't do it. It's like a shrine."

Once Kvancz had Red squared away with the hot dogs and the table, he thought maybe he might have some peace.

No way.

"The anthem," he said. "He wouldn't let up about the anthem."

Red is a navy veteran and, having traveled overseas as much as he has, very patriotic and proud of his country. Once upon a time, every team in every sport stood at attention during the playing of the national anthem. That changed in basketball with the takeover of the sports world by TV. Almost always, television producers do not want to show the playing of the anthem. (That changed for a while after 9/11 but has been a general trend for most of the last twenty years.) As a result, the anthem is almost always scheduled for ten to fifteen minutes prior to the introduction of the starting lineups. Coaches got into the habit of taking their teams to the locker room just prior to the playing of the anthem for their final instructions.

Red was incensed.

"It's wrong," he said. "The anthem should be played after the lineups are introduced and with both teams out there. What is it going to do, kill them to stand there for two minutes? It's an absolute insult. I wouldn't tolerate it."

Red climbed all over Kvancz on the topic. Kvancz would nod and agree and nothing would change because as much as he would like to go to the coaches and TV producers and say, "We're doing it this way because Red says we should do it this way," he can't. "Actually the problem wasn't with my team," he said. "I *could* tell my coach to do it that way. It was the visiting coach. If you have one team out there and not the other, it really looks bad."

Red did understand that. He had also lectured John Thompson, then the coach at Georgetown, on the subject. Finally, Thompson did keep his team on the court for the anthem. The visitors did not and Thompson felt the other team had been embarrassed.

Only after 9/11, with the wave of patriotism, did TV push back the playing of the anthem so that the teams would be on court when it was played. Some schools have slid back since then, but GW has continued to play the anthem after player introductions with both teams on the court. All of which makes Red happy. Sort of.

"It shouldn't have taken that sort of tragedy to get it done," he said. "But at least now at my school they're doing the right thing."

And GW is Red's school. Of that there is very little doubt.

The Celtics, returning to the practice of employing ex–team members, ended up hiring Chris Ford in the spring of 1990. Ford had been a solid NBA player, had been a part of the 1981 championship team, and had coached in the NBA previously — something that made him different than the other ex-Celtics who had coached the team (except for K. C. Jones, who had succeeded Fitch and won two titles in '84 and '86).

Ford did well until Lewis's death and then became a part of the team's spiral. M. L. Carr replaced him in 1995 and did even worse, bottoming with the 15–67 season in 1997. Paul Gaston, who had become the team's owner in 1992, felt he had to do something radical to turn things around. As Gavitt and Red had done, he looked to the college ranks.

Krzyzewski had finally won the national championship — two, in fact, in 1991 and 1992 — but he was no longer the hot college coach, having gone through serious health problems in 1995. The unquestioned star of the college game at that moment was Rick Pitino, who had rebuilt the University of Kentucky's program after an embarrassing NCAA probation, taking the Wildcats to three Final Fours in five seasons, winning the national championship in 1996, and then losing the championship game in overtime to Arizona in 1997.

What's more, Pitino had NBA experience — he had coached the New York Knicks for two seasons in the late 1980s — and he was still a hero in New England, having taken Providence to the Final Four in 1987. Of course Pitino insisted he had no intention of leaving Kentucky (just as he had insisted he had no intention of leaving Providence right before taking the job in New York), and Gaston knew he would have to make Pitino an offer he couldn't refuse.

He did. Pitino was offered $10 million a year and absolute power. He would be the CEO, the general manager, and the coach, and if he wanted he could probably call play-by-play on the telecasts. In many ways it was similar to the power Red had wielded in the fifties and sixties, the differences being the salary and the fact that Pitino would have innumerable minions to do his bidding. Red had a trainer.

Red told Gaston he thought the idea of hiring Pitino to coach — at any price — was a good one. "The guy's a hell of a coach," he said, "at any level." There was one caveat: Red was concerned about Pitino's insistence on complete control, not because it bothered him in principle but because he believed that in the NBA of the nineties it was too much to ask of one man. "If you look at the guys who have tried to do it without help," he said, "they don't usually succeed. I have no problem with the idea of one guy being the ultimate decision maker when there are disputes, but you can't be the be-all and end-all today. When I did it, there were ten teams in the league and no one had scouting staffs. It's a different world."

The only way to get Pitino was to put him in charge of everything. Red understood. Gaston was pretty close to desperate. The team had become an embarrassment. But before Gaston could seal the deal, Pitino had one more demand: he wanted absolute power not just in fact but in name also. He wanted to be president of the team. The Celtics had a team president: his name was Arnold (Red) Auerbach. He had held the title since 1970.

Red had absolutely no intention of trying to tell Pitino how to run the team. He had taken the approach for several years that he was there if the people in charge of day-to-day operations wanted to consult with him, but he wasn't going to give advice he had not been asked for. But when Gaston called to tell him that Pitino had demanded the president's title and he had given it to him, Red was hurt.

"Paul handled the situation as well as it could have been handled," he said. "The first words out of his mouth were, 'I've made a mistake.' He told me how sorry he was but that he had made this commitment to Pitino. I wasn't going to make a big deal out of it, that's not my way. And I knew he was genuinely sorry. The guy has done a lot of very good things for me, a lot of things he didn't have to do, so I wasn't about to give him a hard time about it. But it did hurt me. And even though I tried not to think less of him for it, I did think less of Pitino. I simply couldn't understand why he had to have the *title*. He had the money, he had the power, why did he have to have the title too?"

Anyone who knows Pitino knows the answer to that question. Pitino has an ego slightly larger than the state of Kentucky. Even though he was hurt by what had happened, Red's attitude was pretty much the same as that of everyone in the city of Boston: if Pitino won, he could have the title King of the World for all he cared. He told Pitino he was available anytime he wanted to talk but wouldn't think of making a suggestion unless asked.

Pitino arrived in Boston riding on a white horse, the savior of the franchise. His timing, it seemed, was perfect. With the worst record in the NBA that season, the Celtics were likely to get the first pick in the draft when the lottery was held, and everyone knew that Wake Forest's Tim Duncan, the kind of gifted big man not seen in Boston since the departures of McHale and Parish, would be the first pick.

Pitino coaching, Duncan playing. The Celtics would be back again, and Pitino, president / CEO / coach / God, would be drenched in glory. No one hoped it would happen more than the ex-president of the Celtics, the new vice chairman of the board.

9

Expanding the Circle

"I EVER TELL YOU about the time I met Clinton and Gore? Nice guys. Both basketball fans. Boy, that Clinton really liked to talk basketball. I couldn't get a word in edgewise."

Actually, Pete Dowling tells the Clinton-Gore story better than Red simply because Red is too modest to give it full flavor. "Let me put it this way," Dowling likes to say. "He brought the entire White House to a standstill."

Dowling first met Red in the summer of 1995. By then, he had been in the Secret Service for nineteen years and was one of the special agents in charge of President Clinton's protective detail. Don Casey, then a Celtics assistant coach, was a friend of his. One of Dowling's fellow agents, Joe Conlin, had been a team manager for Casey when he coached at Bishop Eustis High School in Camden, New Jersey. "Joe is six-foot-six," Dowling said. "You would think at that size he would make a great power forward. Actually at that size he made a great manager."

Dowling had met Casey through Conlin when he and Conlin were still in college at Mount St. Mary's in the early 1970s. In the early 1980s, John McDonald, another agent who had once been Gary Williams's teammate and roommate at Maryland, made frequent trips to Philadelphia to scout for Williams, who was coaching at Boston College. Casey was by then the coach at Temple, and Dowling spent time with him whenever he was in Philadelphia. A friendship grew.

In the summer of 1995, Casey was coming to Washington to play in a charity golf outing that had been set up as a fundraiser for families of the victims of the bombing in Oklahoma City. Dowling had been asked to round up some silent auction items, and one of the people he had called was Casey.

"So he knew I was around that weekend," Dowling said. "On Wednesday I get a voice mail from him saying he's coming to town Thursday and he's going to have lunch with Red. He knew I would do almost anything to meet Red Auerbach. He also knew that if I mentioned that I wanted to bring Red Auerbach to the White House mess for lunch, it probably would not be a problem getting a table."

A table was no problem. In fact, a private room was no problem since the guy in charge of the mess at the time was a lifelong Celtics fan. Red and Casey and Dowling were ushered to the room and had a nice quiet lunch until someone came in to tell them that Vice President Gore had heard that Red

Auerbach was in the building. Did the coach have a few minutes to come by and see the vice president?

Of course he did. Red, Casey, and Dowling made their way up to Gore's office. A lively basketball discussion ensued. Gore was especially fascinated by the fact that Red had started his coaching career at his alma mater — St. Albans. On went the conversation until it was interrupted by a phone call. President Clinton had now heard that Red was in the building and *he* wanted to see him.

So Red, Casey, and Dowling bid their farewells to Gore and headed for the Oval Office. Casey was now, according to Dowling, visibly excited. He was on the President's Council on Physical Fitness and Sports, and he was now going to get a few minutes to talk to the president about some of his ideas.

No chance.

"The president just wanted to talk ball with Red," Dowling said. "He wanted to know about the Celtics, about the old Celtics, about what Red thought about some college players. On and on. A couple of times someone buzzed in to tell him that his two o'clock appointment was waiting outside."

Red remembers that part of it. "I was getting a little embarrassed," he said. "I finally said to him, 'Mr. President, I can't tell you how honored and proud I am. Here I am, a kid from Brooklyn, a basketball coach, and the president of the United States has delayed his schedule a few minutes to talk to me. But I do understand, you've got a lot of work to do.'"

To which Clinton replied, "We've got a few more minutes."

It was around 2:30 by the time Red and Dowling convinced Clinton it was perhaps time for them to leave. Casey wanted to stay. He still had agenda items to discuss. "I had to get Case out of there or the president wouldn't have seen *anyone* on his schedule the rest of the day," Dowling said.

The three men thanked the president for his time and courtesy and finally left the Oval Office. As they were leaving, Red noticed the man waiting in the outer office. He looked familiar. Then he realized who it was: Bill Gates.

For a solid thirty minutes Bill Gates had sat and waited because the president of the United States wanted to talk some ball with the old basketball coach.

For Dowling, the entire day was a thrill. He was accustomed to being around the president and the vice president since he had worked for the Secret Service beginning in 1976. But hanging out with Red Auerbach was a different story.

"The Celtics were always the ultimate *team* to me, and Red was the ultimate coach," he said. "Then I became a mediocre basketball player in high school, so Red and the Celtics were the pinnacle to me, even though I was from New York."

Dowling was actually a good deal better than mediocre when he played at Xavier High School. He was recruited by Mount St. Mary's, which was then a Division 2 power under coach Jim Phelan. In those days, there was no such thing as a letter of intent in Division 2. Dowling was actually recruited by a friend of Phelan's, who did bird-dog work for him in the New York / New Jersey area.

"The deal was simple," he said. "I was told I'd be allowed to try out for the team, and if I made it, I'd be on scholarship. If not, I'd be in school but my parents would have to pay my way."

What Dowling didn't know was that the Mount was loaded at the time, with four players who would eventually spend some time in the NBA, including Fred Carter, who would become a starter for the Philadelphia 76ers and Baltimore Bullets. "They were really, really good," Dowling said. "I wasn't surprised when I got cut. But I was crushed." He tried out again as a sophomore and was cut again. "After that I got the message," he said.

It was while he was at the Mount that Dowling began to think about law enforcement as a career. He started off as an accounting major, then switched to English — "because it was as far away from accounting as I could possibly get." It was a television show that made Dowling think he might want to pursue a career chasing bad guys.

"No Secret Service man should admit this," he said, "but my first goal was to join the FBI. Back when I was growing up they had the TV show on Sunday nights, the old Efrem Zimbalist Jr. show, and I thought what they did looked exciting. I liked the idea of catching bad guys. So when I got out of college, that was what I was thinking."

Neither the FBI nor the Secret Service hire many people directly out of college. Knowing that, Dowling went to work as a policeman in Montgomery County, Maryland. While he was there, he kept in touch with another college buddy, Pat O'Carroll, who had interned with and was later hired by the Secret

Service. It was O'Carroll who convinced Dowling to apply to the Secret Service.

"My friends like to tell me I got my job through Squeaky Fromme and Sara Jane Moore," he said. "They both made attempts on President Ford in 1975, and as a result the Secret Service was authorized to hire four hundred more people in 1976. I was one of those people."

Dowling began his career, as all Secret Service officers do, in a field office: Philadelphia. In 1979 he was assigned out of Philadelphia to protect a presidential candidate (all visiting foreign dignitaries and candidates for president are assigned their protection out of field offices) for the first time. It wasn't just any candidate, though. It was Ted Kennedy.

"You couldn't treat him the way you treated most candidates, where you were careful, but not paranoid," he said. "This guy had already had two brothers killed, and you had to think of him as a potential target at all times. I had great respect for the way he and his family handled all that and the way they dealt with us. I was with him for almost a year — September of 1979 until noon on the day after the 1980 convention."

Years later, when Dowling was assigned to then Governor and eventually President Bill Clinton, he crossed paths with Kennedy again. The Clintons visited Martha's Vineyard during a summer vacation in 1993 and spent some time with the Kennedys and with Jacqueline Kennedy Onassis.

"We were up on the bridge of a yacht one afternoon and Senator Kennedy came up there," he remembered. "It was just President Clinton and me up there. He came in and said to the president, 'I want to tell you something: pay attention to these guys' — pointing at me — 'because they have no agenda other than taking care of you.' I really appreciated hearing him say that."

Dowling had moved to the Washington office after his days in Philadelphia and was on Vice President Bush's detail for four years before being assigned to the intelligence division out of Cleveland. He was there in 1992 when he originally got the call to join the long-shot candidate from Arkansas, Bill Clinton.

"I was his first agent," Dowling said. "The first three days we were together, we barely exchanged a word. He was campaigning up in New England. On the fourth day, we were in an airport terminal in Portland, Maine. The governor was having a meeting in the airport with [George] Stephanopoulos and [James] Carville before heading to his campaign stops that day. They were inside a secure room and I was just outside. There was a family there waiting to fly to Disney World. The little boy was a Make-a-Wish Foundation child, and I just started talking to him. My kids were all in his age range at the time.

"The governor came out and we got in a car to go to the campaign stops. That night, coming back to the airport, it was just he and I in the car. He put his hand on my shoulder and said, 'You've got kids, don't you? I could tell seeing you with that little boy in the airport.' After that, we had a great relationship. He was someone you really could sit around and talk to. I always felt comfortable with him. More important, I hope he felt comfortable with me."

When Clinton was elected, Dowling — who had been re-assigned to the Washington office by then anyway — was made assistant agent in charge of the Presidential Protective Division. "It was a challenge," he said, smiling and knowing the wisecracks that come with having been so close to Clinton for almost five years. "President Clinton was younger and more active [insert wise crack here] than Presidents Reagan and Bush. They both liked quiet time at Camp David. He rarely went there. He liked getting out. I can remember once at Martha's Vineyard we had to plead with him not to go out for ice cream one Saturday night because it would have brought the town to a halt. One of the other guys went out and got the ice cream for him."

The one tough moment Dowling remembers from those years came on a Sunday morning in 1995. He was sitting at the breakfast table at 5:30 a.m. reading the newspaper, preparing to go into the White House because a supervisor always had to be in early on Sundays in case the president decided to go out for a run. He was glancing through *Parade* magazine when he came upon a gossip item in the Personality section that claimed the Clintons were going to separate later in the year and Hillary Clinton was going to challenge the president in the Democratic Primary the next year. The information, according to the item, came from "Secret Service sources."

Dowling felt sick to his stomach. "We cannot do our job if we don't have the complete trust of the first family," he said. "It's that simple. Someone puts out an item like that and says it comes from the Secret Service, it gives them immediate credibility. We're a White House institution, people trust us. That was the first time anything like that ever happened to us. I knew it wasn't true, but that didn't matter; it was out there."

Later that day, Clinton called Dowling into the Oval Office and handed him the magazine. "Did you see this?" he asked.

"Yes, sir, I did," Dowling answered. "Seeing it was very painful and I'm embarrassed, but don't you think if someone was going to do something like that, they would put something out there that would be just a little bit believable?"

That seemed to break the tension. Clinton said he understood and never brought it up again. Dowling was relieved, but the memory of that morning remains vivid — even now in retirement. If Clinton didn't completely forgive him that morning, he probably did the day Dowling showed up at the White House mess for lunch with Red Auerbach.

On that day, when they finally left the Oval Office and the White House, Dowling dropped Casey off at his hotel, then gave Red a ride home. When they pulled up to the house, Red told Dowling he wanted to give him something. "Next thing I know, things come flying out of his trunk," he said. "He's got stuff in there all the time. I got a Wheaties box he'd been on, some Celtics stuff, some things for my kids. On and on. Then he turns to me and says, 'Listen, there's a group of us that goes to lunch on Tuesdays at the China Doll downtown. If you can make it next week, come on by. It's at eleven o'clock.'"

Like everyone else, Dowling was a bit nonplussed by the 11:00 a.m. starting time but was thrilled to be asked. He said he would be there. "I walked in and there were all these old guys," he said. "I didn't really know anybody. I certainly recognized Morgan and I recognized Jack Kvancz's name. But that was about it. I just sat there awestruck the whole time, thinking, 'Wait till I tell people I got to have lunch with Red Auerbach.' I thanked him for inviting me, told him it really meant a lot. He gave me the 'aah, forget about it' routine that he does when you try to thank him for something."

Dowling also made the same mistake many people make: he assumed the invitation had been a onetime thing. A week later, on Tuesday night, Dowling's phone rang at home. He recognized the voice right away.

"Where the hell were you?"

"I was supposed to be somewhere?"

"At the restaurant for the luncheon."

"I didn't know I was invited again."

"Well, you are. See you next Tuesday."

Even after he had become a regular, Dowling wasn't certain if he was truly welcome. One day he asked Alvin Miller, a friend of Red's from Woodmont, if it was really okay for him to be there. "I don't want to intrude," he said. "I wonder if Red tells me to come just to be polite because of that one day at the White House —"

"Are you kidding?" Miller said. "That's not his way. He likes having you around. Gives him another target."

By then, Red had started giving Dowling a hard time whenever he got the chance about the work the Secret Service did. The movie *Air Force One*, in which one of the bad guys turned out to be a Secret Service agent, delighted him. "Now," he declared to Dowling one day, "we find out the truth about the Secret Service."

"I got used to being zinged," Dowling said. "If he didn't zing me when I came in, I worried that maybe something was wrong with him."

Red and Dowling became close over the next seven years. Dowling brought his son, Stephen, to GW games and reveled in the notion that the boy was getting pointers from Red Auerbach. "All those years I coached him and now he's sitting there learning the game from Red," he said. "I couldn't help but be thrilled by that." On another occasion Red invited Stephen Dowling and his chauffeur (Pete) to his house to see all his memorabilia. Stephen wanted to know how many championship rings Red had.

"He takes Stephen back to where he keeps them," Pete Dowling remembered, "and pulls all sixteen out, one by one, and tells Stephen the story of each one. What an amazing experience."

Red absolutely adores kids. It is a side of him few people ever get to see. He dotes on his three great-grandchildren and clearly enjoys telling his stories to kids every bit as much as — if not more than — he enjoys telling them to adults.

One night Dowling brought his mother, who is three years older than Red, to a GW game. Each had been through open-heart surgery not long before and they compared notes on the ordeal. At game's end, Cecile Dowling bolted downstairs to say hello to George Blaney, the former Holy Cross coach, whom she had spotted (his son was a GW assistant at the time).

"Red turned around and Mom was gone," Dowling remembered. "She was about eighty-four at the time. We saw her downstairs and Red shook his head and said, 'Man, I'd like to have her on the good side of a fast break.'"

The only thing Dowling could never get out of Red were plays to teach the youth basketball teams he coached — he has two daughters in addition to Stephen and coached all three of his children as kids. "Every year I coached I asked him for plays, and he'd tell me to read his book, that all the plays I wanted were in there. But I wanted him to give me something different, something no one else had, so I kept asking. Finally, my last year coaching the kids, he said he was going to sit down and do it. He never did. I think he figured if I couldn't get it from the book, I wasn't going to get it."

Dowling did get Red to speak at a Secret Service graduation ceremony in 1997. "I remember walking in with him and everyone just kind of hung back a little bit because they were in awe of him," he said. "I was thinking, 'It's amazing that I'm actually friends with someone who is held in such high respect by so many people.' But he's great in those situations, putting people at ease. He said, 'Hey, anybody mind if I smoke?' Of course no one minded. He lit a cigar, chatted everyone up.

"His speech was terrific. He talked about the kind of commitment you make when you join the Secret Service and how much he respects everyone who takes on that kind of commitment. Then at one point he says, 'You know, the one thing I know for sure is that it takes a big set of balls to do what you people do.' I'm sitting next to the assistant director — who is a woman — and she leans over to me and says, 'Well, now I know what to ask Santa for this Christmas.' "

Red also spoke at Dowling's retirement party in the spring of 2002. After twenty-six years, he retired to take a high-paying job in New York working for AXA Securities as the head of their security division. Not only was Red there but the whole China Doll gang as well, seated at a round table. The only thing missing was the chow mein.

"Let me tell you one thing," Red said to the crowd, almost all of them Secret Service agents other than the China Doll group and Dowling's family, "I don't exactly know what Pete's going to be doing on this new job, but I do know one thing for sure: he'll do a hell of a job at it."

Dowling knew that through all the ribbing and teasing, this was the way Red felt about him. "It meant so much to me for him to be there that night," he said. "But also for the whole lunch group to be there. I feel like I've been part of an exclusive club, one that has certain coding that only those inside the club really understand. In that sense it isn't unlike being in the Secret Service. I know that if I was ever in need of help or ever in trouble, I would have twelve instant allies.

"Since I started this job, I try to schedule a meeting every Tuesday at eleven. I want to be busy then, distracted, so I'm not thinking about what I'm missing."

One Tuesday, Dowling called Rob Ades's cell phone during lunch. The phone was passed around the table until it finally reached Red. "Hey, Pete," Red said. "They paying you all that money to sit around all day and BS with us?"

"No doubt about it," Zang said, shaking his head. "Red really misses Pete."

Red really did forgive Paul Gaston for ceding his president's title to Pitino, in large part because he genuinely liked Gaston and because Gaston had gone out of his way to make certain that Red still felt as if he were an important part of the Celtics even after he had stepped away from day-to-day involvement.

"I've been through a lot of owners," Red said. "The greatest of them was Walter Brown. Since then I've had good ones and bad ones. Paul Gaston was one of the good ones."

Red has, in fact, dealt with fifteen different owners during his fifty-four-year association with the Celtics. "When I first came in back in 1950, Walter Brown was almost broke," he remembered. "If he hadn't been able to talk Lou Pieri [who had previously owned the ill-fated Providence Steam Rollers for three seasons] into putting up fifty thousand dollars and coming in with him, we might not have made it through that first season. As it was, there were times when I had to reach into my pocket to pay bills."

Brown's death in September of 1964 crushed Red because he lost a friend who happened to be his boss. Brown's widow, Marjorie, and Pieri took over the team until they sold it the following year to Jack Waldron, who owned Ruppert Brewing Company. That began a revolving door that saw the Celtics change hands twelve times in twenty years, including the famous franchise swap in 1978 in which Irv Levin, then owner of the Celtics, swapped his ownership to John Y. Brown and Harry Mangurian Jr. for their ownership in the Buffalo Braves. Levin then moved the Braves to San Diego — taking four Celtics with him as part of the deal — where they became the Clippers. Thus, in a strange sense, there is a strain of the Celtics in the (now) Los Angeles Clippers, the team that has come to define futility in the NBA.

The Gaston family brought some long-absent stability to the franchise. By then, the Celtics had finally become consistently profitable, selling out nightly for the first time ever after Larry Bird's arrival in 1979. Their presence as owners kept Red from being tempted by some of the offers that continued to come his way even after his flirtation with Sonny Werblin and the Knicks in 1979.

At one point he was offered part ownership in the Atlanta Hawks when Tom Cousins owned the franchise. "He wanted me to come down there, coach for three years, and then be general manager for two. After that I'd be CEO and I'd have a piece of the team. I can't remember how much he offered me, maybe it was fifteen percent, something like that. By then [late eighties] I was too old to coach and I was very happy with the Celtics, so I told him I was flattered but no thank you."

As recently as the nineties, Red was approached by Donald Sterling, the current owner of the Clippers, about taking over the team. "I could have had a place in Malibu," he said, laughing. "I was seventy-five years old. I told him I was too old. He said, 'No, no, you're not. You can do it.' I had to tell him no. If

I'd been sixty-five instead of seventy-five I might have thought seriously about it."

Gaston made Red feel as if he still had an important role to play with the team. He consulted with him often, especially after Gavitt left in 1994. By that time, the lunches had become a weekly part of Red's life and had, as Morgan Wootten likes to say, "taken on a life of their own."

Red mentioned them to Gaston one day, telling him if he ever happened to be in Washington on a Tuesday, he was more than welcome to come and join the group. "Who pays for these lunches?" Gaston asked.

"I do," Red said, not sure why that mattered.

"From now on I want the Celtics to pay," Gaston said.

"There's no need to do that," Red said.

"I know," Gaston said. "And I know you'd never ask. But I *want* the Celtics to pay. Just make sure you talk some basketball every week."

"That's certainly not a problem," Red said.

Since that day, the Celtics have paid for lunch. But not for the takeout. Each week Red orders takeout to bring home to his housekeeper, occasionally to Nancy, and sometimes for himself for later in the week. He always pays for that on a separate credit card. Is there any chance that the Celtics would notice the extra twenty bucks or even care? Of course not. That's just Red's way.

"I have always tried to behave as if the Celtics' money was my own money," he said. "For one thing, there have been times when it *has* been my own money. That's not true anymore, but I try not to take advantage. When I fly to Boston, I use those US Air discount coupons, and I always try to make my reservations far enough in advance so that I don't waste a couple hundred bucks because I'm too lazy to pick up a phone and make a call. I just don't see any reason to waste anyone's money."

In many ways, Red is a classic Depression kid, even at eighty-six. He is more than willing to spend money — especially on his family and friends — but sees no reason to waste money. He was annoyed with himself one day in the winter of 2003 because he had gone to visit someone in Montgomery County and misread a parking meter, thinking he didn't need to pay because it was after 5:00. The meter required feeding until 7:00 and Red got nailed with a $35 ticket.

Could he have gotten out of it? Probably. One phone call to Rob Ades, who works with the DC police union, probably would have led to another phone call and the end of the ticket. Red never made the call, just wrote a check. "I screwed up," he said. "You screw up, you just pay the price and shut up."

Which is what Gaston decided to do after he had handed Pitino the team presidency in 1997. At the end of that year, Red received a check from Gaston for $100,000 — over and above what the team was paying him.

"What's this for?" Red asked.

"It's my way of trying to tell you I'm sorry about what happened."

"You don't have to do that."

"It's because you don't think I have to do it that I want to do it."

Case closed. At least for the moment.

During Pitino's tenure with the Celtics, Red said almost nothing about him in public and very little about him in private. Even at the lunches, when one of Pitino's questionable moves or comments would come up in conversation, Red held his tongue. Part of it was because he thought Pitino deserved time to try to put a mark on the team. But mostly it was out of loyalty to the Celtics.

Pitino's tenure did not get off to a very good start when the Celtics did *not* win the draft lottery that spring. Instead of getting the number one pick and Tim Duncan, they got the number three pick and the number six pick. With those picks, Pitino took Chauncey Billups, a guard from Colorado, and Ron Mercer, a forward who had played for him at Kentucky. Billups has emerged as a star in the last year — in Detroit. Mercer lasted two years with the Celtics before Pitino traded him to Denver along with another player Red really liked, Popeye Jones.

The first decisions he made that Red disagreed with came in the summer of 1997, when he opted not to re-sign Rick Fox or David Wesley. Both were players Red thought the Celtics needed and urged Pitino to keep.

"Rick did ask me what I thought about guys," Red said. "The problem is, he'd ask me, I'd tell him, and then he never listened to me. That's not to say I was always right. But I told him I thought he was crazy to let Fox and Wesley go, that they were the kind of players who might not be stars but would be very solid players for us for a long time."

Fox ended up being a key component on three straight World Championship teams in Los Angeles. Wesley became a star in Charlotte. Three years later, during a radio interview with ESPN's Bob Valvano, Pitino was asked if he regretted not trying to re-sign Fox and Wesley. "Absolutely I regret it," he said. "But you have to understand what was going on. I'd been in the college game for eight years. I was flying blind, so I was dependent on what other people told me when I made those decisions."

At least one person with exactly sixteen more NBA championship rings than Pitino told him to keep the two players. One has to wonder whom exactly he was depending on.

Pitino was smart enough to take Paul Pierce with the number ten pick in the draft in 1998, but Pierce was another guy who had dropped much lower than anyone thought he would because of some less-than-impressive predraft camps. "It was a good pick, to say the least," Red said. "But we never should have gotten him."

Red also was pleased that one of the players who came from Denver in the Mercer trade was Danny Fortson. He thought that Fortson brought toughness inside, a willingness to mix it up, and the ability to get an important rebound. "Winning teams always have a player like Fortson," Red said. "Rick said he was a problem in the dressing room. My attitude was, 'Deal with it. He's worth it.' He disagreed."

So Fortson was traded — twice. The first time, when Pitino tried to trade him to Toronto for the immortal Alvin Williams and Sean Marks, Williams flunked the post-trade physical. So Pitino traded Fortson again that summer to Golden State. The Celtics have lacked toughness inside ever since.

Pitino's biggest problem, regardless of where he has coached, has been his inability to accept responsibility for defeat or mistakes. It is always someone else's fault — frequently the players' fault. Occasionally it might be the officials' fault. Sometimes he is dependent on others because he is flying blind. It is never Rick's fault.

The clearest example of this trait took place in 1994, when Pitino's Kentucky team was stunned in the second round of the NCAA Tournament by Marquette. Marquette had a little guard named Tony Miller who wasn't a particularly good shooter or all that adept at running a half-court offense. But in the open court, he was a jet. Pressure him and he would go by you and create on the fast break. Pitino stubbornly clung to his full-court pressure defense for forty minutes, Miller broke the press all day, and Marquette won the game.

In the postgame press conference, with his three seniors sitting next to him, Pitino said the following: "This was a Kentucky team that lacked leadership, lacked talent, and lacked chemistry all season long."

That team, including the three brokenhearted kids sitting

next to Pitino, had won twenty-seven games. It had been let down that day by the stubbornness of its coach. That thought never occurred to the coach. His motto in defeat has always been "I coached good, they played bad."

Even Red, after another Pitino outburst against his players during his Celtics tenure, shook his head one day and said, "You can't always say the players lose and the coach wins. For one thing, most of the time, it's not true. For another, you lose your players if you keep saying things like that."

Red once tried to tell Pitino a story about himself. "Every once in a while, when we'd lose a ball game, I'd come in and I'd say to the guys, 'Fellas, this one's on me. I had a bad night. I made bad decisions and I didn't have you ready to play. So just forget this one and move on. I'll take the hit.' I did it for two reasons: one, it was probably true — we've all had nights like that — and two, they appreciated the fact that I was willing to take the blame some of the time too. That way, when they really did blow one, I could give it to them good and they'd take it."

If any of that registered with Pitino, it never showed.

Pitino is forgiven this particular foible by most, because he is a wonderful coach. He is extremely adept at getting college players to accept his style and his work ethic and to play their hearts out for him. In the pros that sort of system is rarely as effective. But Red doesn't believe coaching was Pitino's problem.

"The guy can coach," he said. "I've watched him. He's really good. He just fell into the same trap that so many guys fall into nowadays: he wanted everything. That might have worked forty or fifty years ago, but it can't work today. You need guys you can turn to and really depend on to tell you the truth about everything — whether it's good or bad. I don't think Rick ever really trusted anyone but himself, which is really too bad."

It is especially too bad given that the man he deposed as team president was more than willing to help. One can't be helped, though, unless one is willing to listen. And to trust. Not trusting Red Auerbach on the subject of basketball — even at eighty-seven — is a little bit like not trusting Mozart or Beethoven on the subject of great music. When a master speaks, the wise listen.

10

The Greatest
of All Time . . . Sort Of

"I EVER TELL YOU the story about Ted Leonsis and Michael Jordan? When Jordan first comes to town, John Thompson calls me and wants me to go to lunch with Leonsis. I say fine and I go. Leonsis seems like a perfectly nice guy. But at one point he says to me, 'Would you mind sitting down with Michael and talking to him about what it's like to run a team?' I looked at him and said, 'What are you, crazy? You think I'm going to sit down and give advice to the enemy? You guys are the enemy! I'm a Celtic, not a Wizard.'"

Which is really too bad for the Wizards. Maybe, just maybe, if Abe Pollin had thought at some point to go to Red and ask him to take over his team, Red might have done it. After all, Red has lived in Washington almost all his adult life. What's more, he's known Pollin since his teaching days at Roosevelt

High School when Pollin — who is six years younger than Red — was one of his students.

But Pollin never approached Red. "I'd a probably turned him down," Red said, "but you never know. It would have depended on the timing and the deal."

When Leonsis, who had bought the Washington Capitols from Pollin along with a minority ownership in the Wizards, first came up with the idea of bringing Jordan in as CEO of the basketball team, Red was skeptical. "Here's what I think about Jordan," he said at the time. "He's a bright guy, a good guy, I think. But is he *really* going to want to do the work you gotta do to rebuild that team? Is he gonna put in the hours, do the scouting, make the phone calls and the tough calls?

"Maybe he will. But I think it's going to be very hard for him. He's got so much other stuff going on in his life. Plus, this is not a guy who is accustomed to not getting his way. He had such a strong will as a player that he could almost *force* the game to go his way; he could intimidate his teammates into doing what he wanted them to do. It doesn't work that way when you're in management. I think he could be in for some unhappy surprises. I wish I could say I think it will be great for everyone, but I'm not so sure it will be."

All of which is why Leonsis was probably right to want to get Red and Jordan together. Red is one of the very few people on the planet who Jordan might — repeat *might* — listen to.

Red's instincts were proven correct pretty quickly. Jordan spent little time in Washington. When he decided to pull the plug on his coach, Garfield Heard, less than two weeks after taking over the team, he sent poor Wes Unseld, who still had the general manager's title, to deliver the news while he was unveiling yet another corporate venture at the Super Bowl in Florida.

Clue one: Jordan was too busy to do what was now *his* job.

Clue two came very soon after that. Jordan wanted to hire his buddy Rod Higgins as his new coach. But Higgins was under contract to Golden State as an assistant. Jordan was stunned when the Warriors demanded compensation for Higgins if he was going to leave at midseason to coach the Wizards.

Clue two: Jordan couldn't get his way just because he was Jordan.

The real tip-off came at the end of that season. Darrell Walker was brought in to coach the team for the rest of the season. He was not going to be the coach long-term. Jordan decided he wanted to hire Mike Jarvis, who at that moment was riding high as the coach at St. John's. His team had won the Big East title that season and had gone into the NCAA Tournament as a number two seed, meaning the basketball committee saw the Red Storm as one of the top eight teams in the country.

Jarvis, who was making about $1 million a year at St. John's, was very interested in the job. He had always had NBA aspirations, although as a Boston guy it was the Celtics he dreamed of coaching. Still, he had enjoyed living in Washington while coaching at George Washington and the idea of coaching a team run by Michael Jordan sounded appealing.

Jarvis met with his lawyer and told him to discuss the job with Jordan. His lawyer was Rob Ades.

"He wanted the job, but not at any cost," Ades said. "We discussed what it would take for him to do it. Mike thought he should get five years at three million a year because that was the deal Lon Kruger had just gotten to leave a similar kind of job at Illinois for the Atlanta Hawks. Now, when your client throws out a figure of what he wants, you know that's different from what he'll take. We agreed there had to be four years guaranteed at two million a year to make the move worth his while, because with any less than that, he could easily be fired after a year or two if things weren't going right, and my sense was that if things went wrong Michael Jordan wasn't likely to stand up and say, 'This is my fault. Fire me.'"

Ades flew back to Washington and met with Jordan in his new office at the MCI Center. He noticed that Jordan had one thing in common with Red: he smoked a cigar throughout their meeting. The similarities ended there. Once the small talk — which was brief — had ended, Jordan told Ades what he was prepared to offer Jarvis: two years at $1 million a year.

"I was stunned," Ades said. "He was asking Mike to take no more money and less years than he had on his contract at St. John's to take over what had been a bad team for a long time. So I told Michael that we wanted seven years at four million a year. He looked at me and said, 'What're you, nuts?' I told him yes, I was nuts; that we had now both thrown out numbers that were ridiculous on both sides and could we now maybe get down to business.

"He was pissed. Really pissed. We started talking about what some other coaches were making. I mentioned the deal Jeff Van Gundy [another client] had just been given by the Knicks to make the point that I didn't expect *that* kind of money because Van Gundy had taken the Knicks to the finals. This time he really blew up: '*Don't you ever mention that fucking name in my office!*' Now, I'm in shock. I knew he didn't like Van Gundy, fine, but you can't respect an opponent? You can't concede he's a pretty good coach? I guess not."

The two men finally put real numbers on the table: Jordan came up to $1.5 million a year for three years. Ades told him it had to be four years guaranteed and it had to be at least $2 million a year or there was no way Jarvis would take the job.

"At that point he more or less threw me out of his office," Ades said.

Ades called Jarvis to tell him the meeting had not gone well. He told him where the numbers were. Jarvis asked him to make one more attempt at seeing if Jordan would move up one more year. Ades asked him if he would be willing to take three years guaranteed with a buyout option in the fourth year. Jarvis said he would do that if that would get the deal done.

That afternoon Ades drove back to the MCI Center and left a box of expensive cigars for Jordan. The next day he called Jordan and told him Jarvis would be willing to take the fourth year as an option year if the money was $2 million guaranteed for three years, plus the buyout year. "Three years, $1.8 million a year — no options," Jordan said. "That is absolutely as far as I'm going. I will not make another offer."

Ades asked him if he was absolutely certain about that because he did not think Jarvis would accept the deal as offered. Jordan told him in no uncertain terms that this was the end of the negotiation. Ades relayed the information to Jarvis. Smartly, as far as Ades was concerned, Jarvis said no.

"With only three years guaranteed it's too easy to fire a guy after one year, let him take the blame," said Ades in what turned out to be a prescient statement. "I felt I failed Mike because he wanted the job. But Jordan wouldn't budge."

The news that Jarvis would not be the Wizards coach hit the papers on a Tuesday morning. That day, a very disturbed-looking Ades walked into the China Doll at about 11:30. Lunch had just been served amid discussion of what had gone wrong in the Ades-Jordan negotiation. Normally when Ades walks in late, he acts like a political candidate, shaking hands around the table, making comments on everyone's outfit or what they have been up to lately. If there was a baby at the table he would kiss it.

This day was different. "Red, I want you to understand what happened," he said. "I tried everything I could to make the deal happen for Mike."

Ades was aware of Red's fondness for Jarvis, dating back to his GW days. He knew that Red would never question his negotiating tactics on behalf of a client. Nonetheless, he wanted him to hear, firsthand, what had happened.

"Sit down and calm down," Red ordered. Ades, who is often awakened in the middle of the night to go to the scene of police shootings as part of his work with the DC police union, rarely appears shaken. Now he appeared shaken.

He went through everything that had happened in great detail, including the profanity and the proffered box of cigars. Red listened without interrupting or commenting. When Ades was finished, Red said quietly, "Sounds to me like you did everything you could possibly do. I wouldn't worry about it."

Ades was visibly relieved. "It was very important to me that Red understand what had happened," he said later. "I did not want him to think that I had ruined Mike's chances of getting the job with some smart-ass lawyer tactics. He understands better than anyone how negotiations work and that sometimes it is better for your client if a deal doesn't get done than if it does. As it turned out, I think this was one of those times. But at that moment, none of us knew that for sure.

"I was twenty-six when my father died [Ades is now fifty-five] and I'm not going to say Red is like a surrogate father to me, but he is very important to me. His approval is very important to me. I honestly think that's true of all of us in the lunch group. I did not have time to go to lunch that day. Because I'd been working Jarvis and Jordan for several days, I was way behind in all my other work. But I had to tell Red what had happened, and why it had happened and I wasn't going to do it on the phone."

As luck would have it, Jordan's next choice was University of Miami coach Leonard Hamilton — also an Ades client. When Hamilton told Jordan who his lawyer was, Jordan told him that, based on what had happened in the Jarvis deal, he did not think he would be able to get a deal done with Ades.

Hamilton — with Ades's approval — got someone else to represent him.

"I think Michael was right," he said. "There was so much animosity that a deal might not have gotten done, and Leonard badly wanted the job."

Hamilton wanted the job so badly that he accepted exactly the kind of deal that Ades did not think Jarvis could afford — and was fired after one season.

To Red, all these stories simply confirmed what he had suspected: Jordan could not deal with being challenged on any level. The next rumor coming from Camp Jordan didn't surprise him either: Jordan was coming back to play.

"I feel kind of bad for the guy," he said. "I mean, if he wants to play, he should play. But to me, it's a no-win deal for him. He can't be as good as he was. He's three years older and he was already starting to slow down. And he's not going to win a championship with this team. If he was twenty-eight instead of thirty-eight I don't think he could win a championship with this team. So maybe he gets them into the play-offs. Is that going to satisfy him? I don't see how. He's Michael Jordan."

Red has nothing but respect for Jordan the basketball player. He has said publicly that Jordan is the greatest player of all time, hedging the comment only by saying if he was starting a team to try to win championships he might take Bill Russell first because, at least in his day, you couldn't win without a great center.

"I would have loved to have coached Jordan, not just because of his ability but because of his attitude," he said. "The guy would do anything to win. Guys like that make good coaches into great coaches and good players into great players."

When Jordan finally made the announcement that he was going to play, Red shrugged. "He'll have some great nights," he said. "Especially the first half of the season, when his legs are fresh. But the road is going to wear him down, I think. He'll get tired and he might get hurt. When you get older, you're a lot more vulnerable to injury."

Of course Red had that right too. The first half of the Wizards 2001–2002 season was almost like a Jordan victory tour. The team was playing well and, even though Jordan clearly wasn't the player he had once been, he was still pretty damn good. Then, after the all-star break, it began to fall apart. The team started losing. Jordan struggled, then was hurt, missing the last thirteen games of the season. What's more, Red saw serious problems on the horizon.

"I feel sorry for Doug Collins," he said. "I think it's impossible to coach when the boss is in uniform. Who are the players listening to, you or him? I just don't see how it can work."

Jordan had brought Collins in to coach the team after deciding to play again. Collins had coached a young Jordan in Chicago and had been fired — some thought at Jordan's behest — just before the Bulls began winning championships. When Jordan asked him to come back — at $20 million over four years — he couldn't say no.

The second season proved worse than the first. Jordan traded rising star Richard Hamilton to Detroit for Jerry Stackhouse in large part because Hamilton had made it clear he didn't like deferring constantly to the old man on or off the court. Jordan thought Stackhouse, a fellow North Carolina alum, would be easier to deal with. While the Washington media was singing the praises of the trade, Red sat at lunch shaking his head.

"Has he ever watched Stackhouse play?" he said. "The guy needs the ball all the time. You can't have the ball all the time when you're playing with Jordan. Write this down: this is gonna be a disaster."

And of course it was. Jordan and Stackhouse sniped at each other all season, first privately, then publicly. Jordan continued to play well, especially for a man who turned forty in February, but often at the cost of what was best for the team. By the time he reached his fortieth birthday, the team was in almost open revolt against him and Collins. Kwame Brown, the much-bally-hooed Jordan-selected number one pick in the draft out of high school in 2001, had been cowed into a complete shell by Jordan and Collins.

Watching it all happen, Red didn't know whether to laugh or cry. "Part of me feels bad, especially for Collins because I really like him and I think he's a really good coach," he said. "Part of me has to laugh because every time I pick up a newspaper I read how this is everyone's fault *but* Jordan's. I'm amazed at his ability to control the media. I've seen guys who were good at it, but no one like Jordan. No matter what he does, they always say he's right. Hey, good for him if he can do it. But I honestly don't see how he pulls it off."

Red's point was further reinforced when Abe Pollin decided

to fire Jordan, choosing to see Jordan as a failed executive rather than as a playing icon. Almost everyone in the Washington media pilloried Pollin, led by Red's good friend John Thompson, who accused Pollin of "sending Michael back to the plantation."

When that comment and the nearly hysterical bleatings of the *Washington Post*'s Michael Wilbon were replayed to Red (who was well aware of them), he simply spread his hands and said, "What'd I tell you?"

Of course things weren't any happier in Boston during Jordan's Washington sojourn. The Pitino presidency had a very brief honeymoon period. One wonders if Pitino might have reconsidered his decision to leave his job as king of Kentucky to be a mere president in Boston if he had known the Celtics weren't going to end up with Tim Duncan.

As it turned out, the Celtics did improve considerably during his first season — they almost had to on the heels of 15–67 — but still missed the play-offs with a 36–46 record. Pitino continued to move players in different directions like a mad scientist, but the team stagnated, continuing to finish under .500 each season. Even adding Paul Pierce in the '98 draft to a team with Antoine Walker, who had been taken pre-Pitino in 1996, didn't spark the Celtics.

During this period, Red never said a word against Pitino — publicly or privately. Even at the lunches, surrounded by trusted friends, he would change the subject when Pitino's name came up. About the only thing he might say was, "We got too many good players wearing other uniforms." Translation: What was he thinking letting Fox and Fortson and Popeye Jones and Wesley go?

These were not good times for the Celtics. After all, this was the proudest franchise in the history of the NBA, and it had not reached the play-offs since 1995, had won one play-off game since the night Reggie Lewis collapsed in Boston.

"It's hard for me to watch," Red admitted one day. "I'm like any fan. I get frustrated. If I turn it on and we're winning and then the other team starts to score, I turn it off, I figure I'm bad luck. Then I'll start sneaking looks to see how we're doing. It's never easy. Of course it isn't easy when we're good either because then when I watch there's more at stake and that makes me more nervous. Still, this is tough to take. I just want to see us get good again."

While Pitino was struggling in Boston, Phil Jackson was becoming the NBA's marquee coach. He had been the final piece — or so it appeared — in the Chicago Bulls puzzle, arriving in 1990 to succeed the fired Doug Collins. Coincidence or not, the Bulls won their first title the next spring. Then they won two more before Jordan's first "retirement" slowed them in the 1993–94 season. That season may have been Jackson's best coaching job. Without Jordan and with Scottie (I've-got-a-headache-when-it-matters-most) Pippen forced into the role of team leader, the Bulls won fifty-five games and might very well have returned to the finals if not for an awful call in game five of their intense seven-game series against the Knicks.

A year later, after vowing (for the first time) never to return, Jordan came back late in the season and the Bulls lost in the play-offs to the Orlando Magic. That late-season stint was the first — and last — time Jordan changed his number, wearing number 45 instead of 23 — a move many saw as nothing more than a marketing ploy to sell a whole new set of Jordan uniforms. Still getting back into playing shape, Jordan was a shadow of himself in the play-offs that spring, causing Orlando's Nick Anderson to deliver his famous line: "Number twenty-three was a better player than number forty-five."

A year later, number 23 returned and the Bulls went on another three-season winning binge, finishing the 1998 season with six titles in eight years. By then, Jordan and Jackson were in a full-scale PR war with Chicago's famous "Jerrys" — owner Reinsdorf and general manager Krause. Rather than continue to work for the Jerrys, both "retired." A year later both were back, Jackson as coach of the Los Angeles Lakers, Jordan as CEO in Washington.

Once again, Jackson proved to be the missing piece in a puzzle, turning the Shaquille O'Neal / Kobe Bryant Lakers from talented nonwinners into champions. The Lakers won in 2000, then again in 2001 and 2002. During their 2002 run, a number of people looked up and noticed that Jackson was closing in on his ninth NBA title as a coach. Only one other coach had won nine NBA titles. That would be Red. So people began calling Red, always reachable, to ask about Jackson and his assault on his record.

"The guy has done a great job," Red said, believing it, "but he never put a team together. He came in when the pieces were in place. What he's done is a lot different than what I did."

Whoa boy, we've got ourselves a controversy now. The old master was saying that the young master — Zen master, specifically — wasn't in his league. In a sense, that was exactly what he was saying — but not in the way people thought he was saying it.

The NBA was, in fact, a very different league when Red was building the Celtics in the 1950s than it is now. Red was coach, general manager, marketing director, chief (and only) scout, and, at times, literally stood in the lobby of the Boston Garden counting the house before games. Today, the NBA is a multi-billion-dollar business with giant front offices, coaching staffs that sometimes number in double digits, and three times as many teams. There is free agency to be dealt with; capologists to be hired; and agents to be fought with.

What Red did and what Jackson is doing are entirely different except that both involve the same essential ingredient: knowing how to win. "I wasn't putting down what he's done," Red said in the midst of the firestorm set off by his comments. "Obviously, the guy has done a hell of a job. I think the best thing he does is he gets his stars to believe in what he's doing. That's not always easy to do. But what I said is true: he didn't put either one of those teams together. No one has asked him to do that. If people want to get upset with me for saying that, fine. Let 'em be upset."

Red doesn't necessarily buy into all of Jackson's Zen theories and the notion that meditation may be the key to victory in a tough situation. "I was always very simplistic in the locker room," he said. "Personally, I didn't care what my players did until about twenty minutes before the game started. They could play loud music or no music; they could sit off by themselves or they could sit around and talk and tell jokes. We always had people in the locker room before games.

"But with twenty minutes to go, I got everyone out of there and I demanded their complete attention for a few minutes. I didn't say anything fancy. Obviously we didn't scout back then the way teams do now, but we played everyone so many times a year that we knew everyone's personnel. I might remind guys about a particular play or a particular move; I'd remind them of what we did against the team the last time. Nothing fancy. I mean, let's be honest, there are only so many things you can say. If the guys don't understand what's at stake and what it's going to take to win, you can talk all day and you aren't going to win."

There was one pregame ritual that Red did consider vital to the Celtics' success: Russell throwing up.

"He did it before every game," Red said. "I mean he did it very loudly before every game. We had this little tiny locker room in the Garden and he would be in there getting violently sick. It was awful to listen to. But most nights, it worked.

"One year, we're playing the Lakers. Game seven. I give my pregame talk and we go out on the court. We're going through layups and all of a sudden it occurs to me: Russell didn't throw up. I go out on the court and I say, 'Everyone back in the locker room.' They're looking at me like I'm nuts. There's less than ten minutes on the clock until tip-off. I say, 'You heard me. Back inside.' I think the fans thought something crazy was going on. We go back into the locker room and I say, 'Russell, you forgot to throw up! Go do it right now!' Without a word he went into the bathroom and did it.

"And we won the game."

Actually Red won every game seven he ever coached in; he was 8–0, including 4–0 in the finals. Interestingly, Jackson has never coached a game seven in the finals, although his Laker teams have twice come from behind to win game seven in the conference finals, including their 2002 overtime win in Sacramento in game seven.

"You can't argue with the guy's success," Red said. "He would be right at the top of my list of the best coaches ever in the NBA — just look at the record. But I have to say this: I could never understand the things he let Dennis Rodman get away with. I mean people said I had a double standard for Russell. It just wasn't true. If I let him do something, I would let the other guys do it too. I don't understand how Phil could let Rodman do the things he did. But they won, so you have to say whatever he did worked. I just wouldn't have done it that way. Everyone's different."

The only tough thing about coaching Russell, according to Red, was that there were times when he simply didn't want to practice. If Russell loafed, everyone loafed because they took their cue from him. "One day I want twenty minutes of a hard scrimmage," he said. "I tell 'em, 'Give me twenty hard minutes and we're outta here.' We start and Russell's loafing. Everyone's loafing. I yell at them to pick it up. I yell at him to pick it up. Nothing. He just doesn't want to work. Finally I tell them all to get out, I've seen enough.

"But I'm not going to just let them get away with that crap. The next day they come in and we go through all our drills and I haven't said a word about what happened the day before. Finally, it's time to scrimmage. I reach into my pocket and I pull out five new cigars. I say, 'Fellas, it takes me about thirty minutes to smoke each one of these. I have absolutely no place to go this afternoon. I am going to sit over here in a chair and I am going to smoke these cigars. As soon as you guys give me twenty straight minutes of hard work scrimmaging, you're free to go. But any loafing at all and we set the clock back and start again and we're going to stay here until you've given me twenty straight hard minutes. Understand?' "

Red paused and shook his head at the memory. "Russell must have had someplace to go. He plays like it's the seventh game of a play-off series. No one can get a shot off inside eighteen feet. I mean every shot is going back the other way and he's running like crazy to the other end to finish the break. Fifteen minutes in, I had to stop it. They weren't going to have anything left for the game the next night. I said, 'All right, Russell, you sonofabitch, get outta here.' I sent 'em all home."

Red loves to talk about today's coaches. Ironically, the ones he seems to admire the most are at the college level: his longtime friend Bob Knight; Mike Krzyzewski; recently retired coaches such as Dean Smith and John Thompson.

"You know one thing that bugs me?" he said. "Time-outs. They call a time-out and all these coaches gather around in a circle with their staff and talk to *them*. They stand there talking while the kids are just sitting there waiting for someone to say something. You know why they do it? TV! If they're standing there it's easier for the camera to get a shot of them, and some fired coach who is now an expert because he's been made an announcer can sit there and talk about what a great job the guy is doing — because he's talking to his coaches!

"I remember the first time I saw that. It was Digger [Phelps]. He stands there talking and talking and talking. Then, just as the buzzer is about to sound, he goes into the huddle and some kid runs in and puts a towel on the floor where he's going to kneel because he's wearing a two-thousand-dollar suit and he talks for ten seconds and they go back out there. I love Digger, I really do. He was great for the game when he coached at Notre Dame, but are you kidding me?

"These guys are being paid millions. If you are going to be paid millions, or even hundreds of thousands, you do not stand around and listen to your assistants talk during a time-out. You mean to tell me you don't have enough feel for the game or for your team that you don't know what you want to say during a time-out? You look at the best guys — I mean, the very best: Knight, Krzyzewski, Dean when he was still in it — you ever see one of them ask their assistants what to do? Absolutely not! They know exactly what they're going to say and why they're going to say it."

Red can really get rolling when he talks about today's

coaches, especially when it relates to his belief that most of them play to the cameras. "I see these guys standing up there screaming and hollering on every single play," he said. "Now, if they really need to do that, then their team can't be any good. If you've coached guys right in practice, they don't need you up directing them on every play. So why do they do it? TV. Every game is on TV someplace now, so they know if they're up, the camera is going to find them. Drives me crazy. I sit there and say, 'If you've done your job getting your team ready, you should sit down awhile and watch them play. See if what you've worked on has stuck. When Knight or Krzyzewski get up it's for a specific reason: someone screwed up a play or they want to get on the refs.'"

Red smiled, remembering his many battles with officials. "I'll tell you one thing about Krzyzewski. When it comes to the referees, he's an artist. He is on them constantly, even when he's sitting or kneeling. You watch him — he keeps up a running commentary. Dean used to do that too. And yet how often does Krzyzewski get teed up? Almost never. He and [Maryland coach] Gary Williams amaze me. They're on the refs all the time and they almost never get technicals. They're geniuses when it comes to that."

Red doesn't often bring John Wooden into the conversation when he talks about great coaches. The two men share a warm mutual respect, but Red has never been close to Wooden the way he has with Knight or Smith or, in the old days, Adolph Rupp.

"He [Wooden] was always a little standoffish," Red said. "I

think it was the Midwesterner in him. I always got a great kick out of him, though. I remember back in the sixties, he used to come east to play once a season and I'd go out to watch the team practice if I had time because he always had such good players. Whatever year it was when he'd recruited [Lew] Alcindor, I said to him, 'Hey, John, you got Alcindor. Boy, he's really going to be great for you.' And he looks at me and says, 'Oh, you mean the chap from New York? Yes, we're quite pleased to have him.' "

Red believes that Wooden was a superb coach — underrated in some ways. "I hear people say all the time that he had great talent, which he certainly did. Well, there's two things about that: One, you gotta get the talent. That's part of the job. Two, when you get it you gotta make sure you don't screw it up. A lot of coaches — I mean a *lot* — take great talent and screw it up. Wooden took good players and made them very good; very good ones and made them great; and great ones and made them greater. That's coaching."

Red also believes that Wooden's ten national titles will never be touched because the college game is so different today than when he dominated the sport in the sixties and seventies. "For one thing, back then, he never had to leave the western part of the country to get to the Final Four. He played two games on the West Coast, sometimes right on his home court for crying out loud, and he was in the Final Four. Back then there might have been five teams in the entire draw that could beat him — maximum. Today there might be thirty or more and you have to travel and win four games just to reach the

Final Four. Most years when UCLA won they had to win a total of four games — two of them practically at home — to be national champions."

In fact, UCLA won four games to be national champions nine times. When Wooden won his tenth title — in 1975, the year he retired — the Bruins won five games after the tournament field expanded to thirty-two teams. "Don't get me wrong, what he did was incredible, especially since they were everyone's target year after year. But back then, you didn't worry about great players leaving after a year. Today, there's no way [Kareem] Abdul-Jabbar or [Bill] Walton stays in college for four years. They might both have gone straight from high school to the pros. It's all different.

"That's why I think you can make the case that what Knight [three titles, five Final Fours] and Krzyzewski [three titles, ten Final Fours] have done is right up there with what Wooden did. Dean [two titles, eleven Final Fours] was great too. There are so many more factors involved today — not the least of which is just trying to keep your players — that it is much, much harder."

Red smiled. "And I'll tell you one thing about all those guys: they have *never* coached for the cameras. You show me a coach who knows where all the cameras are and I'll show you a coach who doesn't win."

Phil Jackson? "He doesn't know where the cameras are. But he *always* knows where Shaq and Kobe are. Smart guy. Very smart guy."

11

Always a Coach

"HEY, GUESS WHAT? Paul Gaston just called me. He wants me to be president of the team again."

Red rarely shows much emotion but he was clearly excited on this Tuesday in January of 2001. Rick Pitino had resigned midway through what was going to be his fourth-straight losing season as Boss of All Things Celtic. The Celtics were 12–22 on January 8 when Pitino stepped down and were 102–146 in the Pitino era, their best record having been the 36–46 of his first season. Red took no joy in Pitino's failure because it meant the Celtics were failing too. He didn't even dislike Pitino; he simply didn't understand his need to control everything while taking advice from no one and blame for nothing.

"In different circumstances, he could have done well," he insisted. "When he was with the Knicks, even though he didn't *like* having a general manager [Al Bianchi], he did a hell of a job. That was because all he did was coach."

Now he was no longer coaching the Celtics. That meant that the title of president, which he had insisted on as part of his deal in 1997, was open again. Red had the exalted title of vice chairman of the board. Gaston wanted him to add "president" again.

"So, you gonna do it?" Morgan Wootten asked when Red announced the news.

"Of course," Red said. "I know Gaston felt bad about what happened. There's no need to remind him. I just told him I'd be delighted to have the title again. That's the end of it."

"So he gave you back the title," a voice said from two seats away from where Red was about to sit down. "Does this mean you're going to send him the hundred grand back?"

The speaker, of course, was Zang, who could give his brother the needle in ways no one else would. Everyone remembered the $100,000 bonus Gaston had sent Red at the end of 1997 as an apology for giving Pitino the title of president. Red just waved a hand at him in disgust, but he joined in the laughter all around.

In his own way, Zang was at the heart of the lunches as much as Red. Neither brother could ever remember who first came up with the idea for the two of them to get together once a week, but it was Zang who first suggested inviting others, leading to the twelve to fifteen regulars who now circle Tuesday on their calendars every week. In basketball terms, Red was the group's coach — very much the leader, the person everyone looked up to and wanted to play for (or in this case, eat, talk, and listen with). Zang then was the general manager — the organizer, making sure the coach had the players he wanted in place every week. Most Mondays, Zang would call the regulars in the group to confirm that lunch was on. His calls were so expected and so much a part of the ritual that if someone was going to be out on a Monday, he would leave word at home to make certain someone would answer the phone at the time Zang called — he called each person at the same time each week — because Zang wouldn't talk to answering machines.

"Just don't see any point in it," he said simply.

"If he calls late, I get worried," Chris Wallace said. "Part of the ritual of Tuesday is the ritual of Monday night when Zang calls."

It was that way for me too. I often teased Zang if he called at 9:10 instead of 9:05, accusing him of slowing down in his old age. After a while Zang would call at exactly 9:07 and ask to speak to Danny, my son. Danny had answered the phone on a couple of occasions when I'd been out on a Monday — and had pleaded with my wife to be certain someone answered at the appointed time — and Zang had decided that talking to Danny, who was five when the two first began to talk, was far more worthwhile than talking to me.

"What's up, Zang?" Danny would say, grabbing the phone, and they would chat for several minutes. Early on, Danny's regular bedtime was 8:30, but on Mondays he got to stay up until 9:07 to talk to Zang.

Red often spoke wistfully about the fact that he hadn't had

enough money when Zang was young to get him formal training as an artist. There was no doubting his talent. Even at
eighty-one, he could still do watercolors of people that were so
clear and on the money that you did a double take looking at
them. Zang had never had any formal training — "Imagine
what he might have become if he had," Red often said — but
had been very successful as a cartoonist at the *Washington Star*
and doing more formal portraits, mostly of politicians, for various magazines. The only thing that had kept him from his work
had been his drinking, and he had finally given that up years
earlier when his wife, Gertrude, and friends intervened and
demanded that he seek help.

Of course his friends were a tremendous help while he was
at the rehab center. "He was in a program where he could have
visitors once a week," Hymie remembered. "So the second
week, a group of us decided to go visit him. Of course we went
out and got drunk before we went over there. Very inspiring,
no doubt."

Actually, Zang said it *was* inspiring. "When I saw what they
looked like, I thought, 'Oh God, that's what I look like when
I'm drinking? I think I'll stay sober.'"

Which he did.

Although others in the group would argue with Red, Zang
was the most blunt. For all his toughness, Red has a soft spot
for a lot of people, some of them people who have, to put it po-
litely, eccentricities. For instance, ex-Georgetown coach Craig
Esherick, whose eccentricity was a failure to win games. Red
has been friends with Esherick's former boss, retired George-

town coach John Thompson, since Thompson played for him in the mid-1960s. When Thompson retired in 1999 and turned the job over to Esherick, his longtime assistant, a lot of people were skeptical. Five years later — with just one NCAA trip during that time — a lot *more* people were skeptical, including Georgetown's leadership, which finally fired him in March of 2004.

Red stood by Esherick to the bitter end. "Give the guy a break," he would say when someone (okay, me) would criticize Esherick. "He's a good guy and he's a better coach than you give him credit for. He's just had some bad luck."

Esherick had bad luck in most close games. Some would make the case that that wasn't luck. Not Red. If you were his friend, you were his friend, and close losses were bad luck.

Whenever Red would defend Esherick, Zang would roll his eyes. "If you didn't like him, you'd say he couldn't coach a lick," he said one day.

"Not true," Red insisted. "I like a lot of guys who I don't think can coach."

"Name one."

Red looked around the table for a second, broke into a grin, pointed at Pete Dowling, and said, "Pete. He can't coach at all."

"Red, he's coaching his *children*."

"So? That doesn't count?"

No one at the table ever made the claim that Bob Knight couldn't coach. His name came up frequently, though, in part because of his tendency to make news, in part because of his friendship with Red, and in part because of his connection to me. Whenever Red spoke to Knight — which was about once a month — he would walk into lunch with a smile on his face and announce, "I talked to your buddy the other day."

When Knight made news — especially with his firing at Indiana in September of 2000 and his subsequent hiring at Texas Tech in March of 2001 — everyone would debate his merits and his flaws. Red would often stay quiet while Knight was being criticized but would weigh in to make points about how great a coach Knight was — his genuine concern for his players, his loyalty as a friend. Anyone who knows Knight at all knows all of that is true. Naturally, though, once Red would finish making his point, Zang would pounce.

"Say what you want," he would say. "And every word of it may be true. But the bottom line is he's a bully and an asshole."

"You don't even know him."

"Don't need to."

Red's relationship with Knight dates back to 1962 when Red drafted John Havlicek, Knight's Ohio State teammate and close friend, with the last pick of the first round. Knight remembers lying in bed in his dorm room reading a book when Havlicek burst in to say he had been drafted by the Celtics. "I told him that's the best team you can possibly go to," Knight said. "They'll make the most of your abilities. You'll get to play with [Bill] Russell and play for the best coach there is."

Knight had followed the Celtics as a kid in Orrville, Ohio, watching the NBA Game of the Week on Saturday afternoons. "They had a great style even before they got Russell," he said.

232

"Red liked to run the ball dating back to his days playing for [Bill] Reinhart, and I enjoyed watching them. Then, when they got Russell, they went from a good team to a championship team. I have this vivid memory of Russell's rookie year when they played the [St. Louis] Hawks and Red put Russell on [Hall of Famer Bob] Pettit, and Pettit was having a very difficult time playing against him. I knew then that Red had everything he needed and why he had made that trade to get him."

Knight was coaching high school ball in Cuyahoga Falls, Ohio, during Havlicek's rookie year in Boston, but he made the drive on a half dozen occasions to see his old friend play in the Boston Garden. That was when he first met Red. Soon after, he was hired at West Point as an assistant coach and continued his habit of driving to Boston to see Havlicek. But his first real contact with Red came during the summers at Kutsher's, when he had a couple chances to sit and listen to Red talk basketball with Joe Lapchick, Clair Bee, and Frank McGuire. The group would occasionally go over to the office that Bee, who had retired as a college coach by then, maintained at the New York Military Academy — only a few miles from West Point — and Knight and his boss, Tates Locke, tagged along a few times.

The friendship really bloomed after Knight had replaced Locke as Army's coach in the fall of 1965. Army played in the Holiday Festival in Madison Square Garden that December, and Red, as he often did, came down to New York to scout what was then an eight-team tournament. Army won two of three games, beating Villanova, then losing to Boston College before beating Illinois. Knight can't remember which game of the three it was, but soon after one of them, he encountered Red in the hallway under the stands near his locker room.

"Hey, Bob, I gotta tell you something," Red said. "I really like the way your team plays. They play hard and they play smart."

Knight was stunned and thrilled by the comment. To begin with, it came from Red Auerbach. "Here I was, twenty-five years old, trying to learn my way, and he comes up and tells me he likes what I'm doing. That's the first time I can remember someone whose opinions I really valued commenting on the way one of my teams played. I can't tell you how much that meant to me."

Knight has always studied great coaches — in all sports — and he has studied Red's success and come to the conclusion that there were very specific reasons why he won as much as he did. "He was one of the first guys, maybe *the* first guy, who understood the psychology of coaching," Knight said. "He and [Vince] Lombardi probably did it better than anyone. I've always thought the mental is to the physical as four is to one in coaching. Red figured that out before anyone else did. He knew you didn't treat all players the same. Some guys you get on constantly; others you have to soothe. He understood winners. He could take a guy like Frank Ramsey, who may not have had as much pure talent as some other guys, and see greatness in him. Same with [Bill] Russell. Red loved up-tempo basketball, but he understood he was never going to win championships without the great defender and rebounder, so he changed the team's style, risked giving up truly great players for Russell. Most guys in his position, winning consistently every year the way they were, wouldn't have had the guts to do that."

Knight also believes that Red's decision to make Russell the first African-American to coach a major professional team was one of his masterstrokes — but not for social or political reasons. "It may have been one of the most brilliant moves ever made. When he stopped coaching, his biggest concern had to be figuring out a way to keep Russell motivated," Knight said. "Bill respected Red and played for him, but he wasn't necessarily going to do that for the next guy. But you could be damn sure that Russell would play hard for *Russell*. Red knew that. It was great that he gave Russell the opportunity he did, but he did it for practical reasons too."

Red and Knight became close during Knight's years at Army, and the relationship continued after Knight went to Indiana and became a controversial icon. Often, after Knight would get involved in a public squabble of some kind, he would call Red, in part to seek advice, in part because he wanted Red to understand his version of events. "I never tried to lecture him," Red said. "I knew he wouldn't want to hear it. But sometimes I would say something like, 'Try not to always make things so hard for yourself.' Maybe sometimes he heard me, maybe other times he didn't."

The relationship reached another level in 1982 after the tragic accident that left Landon Turner, who had starred on Knight's 1981 national championship team, in a wheelchair for life as a paraplegic. The following spring, Knight attended the pre-NBA draft camp in Chicago as a representative of the National Association of Basketball Coaches. Red was there looking at players prior to the draft. At that time, there were ten rounds in the draft, meaning teams took flyers on players unlikely to make their team in the later rounds.

"We were just sitting there watching a game and I just threw out the idea that it would mean a lot to Landon if the Celtics, as a symbolic gesture, drafted him," Knight said. "I didn't make a big deal of it, just said it once and left it at that. I didn't want to push it too hard."

Several weeks later, when the draft was held, Red stood up and announced that the Celtics were drafting Turner with their tenth-round pick. Everyone in the room knew what he was doing, but he didn't leave the gesture there. He had Turner flown in to Boston, the way first-round picks are normally flown in, and presented him with a Celtics jersey with his name and number on it. "I can't begin to tell you how much all of that meant to Landon," Knight said. "The fact that an NBA team would do that was great, but to have it be the Celtics and Red Auerbach? He still talks about it to this day."

Red never saw it as a big deal. "Bob was the one who came up with the idea, not me," he said. "But when we did it, my attitude was, let's do it right. We drafted him, that makes him a Celtic. I wanted him to feel as if he were part of our family."

Two years later, when Knight coached the U.S. Olympic team, he asked Red to come to Bloomington to talk to the team during the pre-Olympic camp. "I like to have him talk to my teams whenever possible," Knight said. "I've even asked him to make tapes I can show the players. They all know who he is and what he's meant to basketball. If they don't, I make sure to remind them because they should know."

Through all the years and all the turmoil, Knight has made a special point of keeping in touch with Red. Because he has such a prodigious memory, he rarely writes things down. But he keeps a note on his desk at all times to remind himself when he last spoke to Red. "I just do it to make sure I call him once a month," he said. "He's important to me. The only tough thing about being his friend is that he never lets you do anything for him."

Last year, Knight finally got to do something for Red.

He talked to me — seventeen years after *A Season on the Brink,* we had our first conversation that went beyond "Hello. How are you?" since the publication of the book. He did it for one reason: Red asked him to do it.

"I don't think," Knight said, "I've ever had a more special relationship with anyone than the one I've had with Red. He was nice to me for no reason years ago and he never stopped."

The last thing that Knight and I discussed during our conversation about Red was the Tuesday lunches. "Someday, when I'm on the East Coast for something, I'm going to come to lunch," Knight said. "I've heard about them and I'd really like to come sometime."

Knight was like a lot of Red's friends who had heard about the lunches, if not from him, then from someone else. In a sense, as Morgan Wootten said, they had taken on a life of their own for everyone involved. I was no exception. Once Zang called to harangue me about not following up on his invitation to return, I began showing up regularly. Like everyone else new to the group, I did more listening than talking — very unusual behavior for me. It quickly became clear that everyone had a role. Red was the patriarch. Everything about the lunches began and ended with him. He decided when it was time to order and when it was time to go. Frequently, he would sit quietly at the start of lunch, then something would pique his interest and trigger a story — or a series of stories. He seemed to revel in the frequent arguments, whether they were about current events in sports, current events in the news, or the age-old debates about who was better: DiMaggio or Williams? Chamberlain or Abdul-Jabbar? (No one would dare put either in the same sentence with Russell, at least in terms of who you would build a team around.) Jordan or Magic? Bush or Kerry?

What made the lunches so lively, in addition to Red's storytelling, was the diversity of the group. Red, Morgan Wootten, Sam Jones, Jack Kvancz, Karl Hobbs (who came far more frequently than Tom Penders had), and Joe McKeown were basketball people. Pete Dowling and Bob Campbell were from the Secret Service. Rob Ades, Aubre Jones, and I had been around sports all our lives — in different roles. Zang and Hymie knew more about Red than the rest of us because they had known him longer. Reid Collins, Red's son-in-law, had spent more time with him in recent years than anyone. Murray Lieberman, who had become Red's urologist, was someone Red trusted implicitly both as a friend and a doctor. The Woodmont crowd — Stanley Walker, Herman Greenberg, Alvin Miller, and others — knew him just as a longtime friend. Stanley Copeland, Zang's son-in-law, may have been the most hard-core sports fan in the group. He was a graphic designer who went to more ball games — many of them high school games — than anybody in the group.

Every one of us was a sports fan, so not surprisingly a lot of time was spent discussing sports. But frequently the liveliest discussions had nothing to do with sports. Pete Dowling liked to call the side of the table nearest the wall "the Republican side." He, Campbell, Collins, and Aubre Jones frequently sat there and parried with Red, Zang, Ades, Hymie, and me when the subject turned to politics. Collins, who grew up in Wyoming and Montana, usually led the way for the Republican side, especially when the subject of gun control came up. When Chris Wallace left ABC News late in 2003 to anchor Fox's Sunday morning show, he received considerable ribbing from the Democratic side of the table.

Wallace's presence in the group was perhaps the only contribution I made that had the complete approval of the others. I had run into him on various occasions through the years and had always found him very unassuming, not at all like the majority of TV types. Most people who work in television not only think they are important but like to tell you so. Wallace is nothing like that. Perhaps that's because he started his career working for the *Boston Globe*. Or maybe it's because, being the son of a major TV star (Mike Wallace) and the stepson of a major TV executive (former CBS News president Bill Leonard), he didn't see anything particularly special about working for a TV network.

One night, we found ourselves sitting together at a hockey game. At some point during the conversation, the subject of the lunches came up. "Wait a minute," Wallace said, a bit of genuine awe in his voice. "You're telling me you get to eat lunch once a week with Red Auerbach?"

When I explained what the lunches were and how I had gotten involved, Wallace shook his head. "Just once," he said, "I'd love to come and sit in."

Red's basic attitude when group members ask if they can bring a guest is simple: if he's a friend of yours — and he had better be a *he* — he's welcome. Everyone knows there are certain people who simply won't fit in, so each picks his people carefully. Wallace seemed to fit in easily, although he would later admit it took a while to feel completely comfortable speaking up.

"Sports has always played an important part in my life," he said. "To me, Red is a part of my past, almost a kind of golden, hazy past. Those years when he was coaching the Celtics were a time of innocence in my life, a time of uncomplicated allegiances. When he starts telling a story about Cousy or Russell or the Jones boys, it's almost as if my memory turns to black and white listening to him, and I can see all of them running up and down the parquet floor again.

"Of course when I was a kid, I *hated* Red and I *hated* the Celtics and I *hated* that damn victory cigar. I wanted to run up, rip it out of his mouth, and stomp it into the parquet floor. He always won, just like the Yankees always won back then. I was tyrannized as a child by two great dynasties — the Celtics and the Yankees. Now, of course, I see Red as one of the great sports icons of all time. To have the chance to sit and listen to him tell his stories every week is amazing."

The importance of sports to Wallace goes beyond being a fan. His parents divorced when he was very young and his mother remarried Bill Leonard, moving from Chicago to New York when Chris was seven. He was already hooked on the White Sox by then, but since Chicago didn't have an NBA team at the time, he quickly became a fan of the Knicks. When he was thirteen, Chris's family suffered a tragedy when his brother, Peter, five years his senior, was killed while mountain climbing in Greece.

No doubt it was not a coincidence that he and his father reconnected soon after that. Mike Wallace wasn't that much of a sports fan but he knew that his son was. So he suggested that they get together for dinner on a regular basis — at Toots Shor's, which was then *the* place for sports people in New York. "I can remember meeting Howard Cosell and Eddie Arcaro and Mickey Vernon — among others," Wallace said. "Joe DiMaggio was in there a lot too. It was fun for me and it made it easier for my dad too, I think, because he knew I enjoyed being in that atmosphere so much."

Wallace's first brush with his future business came in 1964 when his stepfather arranged for him to work as a gofer for Walter Cronkite in the CBS booth at the Republican Convention in San Francisco. That was Barry Goldwater's convention and Wallace can still remember being in the booth when Goldwater began carving up the media. "I remember when he got to the line about 'sensation-seeking commentators and columnists' that a lot of the delegates started shaking the booth from below," Wallace said. "I also remember thinking what could be more fun than to be at the center of the world, at an event everyone was talking about, working with people everyone was listening to, *and* get paid for it. After that I think I was more or less hooked."

Wallace went to Harvard, had good grades, and did well enough on the LSATs to get accepted to Yale Law School when he graduated in 1969. "I would have been a classmate of Hillary Rodham," he said, smiling. "Somewhere between graduation and the start of law school, I decided I really didn't want to go to school. I wanted to get into the news business. I ended up with a choice between the *Globe* and one of the local TV stations. I sat down with my stepfather and he said to me, 'If you're going to do newspapers, do it now. You'll always have the chance to go from newspapers to TV, but people don't go from TV to newspapers. What's more, you'll learn to report, write, and think better.'"

Wallace took the advice and worked at the *Globe* for four years. "I loved it there," he said. "I covered city hall, wrote a column, and learned a lot. But I guess because of my father and stepfather, the TV bug was always there."

In 1973, Robert Wussler, who had been a producer at CBS and was friends with both Mike Wallace and Bill Leonard, took over WBBM-TV in Chicago and offered Chris a job. He decided it was time to find out about television. He went from there to the local NBC affiliate in New York and then to the NBC network in 1978. He stayed with NBC eleven years before moving to ABC in 1989. He stayed there until the opportunity at Fox came along late in 2003.

But he never stopped following sports. When the network needed a sports feature done, he frequently volunteered because it gave him a chance to spend time around the games he loves and meet some of the athletes and coaches he has admired for so long. That was how our paths crossed and led to his becoming a regular at lunch.

"It's almost surprising to me how important the lunches have become to me," he said one day. "I've talked to my wife about them and I think it has a lot to do with the fact that it's a time every week when I completely forget about my job, about the merry-go-round at home [Wallace has six children — four with his wife and two stepchildren], and all the different things I'm responsible for every week. This is just for me, something I genuinely enjoy and look forward to with a bunch of guys who I like and who have no agenda other than to enjoy one another's company."

He laughed. "And I have to admit, I get a kick out of being

with my friends and being able to say, 'You know, the other day Red Auerbach was telling a story about Wilt Chamberlain and Bill Russell, back when Alex Hannum told Chamberlain not to talk to Russell or Red . . .' "

In September of 2000, just before Red's eighty-third birthday, Dorothy Auerbach died. She had been fighting cancer for two years and her health had slipped badly during her final months. It was never something Red talked about, but the GW people who rode with him to lunch were often with him when he stopped on the way home to pick up her medicine. She died on a Saturday night and Zang made all the phone calls the next day to let everyone know. Naturally, everyone asked the same question: "Is there anything we can do?"

"Yeah, as a matter of fact, there is," Zang said. "Red told me to tell everyone to please not make a big deal out of it. He knows everyone is going to want to say something, but he doesn't want to dwell on it."

No one was all that surprised to hear that. It has never been Red's way to show a lot of emotion or to be comfortable around people directing emotion at him, even those who care about him. But there was little doubt that Dorothy's death, after fifty-nine years of marriage, rocked him. Reid Collins and Red and Dorothy's daughter Nancy were at the hospital the night Dorothy died.

"We went back to the apartment and Red lit up a cigar," Reid remembered. "He was, as you might expect, very quiet.

He hadn't smoked a cigar in the apartment since Dorothy had gotten sick because he knew it wasn't good for her. It was as if he knew she would have wanted him to have the cigar, that, at that moment, he deserved it. Red's had lots of friends through the years, but there's no question whom he was closest to in the world."

Even a couple years after her death, it was not easy for Red to talk about Dorothy. "She didn't like to read the papers," he said with a smile. "Because if there was anything in there about me that was even a little bit negative it made her mad. She was very smart, someone whose opinions I always respected and listened to. But she was also very supportive of whatever I wanted to do, especially in the early days when I was all over the place trying to figure out exactly what I wanted to do and where I was finally going to end up coaching."

The most difficult decision the young couple had to make came in 1950 when Red got the Celtics job and Nancy's doctor suggested that Boston winters would be very bad for her asthma. "We decided to try it the first season with Dorothy and the kids in Washington and with me in Boston," Red said. "I'm sure it was much tougher on her than it was on me. I was always busy, traveling, coaching the team. There was so much to do, especially those first couple of years. I would get home whenever I could during the season, but I know it wasn't easy for her, being there with two young kids like that.

"But she never complained and, after a while, we got used to living like that. In some ways, I think it was better for the family. I was *not* easy to be around during the season. I tried to

245

leave the games at the arena, but I wasn't very good at it. If we lost, I was in a bad mood. Hell, sometimes when we won, I came home in a bad mood because we hadn't played well. Plus, in those days, there were so many more newspapers in Boston and there were times when guys really went after me. Dorothy would not have liked that. This way, she missed most of that."

It was Dorothy Auerbach whom Russell called when Red first told him he was planning to give up coaching. "He thought that she was the only one who might have been able to talk me out of it," he said. "He wasn't wrong. If anyone could have talked me out of it, it might have been her."

When Red stepped down as coach, family life became a lot more reasonable. Red kept the apartment in Boston — he still has it to this day — but only went there when he had to, for big games and for meetings. Friends of the Auerbachs came to understand that phone calls in the evening were frowned upon. That was the time Red and Dorothy always reserved for each other. One of the things people misunderstand about Red is the fact that he has never needed the spotlight. He always accepted it as part of the job and never backed away from doing what he had to do in public for his position. But he never craved attention. In fact, what he craved was quiet time with his family and friends.

"I've always been bothered by coaches who call attention to themselves all the time," he said. "When I was coaching, after the game I would come out of the locker room and talk to the guys [media] for a few minutes in the hallway outside. Then I would say, 'Okay, that's enough. Go talk to the players, they're the ones who played in the game, not me.' I never wanted any-one to think I thought of myself as the star of the team. I wasn't. I was the coach of the team, not the star.

"Nowadays, guys can't get enough of the cameras. Half the reason they get on the refs as much as they do is because they know when they do, the cameras are going to be on them." He smiled. "Of course when I coached I got on the refs pretty good too. But I only did it because I was really mad. Back then, most of the time, there weren't any cameras around anyway."

Dorothy Auerbach liked attention even less than her hus-band. She would come to Boston when she had to, for events such as the hanging of Red's number two in the rafters of the Boston Garden, the celebration of his fiftieth anniversary with the Celtics, and his eightieth birthday party — a huge event held in the Fleet Center, with all the male attendees in black tie. Beyond that, Dorothy was more than content to remain in Washington with her children, with her grandchild, and, at the end of her life, with her great-grandchildren.

Ten days after Dorothy's death, the group gathered again. Naturally, Hymie had called Zang the week before on Monday night. "I know Red can't make it tomorrow," Hymie said. "But can he swing by the restaurant and drop off his credit card?"

Awful as that comment may sound, it was exactly the kind of line Red would have enjoyed, because sympathy was the last thing he wanted. He also knew that no one was more crushed for him than Hymie. When lunch reconvened, there was a somber tone as everyone arrived. All of us had our marching orders from Zang to keep the condolences brief. That was what we did: an arm around Red's shoulder, a few words whispered in his ear. Morgan Wootten brought a card because he was afraid he would break down if he started to say anything, and he quietly slipped it to Red. Each time someone said something, Red's response was soft, very soft, no more than a few words, and perhaps he gave a pat on the back or held on to someone's hand for an extra beat or two. It was still quiet when everyone sat down, no one quite sure what to say, how to break the mood.

Red waited a few seconds to see if anyone was going to say something more. Then he waved an arm toward Emma Lee, who manages the China Doll, and said what he says every Tuesday at about 11:10. "Emma, let's get this show on the road."

12

The New Guys

"HEY, JACK, whatever happened to that kid you asked me to talk to a couple years ago? Kid didn't listen to a word I said, did he?"

Jack Kvancz laughed. Red was talking about SirValiant Brown (yes, his real name), a talented scorer who had spent two years at George Washington during the brief, ill-fated Tom Penders coaching era. At the end of his sophomore season, urged on by his buddies, Brown had decided he should withdraw from school and enter his name in the NBA draft. Kvancz, an old coach himself, knew it was a mistake, that Brown was too small (a slender six-foot-one), and his game had too many holes in it for him to possibly be ready for the NBA. He also knew there was no chance Brown would listen to him or to Penders, especially since his buddies would argue that they both had a vested interest in seeing him return to GW.

"You want me to talk to him?" Red had asked Kvancz.

"Sure, why not?" Kvancz answered. "But there's one thing. When you talk to him, maybe you can bring all your rings with you? Otherwise, I'm not sure the kid will know who you are."

Red laughed. He understands how it is with today's generation of players. He also understands that players in college today were born fifteen to twenty years after he stopped coaching. "Most of them don't remember Russell or Cousy or Havlicek or the Jones boys, much less remember me," he will say. "That's okay, I understand. They all think basketball started with Michael Jordan."

Actually, with Jordan now retired, a lot of the current players think basketball began with Kobe Bryant. Or LeBron James. Kvancz did set up the meeting for Red and Brown one morning in his office. The GW players do have a sense of who Red is. They see him at practice, they know they play in an early-season tournament called the Red Auerbach Classic. (Red attends but doesn't go down on the court to present the trophy. "They never play anybody good," he says. "I'm not going down all those steps until they play somebody good.") And they know there's a plaque with his name on it outside the door that they walk through every day on their way into the Smith Center.

"They know he's somebody," Kvancz says. "But they aren't quite sure who."

Brown listened to what Red had to say. He heard him explain that there are now only two rounds in the NBA draft, and there was a reasonable chance, from what he had heard from scouts, that he wouldn't be drafted. He heard him further explain that only the twenty-nine players chosen in the first round were guaranteed money. He listened while Red told him what he needed to work on in his game and that he believed if he worked on those things for two more years he could be a first-round pick. Red did not lecture about the value of an education.

"I knew *that* was a waste of time," he said.

Brown thanked Red for his time. He then proceeded to turn pro. He was not drafted in the first round or the second round. He didn't make an NBA roster, that year or any year since.

"Coach, I think he's playing in the NBDL [National Basketball Development League] or something like that," Kvancz answered when Red brought him up.

Red shook his head. "It's too bad. You know, the kid could really score. He wasn't a great shooter, but he was a scorer. He found ways to score. If he'd stayed, he might have had a chance."

Because of his remarkable memory, Red keeps close tabs on a lot of players, including almost everyone who comes through GW. He certainly doesn't lecture on staying in school, because he believes there are times when a player should leave early. "You have to look at each case individually," he said. "Brown was a no-brainer. He should have stayed. But [Alexander] Koul [a Russian center who played at GW in the mid-nineties] would have been a lottery pick if he'd come out after his sophomore year. He stayed and ended up not getting drafted because he didn't get any better. In fact, he got worse, got all messed up."

The GW player whose story makes Red saddest is Yinka Dare, a Nigerian center who starred on the school's NCAA Tournament teams in 1993 and 1994 when Mike Jarvis revived the program. Dare had an extraordinary upper body — "He looked like he was chiseled from stone from the waist up," Red said — but had weak legs and absolutely awful hands. "That was the problem," Red said. "His hands were chiseled from stone too."

Dare had potential, though, if he had learned how to play. Like many players from overseas, he hadn't played that much basketball and was learning — and improving — as he went. Then an agent got to him after his sophomore year and convinced him to turn pro. He was drafted by the New Jersey Nets and made good money sitting on the bench for several years but never became any kind of player. A few days after New Year's in 2004, he collapsed at his home in New Jersey and died of a heart attack at the age of thirty-two.

Red hates to see potential squandered. As much as he admires Mike Krzyzewski, he still talks about Tommy Amaker, Krzyzewski's first great point guard at Duke. "I never thought Mike gave him the chance to be the player he could have been," Red said. "I saw the kid play in high school and he could really score. But at Duke, he's with [Johnny] Dawkins and [Mark] Alarie and Mike never really let him shoot the ball. I thought he limited him. I still think the kid should have played in the NBA for ten years."

Amaker was Duke's second leading scorer in 1987 as a senior (after Dawkins and Alarie graduated) but never did play in the

NBA. Instead, he has gone on to become a college head coach himself, currently at Michigan. Hearing that Red had said he could have played in the NBA for ten years, Amaker laughed. "He really said that? Well then, why didn't he draft me?"

"I knew he'd ask that," Red said. "Good question. We were pretty loaded with guards back then. I still think the kid was a pro — a good one — if he'd been allowed to shoot more in college."

One reason Red would bring Amaker up was because he knows Krzyzewski is a friend of mine and he loves to apply the needle. Pete Dowling and Bob Campbell get nailed whenever the Secret Service makes a mistake of any kind; Jack Kvancz is berated for almost any problem involving the NCAA Tournament (he was on the tournament committee for five years); Joe McKeown is often reminded about the limited jumping ability of most female basketball players; Reid Collins hears it when something goes wrong with the Bush White House; and Rob Ades is constantly reminded that today's coaches are overpaid and rarely run clean programs. I get it whenever Duke loses or Krzyzewski makes a mistake.

One day when he started in on Amaker again, I had to respond. "You know, I saw Tommy play for four years in college," I said. "He was a wonderful college player. But he was never much of a shooter. He passed, he defended, he ran the team — but he would tell you himself he wasn't a great shooter."

Red looked at me the way one might look at someone handing out a leaflet on a street corner. "Morgan, you saw Amaker in high school," he said. "How good a scorer was he?"

"Great scorer," Wootten said. "You couldn't stop him."

Red gave me his favorite look of disdain. I stood my ground. "Well, I still don't think he was meant to be a big-time scorer in college," I insisted.

Rob Ades started laughing. "John," he said, "do you realize what you're doing? You're telling the greatest pro coach who ever lived and the greatest high school coach who ever lived that their analysis of a player isn't as valid as your analysis of a player."

I thought about that for a minute. Then I said, "Krzyzewski can't coach a lick."

Red smiled triumphantly and called for the check.

Even though Pitino's resignation meant that Red got back his title of president, he took no joy in seeing Pitino fail. "He fails, it means we fail," he said. "I really think it was too bad the way it all turned out. It might have been different if we'd gotten [Tim] Duncan in the lottery that first year. But you can't depend on things like that. It doesn't happen, you move on. I'm not sure Rick ever moved on from that."

The notion that he might walk into coaching Duncan was undoubtedly one of the things that enticed Pitino away from being king of Kentucky. That and $10 million a year, absolute power, and the title of president. Red doesn't harp on that these days. He liked Jim O'Brien, who succeeded Pitino as coach, and he likes the new ownership troika of Wycliffe Grousbeck, H. Irving Grousbeck, and Steve Pagliuca, who bought the team from the Gaston family in 2002. It bothers him when the team plays poorly, so the 2003–04 season was like water torture for him as the Celtics lurched along, fighting to get within range of .500. When O'Brien quit midway through the season because of disputes with Danny Ainge over personnel, Red was disappointed.

"Coaches today are so insecure," he said. "They need to have everything their way. Jim's a very good coach, he did a very good job for us, I thought. But he likes one kind of player — guys who play defense — and Danny likes another — guys who are creative on offense. The two of them were bound to clash, which is unfortunate because they're both good guys."

I suggested to Red on the night O'Brien quit that this was a perfect time to make a comeback, given all the senior citizens — Jack McKeon, Joe Gibbs, Bill Parcells, Dick Vermeil, Hubie Brown, Lenny Wilkens — who were coming out of retirement to take over teams again.

"Ha!" He laughed. "You know what the toughest thing is for all those guys? Getting in and out of their clothes for practice. I'm not kidding. Once you hit sixty, it isn't easy anymore. All my friends who coached into their sixties will tell you that."

Red doesn't try to interfere in the running of the Celtics at this stage, but he will always offer an opinion if asked. The new owners made a point of coming to Washington to meet with him soon after they took over the team and have encouraged him to come to Boston as often as he can. His presence in the Fleet Center is always a big deal; the fans routinely give him an ovation just for walking to his seat. He watches a lot of basketball — pro, college, and even high school, and even though he doesn't like to admit it, he will steal glances at the GW women's games — and still has very firm opinions about who can play and who can't.

"We've got too many guys who are good players on other teams," he said. "Unfortunately, the most important thing in basketball today might be having someone who understands how to get around the [salary] cap. [David] Wesley and [Rick] Fox and [Danny] Fortson were mistakes Pitino made. But look at some of the others we've lost: Chauncey Billups and Rodney Rogers and Popeye Jones and Ron Mercer. Those guys are all very good players and we couldn't afford them under the cap. You've got to figure out a way to keep your good players once you've got them."

Red often attends college games in the Washington area. He rarely misses a home game at GW, he often goes to Georgetown games because ex-Hoyas coach John Thompson is an old Celtic and an old friend, and he will make the long trip to Maryland when the big-name teams come to town. He's not crazy about Maryland's new arena, the Comcast Center. "Too loud," he says. "Not the fans — all the music and special effects stuff. Who needs it if you've got a good team and a good game?"

Most of the time when he goes to games, Red is accompanied by one or more members of the China Doll gang — and his daughter Nancy. Often Reid Collins, Rob Ades, and Murray Lieberman are in the group. Murray carries one of those pocket computers that allows him to check scores, so if the

Celtics are playing, Red will ask him every three-to-five minutes, "How we doing?" If the news is bad, Murray will often claim the computer isn't working. "Of course I know he's lying," Red says. "I play along because I figure if he doesn't want me to hear the score, it's because I don't want to hear the score."

Red is always checking out players. When Duke came to Georgetown last season, Red spent most of the game focusing on sophomore sharpshooter J. J. Redick. "I knew he could shoot," he said, "but I wanted to watch the rest of his game. He's a better athlete than people think. He works on defense and he's quicker than people give him credit for. I think he'll be a good NBA player."

Like a lot of NBA people, Red worries about what is going on in the league right now. TV ratings have plunged, attendance has gone down, and the popularity of the league has gone south since Michael Jordan's second retirement from the Chicago Bulls. "There are no easy answers," he said. "I think trying the zone defense was a good idea because teams were cheating all the time and playing zone anyway, so why not legalize it? But I think a lot of the problem gets back to the money — not the money the players are making but the money the coaches are making. They're making millions, and because they're making millions, they're expected to win right away *and* keep winning. If they don't win, they get fired. Well, no one wants to get fired from a job that pays him millions, so most of them take the approach that they're going to control *everything*.

"Look, I understand what they're thinking. When I first coached the Caps, a lot of the players were as old or older than I was. I told them right from the beginning that we were going to do things my way, that if I was going to fail and lose my job it was going to be doing things the way I thought best. If it didn't work, it didn't work, but I wasn't going to lose the job because the players weren't listening to me.

"I remember one game I took a guy named Matt Zunic out of the game. He had been a couple years behind me at GW, so we knew each other pretty well. I gave him a shot even though I knew he had a temper. In school we called him Mad Matt because he was always mad about something. He comes out and starts screaming at me on the bench. 'Why are you taking me out now? There's no reason to take me out.' I let him sit down and cool off for a few seconds, then I called him up to sit with me. I'm sure he thought I'd learned my lesson and was sending him back in the game. I said to him, 'Now you listen to me. Don't you *ever* react that way again when I take you out. If I take you out, it's for a reason and it's because I think it's best for the club at that moment. I don't owe you an explanation for anything. If you don't like it, you can quit. If you do it again, you're fired. End of story.'

"That kind of control I understand. You have to have it and nowadays it can be much harder to get it. But you have to know where to stop. You can't control every single play. Coaches today figure you can't control a fast break the way you can control a half-court offense. These guys don't want a running game because they lose control if they have one. They want to walk the ball up the court so they can stand up and control every possession, every pass. They feel more secure that way. That's why we're getting all these games now with teams scoring in the sixties and seventies and even the fifties on occasion. It's ridiculous. As a coach, you have to go out and get the best players you possibly can, coach them as well as you possibly can, and then, ultimately, like it or not, trust them to know how to play. You can't micromanage the game. One thing [Phil] Jackson does well is he trusts his players, which is one of the reasons they play for him. He's not up on every play pointing to where the next pass should go. And then, when the Lakers lose, people get on him because he wasn't up screaming or calling a time-out the minute the other team scored two straight baskets. A lot of coaches get up and scream or call time-outs so they *look* like they know what they're doing. It's all about image these days.

"Does it work? Maybe for some guys, but the thing that always works best is winning. You can be the best-dressed guy in the world, be great with the media, be popular with your players — if you don't win, you're gonna get fired. Look at the Eastern Conference right now. There's no one who was coaching his team at the end of the '03 season. That's the problem with making a lot of money: people aren't going to be patient with you. You're expected to produce *now* or you're gone.

"There's so much money at stake because the salaries have gone so high. Of course it could be worse. We could be baseball."

Red was good friends years ago with Dick O'Connell, who was then the general manager of the Red Sox. "O'Connell used to laugh at me when our salaries started to skyrocket," he said. "He would say to me, 'You guys are clueless, you don't know what you're doing, you're ruining your game.' I told him to just wait. The same thing would happen to baseball, only worse. Of course it did and the owners handled themselves in such a way that the players union dug in and said it was going to bleed every last cent out of the owners that they could. In basketball, as bad as things may have gotten, David Stern and Larry Fleischer were able to get together and come up with the salary cap that saved us.

"So when the salaries went crazy in baseball, O'Connell comes to me and says, 'What should we do? What should we do?' I said, 'Dick, take two and hit to right.' "

The list of people Red has known through the years is mind-boggling. Almost anytime someone mentions the name of someone famous, Red not only knows them but has a story about them.

"Cardinal Cushing," he said one day. "Now that guy was a piece of work."

Cushing was the longtime archbishop of Boston. As Red tells it, their friendship came about because of an offhanded remark he made one day after giving a speech at DeMatha as a favor to Morgan Wootten. "I was walking out and one of the priests at the school stopped me and asked me why the number they had raised in my honor at the Boston Garden was the number two instead of the number one. Well, everyone who knows the history of the Celtics knows that the number one we've got up there is for Walter Brown. But I was in a joking mood, so I just said to him, 'In Boston, there's only one guy who can be number one and that's Cardinal Cushing. The rest of us are in line to be number two.'

"Never gave it a second thought. Next thing I know, I get a letter from Cardinal Cushing! He's enclosed a clip from a story that ran in the national Catholic newspaper quoting me on what I said at DeMatha. He writes that he's incredibly flattered that I said what I said and he hopes we can get together sometime since he's a big basketball fan. After that, we became pretty good friends."

Red once asked the cardinal if he thought it helped players to cross themselves before they shot free throws. "I think it does help," Cushing answered, "if they're good shooters."

Red has a slew of famous friends from outside the sports world, many of them, not surprisingly, from Massachusetts. He was very friendly with Tip O'Neill, the late Speaker of the House of Representatives, and has known the Kennedy family for years and is good friends with Senator Edward M. Kennedy. He's also close to Senator John F. Kerry — "a real ball fan" — and talks often to Representative Ed Markey, whose basketball fanaticism extends down to the high school level. "Of all the politicians I've known, Markey knows more about basketball than any of them," he said, laughing. "I think he likes basketball more than I do." Politicians frequently come to Red seeking his support. In 2000 Red was approached by Al Gore's people to see if he might be interested in helping the Gore campaign. Their angle was the St. Albans connection — Red coached there and Gore graduated from there. Red was willing. "Gore seems like a good guy," he said. "It never worked out, though. I think they got bogged down in other things."

Red was close enough to Ted Kennedy that he called him when his twelve-year-old son Ted Jr. had to have part of his leg amputated due to cancer. He volunteered to visit him in the hospital. "I took [John] Havlicek with me the first time we went," he said. "I think the kid got a real kick out of it. We spent about three hours with him and talked hoops. He was an amazing kid. About a week after the surgery, he was at a game with his dad, acting as if nothing at all had happened to him."

Kennedy had a town house in those days that wasn't far from the Boston Garden, and he frequently had everyone from the Celtics organization over. "He loved sports," Red said. "Came to as many games as he could. I think he had the Bruins and Red Sox over whenever he could too. It was a distraction for him to talk about something that was a lot less serious than what he was dealing with in the Senate all the time."

Red was also friends with President John F. Kennedy and later with his son John F. Kennedy Jr. In fact, when John Jr. was editing the political magazine *George,* he came to Washington to interview Red for the magazine. "He kept wanting to talk about basketball. I wanted to talk about politics," Red said. "He was a smart kid. I was curious to know what he thought about things. He kept asking me what was wrong with the Knicks. He was a real fan."

In fact, according to Ted Kennedy, he more or less "inherited" his friendship with Red from his older brother, the late president. "I was in college when Red first came to Boston, and of course we all became fans of his because he did such an amazing job turning the Celtics into a power," he said. "I met him through my brother and I was always impressed with the fact that he thought it so important to have his team involved in the community. He did it back in the fifties and he was still doing it in the eighties. I can remember Red arranging to have Larry Bird make appearances with me at public schools around the state the same way he had Cousy and Sharman and Heinsohn and Russell doing things like that back in the fifties."

Not surprisingly, Ted Kennedy's most vivid memories of Red center on the time period when his son was sick. "The first visit meant so much to Teddy because he loved the Celtics," he said. "To have Red Auerbach and John Havlicek walk in with a signed basketball from the team and then spend all that time with him, well, you can imagine how much that meant to a twelve-year-old boy fighting cancer."

Kennedy paused. "It's tough, even now," he said, "to talk about this." (Ted Kennedy Jr. is forty-one now, healthy and married with two children of his own.) He took a deep breath and went on. "After the surgery, Teddy had to go to Mass General on a series of Fridays for treatments that were very painful. In essence, he knew every time we went there he was going to spend thirty-six hours in extreme pain. The way we got him through those weekends was that we scheduled them around Celtics games on Sunday afternoons. He would know that was waiting for him at the end of the treatment, and I honestly believe that's what got him through those weekends.

"Red would always make a point of coming over to check up on him when we went to the games. Another time he had Dave Cowens come to the hospital to see him. If there's one thing I've learned having been on the Health Care Committee for many years in the Senate, it's that how children mend in the midst of a medical crisis depends a lot on their attitude and on their disposition. If their minds are set and there is a sense of inspiration and happiness, they have a much better chance to recover. Teddy had that, and Red and the Celtics were a big part of it. I'll never forget him for that."

Kennedy remembers that when Red and the Celtics would come to his town house, people would crowd around Red to hear him tell stories. "He's one of those people everyone wants to be around. Listening to his stories wasn't just good entertainment. You almost always learned something by listening to him."

As much as he has enjoyed his associations with people such as Ted Kennedy and others in politics, Red's closest friends through the years were people associated with sports. Even though he battled often with the media, some of his most trusted friends were media members: the late Will McDonough of the *Boston Globe* was one of his confidants, and so was Marty Glickman, the legendary New York broadcaster. "Marty and I got to be friends when he was doing the Knicks," Red said. "Even though he worked for them, he was so good and so professional that I came to really respect him, and that started the friendship. He would come up to Kutsher's in the summer and we would spend time together then."

Glickman was arguably the best athlete ever to become a play-by-play man. He was a sprinter on the 1936 U.S. Olympic team that went to Berlin and was supposed to be a part of the American 4 x 100 meter relay. Glickman was one of two Jewish athletes scheduled to run on the relay. At the last minute, Avery Brundage, the chairman of the U.S. Olympic Committee at the time, decided to replace both Glickman and Sam Stoller so as "not to offend" Adolf Hitler, whose anti-Jewish policies were well known to the U.S. contingent. That relay produced Jesse Owens's fourth gold medal.

"I'm not sure Marty ever got over that completely and I don't blame him," Red said. "Back then, you really only got one shot at being in the Olympics because you had to go out and earn a living. It isn't like today, where you can get paid to be a track star and just keep coming back one Olympics after another. That was his one chance and he didn't get it because the fact is, Brundage was an anti-Semite. Marty was always convinced Brundage was glad to have the chance to pull him from the relay. He hated the man with a passion. After the Olympics were over, the track team toured Europe and Marty was restored to the relay. No one came close to beating them. There's no way they wouldn't have won the gold medal. He had that stolen from him by Brundage."

Red and Glickman staged their own one-on-one Olympics each summer at Kutsher's. "We had a 'decathlon': tennis, rowing, handball, basketball," Red said. "I wouldn't do any-thing that involved running or swimming — he would have killed me in both of them. I beat him in basketball and hand-ball, he beat me in rowing, and we were pretty even in tennis. Of course if we *had* done any running events, it would have been no contest."

Red's respect for Glickman is perhaps best illustrated by the fact that he was the only person who ever convinced Red to change his coaching style. "He came to me at one point and said he thought I was hurting the team and my image because I was up so much during games and on the refs so often," Red said. "I knew he was genuinely concerned, and since I re-spected his opinions, I was willing to give it a try. For two games I never got up about a call, never got on a ref, never re-ally got on the players except during time-outs. We got blown out in both games.

"After the second one, Marty came to me and said, 'I was wrong. You have to be into the game emotionally. You need to stay on the refs for your sake and for your players' sakes.' So I went back to doing what I had always done."

During his career, Glickman was the radio voice of the Knicks, the New York Giants, and later the New York Jets. He also did a high school football and basketball game of the week on local television and was the track announcer for twelve years at Yonkers Raceway. "I always thought his biggest mis-take was staying at Yonkers all those years," Red said. "I mean he was good at it and he enjoyed it and they paid him well. But because he was committed to Yonkers, he couldn't travel and do national games for the networks all those years when he was at his peak as a broadcaster. He should have been doing national games because he was as good as it got back then. He should have been the number one guy on football for one of the networks — basketball too — and he could have done baseball if he wanted to do baseball. But he liked being at Yonkers so it never happened, which I think is a shame."

One thing Red and Glickman never agreed on was football. Glickman enjoyed the sport so much that, in addition to his NFL work, he voluntarily did 11:00 a.m. high school games on local New York TV on Saturdays. Red always respected football players but never really saw the allure of the sport. "I remember years ago I went to a game at Boston College," he said. "I had great seats: eighth row, fifty-yard line. The game starts. On the first play everyone in front of me stands up. I figure, 'Okay, it's the first play.' Next play they all stand up again. By midway through the first quarter, it occurs to me that the only way I'm going to see the damn game is if I stand up on every play too. So I stood up — and left.

"Years later, Marty convinced me to go with him to a Giants game. He told me I could sit up in the booth with him and no one would block my view. I would have a perfect seat. He was right, it was perfect. I sat in an armchair, there was food right there, it was nice and warm. Only problem was I fell sound asleep."

Red's other great broadcasting friend was Johnny Most, the legendary voice of the Celtics throughout the glory years, from Russell right through Bird and beyond. "The only time I ever had a problem with Johnny was when he sent his kid to my summer camp," Red said. "Johnny was the perfect broadcaster for us. People tell me all the time, 'He was a terrible homer. The Celtics never committed a foul when he was doing a game.' I would tell them, 'You're darn right we didn't. That's just the way I wanted it!' I told Johnny, 'This is the Celtics network, listened to by Celtics fans, and you do the game the way a Celtics fan would do it.' I guess you could say he took instructions pretty well."

Red is not a big fan of color commentators. "Most of them are fired coaches," he said. "If they know the game so well, then why'd they lose their jobs coaching? It's amazing how you can fail as a coach, they give you a microphone, and all of a sudden you're the world's greatest basketball expert. Some of them are okay. I like Doug Collins because he explains the game. He doesn't sit there and second-guess every move the coaches are making. I can't stand that. It's crazy what stars we make of some of these guys. Al McGuire was pretty good because he was funny and he never tried to sound like he was a coaching genius. Of course he wasn't fired, was he? He retired."

One coach whom Red counseled to stay away from a microphone was Bob Knight. In 1981, after Knight had won his second national championship at Indiana, he seriously considered an offer from CBS to give up coaching and become the network's number one analyst after it had wrested the rights to the NCAA Tournament from NBC. Knight called Red, seeking his input while trying to decide what to do. "I told him he was crazy to do it," Red said. "First of all, he's a great coach, he loves it, even if at times it frustrates him. Everyone gets frustrated. But beyond that, if he'd gone into broadcasting, the media would have killed him. They could never really criticize him as a coach because he was so good, but as soon as he was in broadcasting, they'd have nailed him for anything he did wrong. All those years of him going after them, this would have been their chance to get even. And don't think they wouldn't have done it. That's what I told him."

In spite of his many friendships with media people, Red is like most players and coaches in that he tends to view the media with suspicion. He has certainly had his battles with reporters, dating back to his early days in Boston when a lot of the local columnists were disdainful of the NBA, disdainful of the Celtics, and disdainful of the brash young coach who had the nerve to call Bob Cousy a "local yokel," even if he did later admit he had misjudged Cousy. He is old-fashioned enough to still oppose the idea of female reporters in the locker room, even though he is close friends with and has great respect for Jackie McMullan of the *Boston Globe*.

Red also likes to put reporters on sometimes. Last year, on the fortieth anniversary of President John F. Kennedy's assassination, a network TV crew came to his office to get him to talk about his friendship with Kennedy. "A bunch of guys came in and put up all these lights," Red said. "Took forever. I had to sit there while they worked, which made it hard for me to get anything done. Okay, fine. Then the woman who is supposed to interview me shows up — late. We're all waiting for her. She comes in, no apology, then she says she needs a few more minutes to go do her makeup. Fine. At last, she comes back, then she starts wanting to adjust the lights. I wait some more. Finally, she's ready. She has a clipboard with all these questions. She looks down at her clipboard and comes up with the first question: 'Where were you when you heard President Kennedy had been shot?' "

According to one of the technical men working the interview, Red's description of the morning is completely accurate. He then describes what happened next. "So she asks the question. Red's eyes go wide, the cigar drops out of his mouth, he leans forward and says, 'You mean they shot Kennedy? Nobody told me!' I thought our reporter was going to faint."

Red's closest friend in the media might very well have been Will McDonough, the *Boston Globe* columnist who may have had more important sources than anyone in the history of sportswriting. "The reason we were able to stay close through the years was I never gave him a scoop," Red said. "I never misled him and I made sure he was protected if a story was breaking, but he never came to me and asked me to give him the story. Of course he was so good that he'd get the story with or without me most of the time. I knew I could bounce something important off of Will and get his input and it wouldn't show up in the paper. Conversely, he knew that when the time came, he was going to get the story first, that I would never put him in a position of having to explain how he could know about something and not be the one to break the story."

McDonough's death early in 2003 was crushing for Red because he lost one of those friends who he always felt he could call at any hour, day or night, just to talk. As many people as Red knows, there are only a handful that he feels that comfortable with, and McDonough was one of them. A few weeks before his death, I talked to McDonough about Red.

"You have to understand a couple of things about him," McDonough said. "First, he's smarter than you, he's smarter than me, he's smarter than just about all of us. He's got an amazing feel for people. That's what made him such a great coach. People say he had great players. Who do you think chose the players? Think about the notion of winning nine championships in ten years today. Forget free agency tearing a team apart, what about egos? Look at who he had in that locker room — Russell, Cousy, Sharman, Heinsohn, then Havlicek, Sam, and K. C., and on and on. Every one of those guys is in the Hall of Fame. But every one of them listened to Red and did whatever he told them they had to do in order to win. That's why he always says that he never 'handled' players. He never tried to handle anyone. He was completely honest with them, told them what was expected of them, and gave them a choice: my way or the highway. There was never any ambiguity."

Red laughed when told of McDonough's description of his style. "I used to tell the guys they had two options: they could do it my way or they could be shipped to Siberia — Minnesota."

Beyond that, McDonough said, those who spend time with Red come to understand that under the gruff exterior is someone who is compassionate and loyal to the people in his life. "The hardest thing about being his friend is trying to do him a favor," McDonough said. "I almost hated asking him for anything because I knew the answer would be yes, but I knew if I tried to do anything for him it would be almost impossible. For one thing, he just doesn't need very much. For another, he doesn't like to ask for things even if he does need something. It's just not his way."

Most of Red's friends voice the same complaint about him. At the end of my conversation with Bob Knight, I thanked him for the time and said, "Bob, I know you did this for Red, but I want you to know I'm grateful."

Knight answered without any hesitation. "No," he said, "I should thank you. I don't get many chances to do something for Red. I'm glad to have had the chance. It means a lot to me."

Just as Red means a lot to him. And to so many others.

13

Still the Man

"COACHES TODAY DRIVE me just a little bit crazy. When I hear one of them say after a game that he's going to have to look at the film to figure out what happened, I bust out laughing. I mean, who do they think they're kidding? You lose a game, you know exactly why you lost the game. You know who screwed up, and if you don't, you shouldn't be coaching in the first place. When I coached, we didn't have film or tape or anything like that. You think I didn't know who could play and who couldn't play? These guys today want you to believe that what they're doing is some kind of science. Coaching is simple: you need good players who are good people. You have that, you win. You don't have that, you can be the greatest coach who ever lived and you aren't going to win."

Red respects a lot of today's coaches and readily admits that there are added pressures now that didn't exist when he was coaching, notably all the media demands that are a daily part of the job. But he laughs when he hears coaches act as if they're splitting the atom while trying to concoct a good man-to-man offense. "Here's what bugs me. You got thirty seconds to go and a coach calls time-out to call a play. First of all, if he's any good, he doesn't really need the time-out because when you call time, you let the defense set up. But sometimes you have to call it or maybe the other guys call it. Okay. But then he pulls out a clipboard and starts drawing a play. Are you kidding me? You think with all that adrenaline pumping in a close game, the players are going to be looking at what he's drawing and get it? Take a look sometime and see if the players are paying attention. They're not. And half the time the coach doesn't even care if they're paying attention. He's drawing the play up for himself so he can say afterward, 'Well, I called this play and it should have worked . . .' You have to have a play for that situation and the players better know it. You want a certain guy to get a shot with the clock running down and you need a second option in case they double your first guy. That's it. Then you go to the boards for a rebound.

"The biggest mistake coaches make is overcoaching. When you see a guy up, especially in the pros, trying to control every play, that's overcoaching. If your guys don't know where to throw the ball or who they're guarding or where they're supposed to be on defense once the game starts, you're in trouble. Like I said, though, it's about control and about *looking* like you're in control.

"That's not to say you don't pay attention to detail. I used to always go out with my team for warm-ups because you never knew what you were going to pick up by watching the other team. Maybe someone is limping just a little. Maybe someone looks listless, like they're sick. Maybe you see that something looks wrong with one of your guys. You never know.

"The other thing you have to do, especially in the NBA, is pick your spots. I mean you can't get all over your guys and try to pump them up for every game. The big games, you really don't have to do anything. When we used to play the Lakers or the Sixers with Wilt or any of the top teams, I didn't have to say a thing. I knew the guys would be ready to go. The games where you really have to get after them are the ones against the bad teams because they're apt to come out flat."

He laughed. "Of course you can screw up there too. I remember one year we had won seventeen straight games — tied the record for most wins in a row. Our next game was on New Year's Day against Cincinnati. They were terrible. I wanted to make sure the guys didn't go out, have a big night on New Year's Eve, and not be ready to play the next day and blow the streak. So I told 'em we'd all get together in my room and have our own party: play cards, watch TV. Everything was on me — food, drinks, the whole deal. The point was I wanted to know where they were and make sure they got to bed at a reasonable hour.

"So they all come to the room, we have a nice time, everyone goes to bed early. Next day we got killed. I mean hammered.

Why? Because I made too big a deal out of it. They knew what I was thinking and they also knew I rarely made a big thing out of a regular-season game. So they started thinking about the record, went out, and were awful. Talk about overcoaching! If I had just left them alone and let them do whatever they wanted to the night before, they would have taken care of themselves, not given a second thought to the record, and we'd have won by twenty. That was one time I really blew it.

"Most of the time before a big game I would tell the guys that being nervous was a part of the deal. I'd say to them, 'Look, I'm nervous and I know you're nervous. We should be nervous. But think about the other guys. They have to play *us*. Imagine how nervous they must be!' "

Overcoaching was something Red was rarely guilty of. His ex-players still marvel at the simplicity of his system — usually the Celtics had about seven basic plays and that was it — and his ability to get the most out of them without making them feel as if he were pushing them to the wall except when it really mattered.

"When I coached, during the season, my practices always got shorter and shorter," Red said. "Why? First of all, you have to rest guys as the season goes on so they can be fresh for the play-offs. Second, they shouldn't need as much practice late as they do early. You can only go over things so many times before they stop listening. Now if the guys didn't come in prepared to go hard, I might keep them longer. But they knew that. They understood as long as they came in ready to give me their best effort, we were going to be out of there in an hour and a half tops, maybe less than that late in the season.

"I go to college practices and I see a guy in January or February keeping his team out there three hours. That's crazy. And, by the way, if you believe any of the college coaches follow those NCAA rules [limiting practice and meeting time to twenty hours a week], I got some very expensive land I'd like to sell you. Who does anyone think they're kidding with that stuff?

"Another thing that bugs me: coaches who never take the blame. You know what? Sometimes it's *your* fault. I love coaches who scream at the kids sitting on the bench. The easiest thing in the world is to scream at subs. Makes you look like a tough guy, I guess. You called the wrong play or the wrong defense or had the wrong guys in the game. Or maybe you've got the wrong players. No matter how much homework you do or think you've done, you can still screw up picking players. I remember one year [1963] I saw a kid named Bill Green play for Colorado State. Went and saw him play twice because sometimes once isn't enough. You catch a guy on a good night, a bad night, you never know. I thought he could really help us. He was six-eight, he was strong, he could run. So I took him in the first round. He comes to camp and tells me he doesn't like to fly. In fact, he hates to fly.

"Look, I can sympathize. I remember when I first started flying early on, I had terrible problems with motion sickness. I tried everything — sitting up front, sitting in the back, putting a pillow over my head. Nothing worked. But if I was gonna coach in the NBA I had to be able to fly. It was simple as that. I just had to fight my way through it. I told the kid I understood, but there was no way he could be in the league without flying. I mean, what was he gonna do, take the train to LA? San Francisco? He said he understood. Our first couple of trips during the exhibition season, he told me he wanted to take the train but that he'd be ready to fly by the time the season started. I cut him some slack. Finally, our last exhibition game was in St. Louis. I said to him, 'Bill, the time has come. You gotta fly with us.' He said he knew but asked if he could please take the train out and then he would absolutely fly back with us. I said okay. We play the game and he comes to me afterward and says, 'Coach, I'm just not ready. I have to take the train home. I can't do it.'

"I said to him, 'Bill, I can't start the season with someone I can't rely on to get to games rested and ready to play. If you can't get on this plane now, I'm gonna have to cut you.' I figured at that point if that threat didn't work, there was nothing that was going to get him on a plane. He said he just couldn't do it. He took the train home and cleaned out his locker a day later. It never occurred to me before I drafted him or anybody else to ask if he was afraid to fly. Nowadays everything is so detailed you know what a guy ate for lunch when he was in kindergarten. Even with all that, we *still* make mistakes on guys."

Red has always believed that the best way to deal with any mistake is to simply admit you made it and move on. That's not to say he admits to many mistakes, but when he does make one — as with Bill Green — he takes the hit. Three years ago, he encouraged the Celtics to use one of their three first-round draft picks on Joseph Forte, a silky smooth guard from North Carolina who opted to leave school after his sophomore year. Red liked the low-key way Forte played the game, finding openings to get his shots, and, because he had played for Morgan Wootten at DeMatha, Red figured he would bring a certain amount of maturity and toughness with him.

He was wrong.

"What did we miss?" Red asked Morgan at lunch one day after Forte had been traded and eventually cut after run-ins with teammates and then the law. "I really thought that kid would help us."

"You never know who is advising a kid," Morgan said. "When he left us, I would have sworn he was going to have a great career. Still looked like it the first year — plus he was at Carolina. Then something went wrong, although I'm not even sure exactly what it was."

Red and Jim O'Brien both believed that Forte would be the Celtics point guard for at least ten years. "I knew we were in trouble when he showed up at practice one day wearing a Lakers T-shirt," Red said. "You can't do that, especially when you're the new guy. I called Morgan and asked him to get a hold of the kid and talk to him. He tried to call him and the kid didn't call him back. That told me he was listening to people he shouldn't be listening to.

"That's the problem today," Red said. "These kids get so much so soon that a lot of them don't know how to deal with it.

And that's the kind of thing you can't predict or see." He sighed. "I got that one wrong."

Of course if you add up the rights in Red's career versus the wrongs, one is a mountain, the other a molehill. Like all competitive people, he tends to remember the rare mistakes longer than the frequent good calls. "It's funny, though, how luck can play into it," he said. "The worst scouting report I ever got was from that Bradley coach who told me that Chet Walker was gutless. That was forty years ago and I still haven't figured out what the guy was talking about. Of course I was going to take Havlicek if he was still there anyway, but what if he hadn't been there and I had passed on Walker? How would I have felt then?"

Forte aside, Red's instincts about players remain uncanny to this day. He took one look at Pau Gasol after the Memphis Grizzlies acquired him and declared Michael Jordan crazy to have taken Kwame Brown over Gasol with the first pick in the draft. He said flatly that the New Jersey Nets had "absolutely quit" on Byron Scott weeks before Scott was fired. The team was 21–20 when Scott was fired and proceeded to win its first twelve games under interim coach Lawrence Frank — eleven by double-digit margins. He saw Stanford play a game on TV early in the 2003–04 college season and said they were the best team in college basketball. He watched Maryland *win* a game at home against North Carolina in January and declared the Terrapins to be in trouble. "They can't shoot," he said. "You can coach guys to play defense, to run your plays. You can't make them into shooters during a season." Maryland went on to have its worst shooting season in eleven years.

Red has always believed that the key to success for an NBA owner is to trust the basketball people hired to know basketball. The main reason he left the Tri-Cities Blackhawks in 1950 was that team owner Ben Kerner ignored him and traded backup center John Mahnken just prior to the start of the play-offs.

During fifty-four years with the Celtics, Red came close to leaving just once — when Sonny Werblin, then the president of Madison Square Garden, wined him and dined him in the late 1970s. "I still remember getting in a cab to go to the airport in Boston for my second meeting with Werblin," he said. "The story had been in the papers that I was talking to the Knicks. I get in and the cabbie looks in the mirror and says to me, 'Red, you aren't going to leave us for New York, are you? You can't do that after all these years.' You know what I think? Right then and there I knew I wasn't going to take the job. The guy was right. I grew up in New York, but my heart was in Boston. If it had come down to it, I'm not sure I could have actually pulled the trigger."

The only way it might have come down to it would have been if John Y. Brown hadn't met Red's ultimatum to sell his share of the team within fourteen days. No doubt part of the reason he sold was because he knew his life as owner of the Celtics would have been a living hell if he had been the owner who drove Red Auerbach from the Celtics — and, even worse, into the arms of the Knicks. "I really wasn't blackmailing him," Red said. "I just didn't want to work for him anymore — couldn't work for him anymore.

"You know, coaching was always something I wanted to do. Even when I was a kid, I always thought I'd go to college, become a teacher and coach. For some reason, coaching was what I really wanted to do. I liked studying games and I liked dealing with people. It was never going to be anything but basketball. We didn't have any football and there wasn't a blade of grass anywhere close to where I lived, so the only baseball we played was street ball. It was basketball and handball, that was it. I remember when I was in high school, one of my teachers grabbed me in the hall one day, pushed me up against the wall, and started screaming at me. 'Auerbach! You think you can go through life just playing ball and caring about sports? You got that *wrong*. You better figure out there's more to life than sports real soon or you're gonna be in big trouble.'

"I guess I never really figured it out, did I?"

One of the most remarkable things about Red at the age of eighty-seven — other than his amazing memory — is his handwriting. It is so neat that it reminds you of the girl you sat next to in the fourth grade who spent all day practicing her letters to get them exactly right. "I need to write neatly so I can read what I've written," he will say. "People with bad handwriting drive me crazy. You can lose your mind trying to read what some people write."

Thank goodness Red and I don't have to communicate through handwritten notes. He would never have any idea what I was trying to tell him.

Poor handwriting is one of Red's pet peeves. In fact, he keeps a list in his desk — in neat handwriting of course — of "things that bug me."

Some he talks about often: preening coaches, teams that don't stay on court for the national anthem, players who won't listen, people today who don't respect old-time ballplayers. "There's no tape on guys like Pettit and Cousy and even Russell when they were at their absolute best," he said one morning. "I remember someone once asked Russell how he thought he'd do against Shaq. You could tell the question made him mad. He looked at the guy and said, 'The question is, how would Shaq do against me?' I said, 'Damn right, Russ,' because I'll tell you what would happen: Russell would run him until he dropped. Guaranteed."

Red is not one of those older guys who sits around and says things were better in the old days. He just bridles at those who think nothing important happened until the media explosion that has turned athletes into megacelebrities. "It's amazing to me the way guys get treated now," he said. "One thing I give all the NBA commissioners credit for is making the league into a legitimate big-time enterprise. My first few years in Boston, I would take the guys to the parking lots outside supermarkets — there were no malls back then — and we'd set up a bucket on the back of a truck and demonstrate the game to people. I mean, they all went, every one of them. No one got paid extra, it was part of the job. We had to sell the game and explain the game to people. Now, can you imagine asking a player to go to a shopping mall to demonstrate the game to people — for nothing? Ha. I mean, nowadays you have to beg guys to go to practice.

"I'll tell you one of the biggest differences, though, really big, is security. Everywhere you turn now, there's security. Guys have personal bodyguards all the time, sometimes several of them. When a coach walks on or off the floor, he's got like five guys with him all the time. I had a personal bodyguard once. I had a friend when I was in college named Pete King. He went on to work for the FBI. He was working in St. Louis, a real hotshot in charge of robberies and kidnappings in the Midwest. So when we went to play out there, I said to him, 'Come to the game and protect me,' because I had a lot of fans getting on me. Maybe they were still upset because we ended up with Russell. Actually it was just a really good rivalry back then. So he says okay. Game ends, we win. Some guy comes out of the stands, walks up to like three feet away from me, and throws an egg in my face. Got me right in the forehead. It was actually pretty funny because I wasn't hurt or anything. Guy throws the egg, runs straight up the aisle, jumps a few seats, and he's gone. Pete chased him but couldn't catch him. I said to Pete, 'You call that protection? Guy could have walked right up to me and killed me if he wanted to!' It's a good thing he wasn't in the Secret Service. The president could have been in trouble." Red was involved in numerous similar incidents during his early coaching days. "When the game ended, you just more or less made your way through the crowd to the locker room," he said. "It wasn't always easy."

In fact, on four different occasions, Red was involved in postgame altercations with fans that led to the fan filing a lawsuit against Red. "I was never shy if a guy came at me physically," he said. "How do I know what he's gonna do? Most of the time the guys were drunk, so I had to defend myself, which I did. One time we won a close game in Cincinnati, where they really hated us because we beat them all the time. Guy jumps out at me screaming in my face that the Celtics get away with murder, that I stole the game by intimidating the referees. He won't get out of my way. So finally I just popped him in the nose. Knocked him down and kept walking. A few minutes later the guy comes into the locker room with the police. He wants me arrested for assault. I've got Havlicek sitting right next to me, so I say, 'Assault? What are you talking, assault? The guy kicked me. It was an act of self-defense. You saw it, right, John?' Havlicek looks confused for a minute. So I leaned over and said, 'John, you saw the guy kick me, right? Me, *the guy who signs your paychecks.*' John looks at the cops and says, 'It was awful. I'm amazed Red can even walk.' "

Not all of Red's confrontations ended that simply. None of them actually went to court, but on the four occasions when papers were actually filed, he ended up settling the case by giving his "victim" $500. "It was amazing. They all took the same amount of money and went away," he said. "I think they just wanted to be able to say they got me to pay them something. Still, it annoyed me. These guys come up and scream all sorts of profanities in my face and I'm just supposed to walk away? I was at a party once years later and I started talking to Supreme Court Justice Brennan. I asked him why it was that I could get sued for responding to someone screaming at me like that, and he said under the law verbal abuse does not give you the right to respond physically. Bad law, if you ask me."

Red remembers being nervous in a crowd once in his career. "It was back in the winter of fifty when I was coaching Tri-Cities," he said. "There was a team in Sheboygan. You could not win in there, no way. They played in a high school gym with a stage at one end and a wall at the other end. The benches were up on the stage. They would put all the ushers down by the wall, and if you were going for a loose ball down there, the ushers would grab you just long enough so you couldn't get to the ball. We went in there to play, and I said I wasn't playing until they got all the ushers out of there. So they did. The game starts and the fans are throwing paper clips at me. I have no idea where they got 'em. Every time-out, I'd have to jump off the stage to talk to the players. Then I'd hold my hand up and the guys on the bench would pull me back up. It was too high to jump or climb.

"This one night, one of the refs can't make it in because of the weather. So they have a substitute ref who is a local guy and he's just killing us. I start screaming at him that he's cheating us and he tees me up. I'm still on him. He walks over to me and says, 'Now you listen to me. I'm a cop and if you don't shut up, not only am I going to throw you out of the game, I'm going to lock your ass up in a place where they'll never find you.' I say,

'F@#$ you.' He says, 'You're out of the game. Get out of the building.' I'm not leaving the building — it's three degrees outside. He tells the guy in charge of the locker room not to let me in the locker room. I have no choice. I have to go sit up in the balcony. It's the only place I can go. The fans are all over me. Finally, a guy named Mike Todorovich fouled out of the game for us. He was a local. So I waved at him to come up and sit with me so I'd have a bodyguard. I felt safer after that.

"Of course we lost the game."

Fortunately for Red, the Sheboygan team folded at the end of that season.

14

Never a Dull Moment

"HERE'S A QUESTION for you: How many NBA teams today do not have cheerleaders or a dance team?"

Red pulled the cigar out of his mouth and smiled. "The answer is one. The team is the Celtics. The reason is me."

The reason, according to Red, is simple. "Too many potential problems," he said. "Best-case scenario, there's not a thing going on between any of them and your players. The wives are *still* pissed off. Worst-case scenario, and you know as well as I do it happens, something *is* going on, and then, eventually, everyone ends up pissed off. So I've always insisted that we don't have cheerleaders. I'm sure the day I die they'll go out and hire one hundred of 'em."

With luck, they will have to wait a while. Even today, at eighty-seven, Red remains a force — in his own way — in Boston. To say that he is revered in the city is like saying people there care about the Red Sox. In December of 2003, even though he wasn't feeling well, Red flew to Boston for the ceremony when the team retired Cedric Maxwell's number. Red had traded Maxwell in 1985 after Maxwell's agent told him that Maxwell couldn't come back to Boston to have an injured knee tested — he had missed most of the previous season — because he was busy building a house.

"Who is paying him the money so he can build the house?" Red had barked and then traded Maxwell for Bill Walton, a move that probably cemented what turned out to be the Celtics' final championship the following season.

Red went to Boston even though he had been sick because he wanted Maxwell to be certain that he approved of his number being retired, that a Celtic is still a Celtic and that he wouldn't miss being there even if he didn't feel well.

The only problem was that Red's ovation during the ceremony lasted about four times longer than Maxwell's — or anybody else's.

"I guess you could say I have a few years of equity built up," Red said, laughing.

The evening didn't end on a high note or a funny one. As he often does when he goes to Boston, Red had taken Murray Lieberman with him. Having Murray on a trip is a twofer: Red enjoys his company and Lieberman's his doctor. At the game, Murray and Red were joined by Red's longtime heart surgeon (he had open-heart surgery in 1993), Dr. Roman DeSanctis.

Red feels close to both men. They are friends first and doctors second — sort of. In the summer of 2003, when Red, along with several other Boston icons, spoke during a dinner at the Fleet Center, he followed hockey great Phil Esposito in the speaking rotation. Esposito had talked about coaches and friends and teammates who "made it possible for me to be here tonight."

When it was Red's turn, he talked about all the Celtics who had made the team into the dynasty it had become. "But in conclusion," he said, "I'd like to offer special thanks to two men who, if not for them, I can honestly say I absolutely would not be here tonight: Roman DeSanctis, my heart surgeon, and Murray Lieberman, my urologist."

Late in the Maxwell game, Red admitted to his friends/doctors that he didn't feel very good. Neither man liked the way he looked. Since they were basically across the street from Mass General, they decided to go there as a precaution.

"We just wanted to be sure his heart was okay," Murray said later. "We ran tests and it was fine. The only reason he had to stay in the hospital for a couple days was some concern we had about one of his kidneys. Red has one bad kidney. This was the good one. Needless to say no one wanted to take any chances with that."

Whenever Red doesn't feel good, word spreads quickly among the China Doll gang. In this case, everyone checked first with Murray, since he had been there, and he assuaged everyone's fears by saying that it wasn't heart related and Red would almost certainly be out of the hospital in a day or two. Once word came back that Red had insisted that Celtics PR director Jeff Twiss and his nephew, who lives in Boston, sneak Chinese food into the hospital, everyone knew he was okay.

"You can only eat that crap they give you in the hospital for so long," Red said.

In this case, he had lasted almost a day before sending out an order for Chinese food.

Two of the new Celtics owners, Wyc Grousbeck and Steve Pagliuca — who took over the team late in 2002 — have taken a similar approach to Red that Paul Gaston took. Both are in their forties, men who made a lot of money in business in their thirties (the sale price of the team was $260 million), but at heart they remain hoops junkies. Even before they officially took control of the team, they flew to Washington to meet with Red, to solicit his opinions, and to let him know they still consider him an important part of the franchise. "They were really good," Red said after the meeting. "You know, believe it or not, I was nervous about it. All these years, all the owners I've been through, I still don't know what I'm gonna get with new guys. They told me they'd like me to come up to Boston more often, and if it makes it easier for me, they'll send their plane for me. I thought that was real nice."

Grousbeck and Pagliuca are both huge basketball fans, life-long Celtics fans, and, as a result, lifelong Red fans. "Just to sit in his office across a desk and talk basketball with him was a thrill for both of us," Grousbeck said. "This is the man who built the Celtics. We wanted to make it clear to him that we want his involvement to go beyond a title. We wanted his input."

Red is always willing to have input. Before he started,

though, he had to test the new guys. Grousbeck had mentioned that Pagliuca was the real hoops guy in the group (there are four owners altogether — Wyc's dad, Irv Grousbeck, and Bob Epstein are the other partners), having played JV basketball at Duke in the 1970s. "Who do you like for the NBA title this year?" Red asked.

"Sacramento," Pagliuca replied.

"Turns out I got it wrong," Pagliuca said. "But Red seemed to think I was right. So I passed that test."

Grousbeck grew up in Boston and is proud to say he is a four-sport season-ticket holder. Pagliuca was born there but moved to New Jersey when he was four. Still, he grew up a Celtics fan. Together, they are the first locally based owners of the Celtics since Walter Brown's death forty years ago. The idea to buy the Celtics was Grousbeck's, but he contacted his friend Pagliuca about investing. "He showed up at my house on a Sunday morning dressed head to toe in Celtics gear," Grousbeck said. "He said, 'I'm in. You got me. How much?' We went from there."

Grousbeck and Pagliuca had been warned by people in Boston that they were going to hear Red's "list" — no cheerleaders, no loud music during time-outs, keep the staff intact — and they did. "Which was absolutely fine," Grousbeck said. "If we don't listen to Red, who in the world would we listen to?"

Pagliuca's son is a sophomore walk-on for the Duke basketball team. When Duke played Georgetown last season in

Washington, Red sat with Pagliuca during the game. Both were delighted when Duke got far enough ahead that Joe Pagliuca got to play. "He needs to be aggressive," Red said to Pagliuca. "Take a risk. Show Coach K what he's got."

Joe Pagliuca never looked at the basket in the final two minutes, getting the ball to a teammate quickly whenever he touched it. Afterward he told his father that Mike Krzyzewski had ordered his players not to look to shoot since the game had long been decided. "It would have been a bigger risk for him to not listen to Mike than it would have been for him to take a risk," Pagliuca said, laughing.

The Celtics' awful 2003–04 season clearly weighed on Red. He can be teased on most subjects but not on the subject of the Celtics playing poorly. He doesn't hide from it or make excuses, but he clearly doesn't see it as a laughing matter. "It hurts when we play like this," he said during a 1–9 stretch that began right after O'Brien quit. "We've made a lot of changes and I hope these deals Danny has made work out. A lot of people are on him, which is understandable because we've been in the play-offs the last couple of years and we're not looking like we're going to make it this year. But you can't judge a trade right away. In the [Antoine] Walker trade, we got two first-round draft picks. Until we know who they are, how can we judge the trade?"

Not only is Red still emotionally involved with the Celtics

but he still follows the entire league closely. Most nights he stays up late watching games — all games, not just the NBA — and still gets angry when he sees something he doesn't like or thinks is unjust.

"Did you watch the Lakers and Nuggets last night?" he asked one morning, knowing the answer was no. "Boy, was that game ever stolen. Late in the game, Denver's up two with the ball and they throw up a shot with two seconds on the shot clock and under twenty-four on the game clock. It grazes the rim — clearly gets it, though: you can see it change direction — and [Denver star rookie Carmelo] Anthony gets the rebound. Guy blows his whistle and says, 'Twenty-four-second violation.' No way was it a violation. They huddle up and finally decide it's a jump ball. Jump ball! That's ridiculous. Of course the Lakers are going to get the jump with Shaq in there. So they get it and win the game. It was robbery! Hell, if I'd still been coaching I'd have been out there screaming and yelling and going crazy. In today's market, it probably would have cost me twenty grand in fines before I got finished with that guy."

Of course, in today's market, Red would be making about $8 million a year.

"Good point," Red said when that was noted for him. "Maybe I'd have gone for fifty [thousand]."

Apparently the NBA agreed with Red's analysis of the play because the referee in question, after claiming he had blown his whistle "inadvertently," was suspended for three games.

Red was happy with that ruling but often disagrees with the league on the way it handles controversy. "I thought they came down on [Dallas Mavericks owner Mark] Cuban too hard," he said. "I'm not saying he didn't do anything wrong [criticizing referees constantly, once actually going onto the court during a skirmish, among other things], but what you do in a situation like that is talk to him privately, make it clear that what he's doing isn't good for the overall good of the league, and try to bring him into the tent a little. Make him feel he's a part of what you're trying to do, not fighting against what you're trying to do.

"We've got an image problem right now. How does it look when you've got players who just refuse to go to practice? I mean, you're a ballplayer, you go to practice — period. Fining 'em doesn't do any good, they're too rich to care. Again, you've got to get them in private and say, 'Look, this is unacceptable. I don't want to bench you because that hurts the whole team, not just you. But if you can't follow our rules, we're gonna trade you.' If a guy doesn't respond to that, then you need to trade him anyway.

"Too many guys today get special treatment from their teams. One time Cousy asked if he could take a day off from practice to go to New York to make a commercial. He was gonna get paid five grand to do it. In those days, that was a lot of money. The guy has never given me any trouble in ten years and he needs one day off. Of course I'm going to give it to him. But do you do it once a week? No."

Red admits he doesn't understand a lot of what coaches do today. "I watch a lot of college practices," he said. "First of all, they're too long. Kids can only concentrate for so long, especially if they're actually being asked to go to class and study too — which a few schools actually insist on. And even though they keep 'em out there forever, they never seem to teach them fundamentals. You watch games today, how often do you see guys screw up a simple box out?

"I always believed that you teach guys to do what they can do. Cousy and Sharman couldn't jump. I mean, neither one of them could dunk the ball. So I never asked them to do anything that involved jumping. But I did insist that they learn how to box out. You don't have to be able to jump to do that. These days, everyone has all these assistant coaches. Honestly, I don't know what they all do. I look at some NBA benches now and there are ten guys over there. Ten guys! That's almost one coach for every player. So why are they all so weak on fundamentals? The college coaches blame it on the high school coaches, the pro coaches blame it on the college coaches.

"Why is it that the kids who played for Morgan at DeMatha are all sound fundamentally? You think that's coincidence? Or Knight's guys or Krzyzewski's. Coaches accept too much crap from players. I know you can still teach guys. Larry Brown does it. Lenny Wilkens does it. You just can't accept a guy saying he doesn't need fundamentals. Everyone needs them. Guys don't want to learn to box out because it isn't sexy. A good box out doesn't get you on SportsCenter, does it? But it wins games. A good pass — a simple one — doesn't make the highlights either. Only the spectacular one."

Red also believes there are problems with games themselves. "I told Stern a few years ago that the illegal defense

[zone] call was ridiculous because people were going to keep doing it no matter what. He said, 'You're right. We ought to change that.' To his credit, he got it done. But there's more to it than that. We have to get away from this style of ball we've been playing the last few years: throw it in the post, the defense doubles, and the big guy either forces a shot or pitches it out to someone who shoots a three. There's only so much of that you can watch.

"You know, the great irony is that they put in the three-point shot to increase scoring," he said. "It hasn't done that. The reason is guys have become so much more one-dimensional on offense. Now, everyone just wants to spot up on the three-point line. No one wants to get in the middle and shoot a pull-up jumper. Guys aren't as dangerous as they used to be because they've just about given up one aspect of their offensive game. Now, they either shoot the three or try to go to the basket and dunk. We should probably either get rid of the three-point line altogether or move it back some more. Of course you can't move it back on the sidelines because, as it is, guys are practically out-of-bounds."

He laughed. "Maybe that's an idea. Put the three-point line out-of-bounds.

"It's very easy to criticize, to bring up the problems, and they're real problems — I know that. But it isn't as easy to come up with solutions." He smiled. "Hell, if it was so easy, I'd have taken the job as commissioner when they offered it to me all those years ago. A couple of the owners came to me after Walter Kennedy retired. I'd stopped coaching by then, and they asked me if I wanted to do it. I remember one of them saying, 'You've always run the league anyway. Why don't you get paid to do it?' I told 'em there was no way I wanted the job. You work seven days a week, you have to live in New York, and you're wrong at least half the time in the eyes of half the people. It's not worth the trouble.

"I think that's one reason why, even though I've fought with all of them at different times, I've always gotten along with all the commissioners we've had. I respected them, they respected me, and I always understood that they didn't have an easy job. If I've had one consistent complaint, it has been the bias toward New York. Look, I know we need a strong franchise there and we especially needed it in the old days. But I thought everyone, even Walter Brown, went too far at times. That's why I always kid [David] Stern about being a Knicks fan, just to remind him not to bend too far backward to help the Knicks. If I *really* thought he was that biased, believe me, I wouldn't just kid him about it."

For his part, Stern loves the give-and-take with Red. "I also try to listen to what he's telling me because if I didn't I wouldn't be very bright," he said. "For one thing, he's one of the last guys left who has been around the entire time the league has been around. For another, he's still as smart as anyone in the game and he cares deeply about what's good for the league. The Celtics first, of course, but the league runs a close second."

Stern likes to tell people that the first few years he was commissioner, he was fairly convinced that his name wasn't really

David. "It was 'Stupid,'" he said, as in Red calling and starting most conversations with, "'Hey, Stupid, let me tell you what you've screwed up now.'"

Red also took a good deal of pleasure in telling Stern whenever he had the opportunity that he had "no balls." No matter which way Stern went on a decision, or so it seemed, Red's verdict was that it proved he had no balls. Finally, Stern made a tough decision on something — neither man can remember exactly what — and Red called him and said, "Okay, you've got balls."

"It was my validation as commissioner," Stern said. "After that, I felt like maybe I could hang on to the job for a little while."

Red's first real battle with the league, the one he brings up all the time, dates back to the summer of 1950, soon after he had been hired to coach the Celtics. "I wanted to sign Sweetwater Clifton," he said. "I had seen him play a lot because the [Harlem] Globetrotters played games in our buildings all the time and I knew he was just the kind of guy who could help us. I found out that his contract with the Globetrotters was up and I drove to Pennsylvania to meet with him to see if I could sign him."

At that moment, the NBA still had not integrated, although the Washington Capitols were in the process of trying to sign Earl Lloyd. Red wasn't trying to make a political statement — that has never been his thing — he was just trying to sign a player he was convinced would help his team. He had already drafted an African-American, Chuck Cooper, in the second round of that spring's draft, so the Celtics were going to have a minority player on their roster that fall one way or the other. Clifton and Red agreed to a deal that would pay Clifton $7,500 to move to the Celtics. The Celtics sent the contract to the league for approval, assuming it would be rubber-stamped the way all contracts were rubber-stamped. Only this one wasn't. Commissioner Maurice Podoloff refused to sign off on it.

"He told Walter Brown that he didn't want to upset the Globetrotters by signing their best player," Red said. "In those days, the Globetrotters played a lot of doubleheaders with NBA teams, and, in most cities, about the only time we'd sell out or get close to a sellout was when the Globetrotters were in town. Podoloff told Walter he was afraid [Globetrotters owner] Abe Saperstein might pull out of our deal with him if we signed Clifton. I told Walter that was nuts, where was Saperstein gonna take his team if not to NBA arenas? The deal worked well for both sides, not just for one side. But Walter didn't want to fight him on it. I was a new coach, I didn't have the kind of clout I had later, so there was nothing I could do.

"A couple of weeks later, I pick up the paper and there's an item: CLIFTON SIGNS WITH KNICKS. I went crazy. I went in to Walter and said how can this possibly be? What happened to Podoloff not wanting to upset Saperstein? 'He made a deal with Saperstein,' Brown explained. 'The league is going to give the Globetrotters a couple of extra appearances in [Madison Square] Garden the next couple years, which is good for them. In return, Saperstein agreed to let Clifton go to the Knicks.'"

Red was furious — with everyone. He thought Podoloff was trying to help the Knicks at the Celtics' expense and that Brown was allowing himself to be rolled at a time when the Celtics could least afford to be rolled. He was also angry because the beneficiary of all the wheeling and dealing was Ned Irish, who was president and general manager of the Knicks at the time.

"Now there's a guy I held a grudge against," he said.

The grudge — which Red still holds today, more than thirty years after Irish's death — dates back to 1940, Red's senior year at George Washington. The Colonials believed they were going to receive a bid to the NIT that year, which in those days was *the* prestigious postseason basketball tournament because it was played in New York at Madison Square Garden. According to Red, Irish had guaranteed a bid to Bill Reinhart and then, at the last minute, changed his mind and reneged on the commitment because he decided GW might be too good for the New York teams in the tournament.

"Remember, I forgive, but I don't forget," Red said. "Now, I actually liked Irish. He was a good guy, someone who usually kept his word on things. But he hadn't kept his word that time, and we didn't get to go to the NIT. We had a hell of a team that year. So I always held it against him that we didn't get a chance to play because he let politics get involved and protected the New York teams."

Lloyd ended up becoming the first African-American to play in the NBA — because of scheduling. The Caps began their season that fall on October 31 with Lloyd in the lineup. The next night, the Celtics and Knicks began their season with Cooper playing for the Celtics and Clifton for the Knicks. Of the three, Clifton had the most notable NBA career. He played for seven years with the Knicks until injuries shortened his career. "To show you what kind of guy Walter Brown was, he stepped in when Sweetwater got hurt and helped him buy a cab in Chicago," Red said. "That was always what he had wanted to do when he stopped playing, drive his own cab back home in Chicago. I think he ended up owning two cabs and doing very well. But it was Walter who helped him get started. Things like that made it hard for me to stay mad at Walter."

Everyone who follows basketball knows that Red played a major role in integrating the game. In addition to being one of the first teams to sign a black player and draft a black player (same year), the Celtics were the first team to start five black players. And, of course, in 1966 Russell became the first African-American head coach in a major professional league. It wasn't until 1974 that Major League Baseball had a black manager and, remarkably, it wasn't until 1989 that the modern NFL had an African-American head coach. Red laughs when the subject of breaking down racial barriers comes up.

"Look, that's not what it was about for me," he said. "Where I grew up in Brooklyn, race was never an issue. Jews, blacks, Catholics — no one ever paid attention to what you were when you played ball. The only thing that mattered was if you could play. That's one of the great things about sports. When you're choosing a team — whether it's in the school yard or in the NBA — no one asks what color you are or what religion you are. Those who do are doomed to fail on every level anyway, so who cares what they think?

"My thing was always winning. If a guy was white and could

play, I wanted him on my team. If he was black and could play, I wanted him on my team. But I also cared about character. Same thing held there. A bad guy is a bad guy; a good guy is a good guy. I never thought I deserved any special credit for starting five black guys. I did it for one reason: I thought it gave us the best chance to win. Period. Same with hiring Russell. It was the best thing for the team."

"There's one more thing coaches do that bugs me," Red said one morning. As always, he had been up late watching games, college games on this particular night. "Actually this isn't just coaches, it's everyone. The other night, I'm out at Maryland when they play North Carolina. Now, before the game and during the game, they're doing everything they can to create a hostile atmosphere and demean the visiting team. This isn't just at Maryland, it's at most places. But it's worse at Maryland than a lot of places. They boo, they use profanity. Then, when they introduce the teams, they practically mumble the names of the visiting players and then they turn out all the lights, have some kind of light show, boost up the PA so that it hurts your ears, and introduce the home team as if they just saved the planet. Then, during the game, the fans are screaming on every call, the coaches are screaming on every call.

"It's hostile. You can call it what you want, but it's a hostile atmosphere.

"Okay, the game ends. Now, everyone lines up to shake hands. I *hate* that. They shouldn't do it."

He lit his cigar. I couldn't resist. "You hate sportsmanship?" I said.

He almost threw the cigar at my head. "Sportsmanship!" he said. "That's not sportsmanship. That's phony, fake. They don't mean it for a second. What's more, it can lead to trouble. Guys are still hot when a game ends, especially a close game. Suppose two players say something to each other. Suppose the fans start to throw things — which you know happens. If the two coaches really are friends, they can wave at each other going off. That's what I used to do if a guy was a friend or someone I got along with okay. But this idea that you have to line up and everyone has to shake hands when most of the time they can't stand one another is a joke."

There is a good deal of phoniness on the big-time college level. In fact, during the NCAA Tournament, when coaches are given a pregame schedule, it includes a notation that says, "When you are introduced by the PA, please walk to the scorer's table and shake hands with the opposing coach."

"That's dumb," Red said. "That's all about image. I'll tell you another thing that's silly in the college game: when the referees all go over and shake hands with the coaches before the game starts. That's phony too. I don't want to shake hands with a guy whom I may need to yell at fifteen minutes later. You aren't supposed to be friends with the referees anyway. They have a job, you have a job. Do your job and leave it at that."

15

Missing Zang

"THE HARDEST THING about being old," Red said one day during the frigid winter of 2003, "is that a cold isn't just a cold. A virus isn't just a virus. The flu isn't just a flu. You get sick, you really get sick. And it scares you."

For once Zang agreed. "Tell me about it," he said simply.

While Red had been through sundry health problems, including open-heart surgery and vertigo, he wasn't nearly as frail in appearance as Zang. Part of that was just size: Red is close to six feet tall and weighs about two hundred pounds. Even at eighty-seven, there is still a sturdiness to him. Zang, several inches shorter and at least fifty pounds lighter, always looked wispy by comparison. Still, he was always the first one to arrive on Tuesday, never backed down from an argument, and refused to even consider the notion that his health might be a problem.

In fact, Zang always parked several blocks away on Tuesdays because his doctor had told him that walking was good for the circulation in his legs. Even on the coldest days, Zang made the walk to and from his car while everyone else parked as close to the restaurant as possible.

It was in January of 2003 that everyone started to become concerned about Zang. He was clearly walking with more difficulty, not moving any faster than Red, who still used a cane for balance most of the time. He was quieter during lunch, eating only soup, refusing to give anyone a serious answer when asked about his lack of appetite.

"Don't need to eat today."

"Why not?"

"Did it yesterday."

Then the coughing started. Zang was a reformed smoker, so occasional coughing bouts weren't that unusual. But this was worse, more prolonged, deeper. Stanley Copeland, his son-in-law, tried to convince Zang to let him pick him up and drive him to the lunches. Zang wouldn't hear of it. "Problem is he's the only person on earth who may be as stubborn as Red," Stanley said.

Zang probably should not have been coming on some Tuesdays. The weather was awful and his cough sounded worse each week. But he wouldn't even think of missing one of the lunches. "What am I going to do?" he asked one week. "Lie around in bed and cough? That doesn't do anybody any good."

On the first Tuesday in February, with the temperature in the teens and the wind whipping, Zang walked into the restaurant looking pale and sick. He sat huddled over his soup, coughing and shivering.

"Where'd you park your car, Zang?" Stanley said.

"Where I normally park," Zang answered.

"Fine," Stanley said. "Give me the keys and I'll bring it to the front door for you."

"The hell you will. Don't try to baby me —"

"Hey, Zang, do me a favor. Give him the keys."

It was Red. He was the last person to publicly baby his younger brother and he also empathized because he didn't like it when anyone babied him. But he was clearly concerned now.

"I'm all right."

"Look, Zang, I'm old too," Red said. "I know how lousy you feel right now. Give Stanley the keys."

"Don't trust him to drive my car."

Everyone at the table immediately volunteered to replace Stanley as the driver. It was Bob Campbell, the Secret Service agent, who leaned over and said quietly, "I'll get the car, Zang. You can trust me."

Grumpily, Zang gave up the keys.

There was a good deal of talk during the following week among the lunch group about Zang's health. It was finally decided that only Red could convince him to go see a doctor. The rest of us would be told in no uncertain terms what to do with the notion of seeing a doctor. Red agreed to talk to Zang — and did. Zang said he would think about it, which meant he had gotten the message.

The next Monday night, on cue, the phone rang at 9:07. Danny, as had become tradition, answered it.

"My dad wants to know if you're taking care of yourself," Danny said.

I couldn't hear Zang's answer, but Danny said it was something about telling his dad to worry about himself. When I got on the phone Zang's opening comment was to the point: "You tell Danny, I'm going to dance at his wedding, okay?" Zang said.

I laughed and told him I'd tell Danny that, but something in my gut told me Zang was thinking he might not talk to Danny again. Still, he sounded stronger and insisted he felt much better. "I'll see you tomorrow," he said. "Don't be late."

He looked better the next day than a week earlier, although he still ate only soup. He didn't argue this time when Bobby asked for his keys. That was the part that worried me. I asked Red as we were leaving if he thought Zang was okay.

"I hope so," Red said. Then he repeated his line about how much tougher it is to be sick when you're old. He said he would remind Zang about seeing a doctor.

The next night I was at a basketball game in Easton, Pennsylvania. When I called home after the game, Mary, my wife, said that Stanley had called. A chill ran through me. "Is it Zang?"

"He's in the hospital," Mary said. "They think he's had a heart attack."

I wish I could say that I was surprised. Maybe, though, it wasn't that serious. At least, I thought, Zang was finally seeing a doctor, although this wasn't exactly the ideal way to get him to one. As soon as I heard Stanley's voice, I knew any optimistic thoughts were foolish. "If he makes it through the night, he may have a chance," Stanley said. "But I suspect it's a slim one. The only good news is that he's stabilized for now."

Zang had apparently collapsed at home, and Gertrude, his wife, had called an ambulance, which took him to Holy Cross Hospital in Silver Spring. She had called Stanley and Emily, her daughter, and they had called Red. Red immediately called Murray Lieberman and asked him if he could go to the hospital so that there would be at least one person in the emergency room Zang would know. When Murray arrived, Zang was being wheeled out of the emergency room. He was stable and conscious. Murray had already talked to the doctor who had examined him and knew the situation was critical. Still, he walked up to the gurney Zang was on with a smile on his face.

"Listen, Zang, these guys are going to make you feel better, so listen to them," he said. "You're going to be just fine in a little while."

Zang looked up at Murray. "I'm going to be just fine?"

"Absolutely."

"Murray, you're completely full of shit."

Murray had to stifle his laugh. Zang knew what was going on and, as always, didn't want to hear anything but the truth.

"Get some rest," Murray said.

"As if I have a choice."

✿   ✿   ✿

Red made it to the hospital early the next morning, accompanied by Reid and Nancy. Zang was still hanging on, but he wasn't conscious at that point. Red stayed a few minutes, looking at his brother, hoping he would somehow open his eyes and start giving him a hard time. The doctors had told everyone by then that it wasn't likely he was going to regain consciousness. "I need to go," Red said softly, implying that he had someplace to go even though that clearly wasn't the case. It had been a little more than two years since he had sat in a hospital and watched Dorothy die. He couldn't bear sitting around and waiting for a doctor to come out and tell him that his brother was gone.

Throughout the morning, different members of the lunch group came to the hospital or called to find out what could be done. Stanley, who was handling the job of keeping everyone updated, told people they probably shouldn't come to the hospital. "He's not conscious. It isn't as if you can talk to him," he said. "It's just a matter of whether you want to see him now . . . like this."

Even in his final hours, Zang managed to make us all laugh. Stanley and Zang's son John remembered the last time Zang had been in the hospital, for neck surgery. "He woke up and we all said, 'How you doing?'" John remembered. "Right in front of him, on the wall, was one of those wooden things with Christ on the cross. Dad looked up, pointed at Christ, and said, 'I guess I'm doing a whole lot better than he is.'"

Rob Ades and I both made it there to see him one final time. Stanley was right: the sight of Zang hooked up to a machine, unable to breathe without it, was jarring. Chris Wallace was in New York. He called frequently for updates. Morgan was trying to make it back from a speaking appearance. Bob Campbell was going to stop and bring food for everyone as soon as he could get away from the office. Jack Kvancz was at league meetings. "I'll be back tonight," he said. "I'll come over as soon as I get there."

There was no need. Zang died at 3:30 that afternoon, February 13. No doubt he didn't want to hang around for Valentine's Day. "Not his favorite day of the year," Gertrude said, somehow forcing a laugh.

Zang would have hated an elaborate funeral or a parade of eulogists — even though there wasn't anyone who had known him for more than fifteen minutes who would not have had a story to tell. A memorial service was scheduled for Monday, February 17, but a huge snowstorm hit Washington over the weekend, making travel — whether from out of town or locally — impossible. The service was pushed back twenty-four hours.

Throughout the weekend, everyone kept tabs on Red. As with Dorothy, he didn't want people going on at great length about how sorry they were for his loss. But it was clear that he wanted to hear people's voices. As always, the subject would turn quickly to basketball because staying on the subject of Zang was just too difficult, regardless of how tough Red appeared to be. He never cried, but his voice was very soft when he talked, almost gentle. No doubt hearing his brother talking that way would have annoyed Zang to no end.

The weather was still lousy on the morning of the memorial service, which was held at a funeral home not far from where Zang lived. All his grandchildren had come to town for the service, and many of his longtime friends from the *Washington Star* were there too. The entire China Doll gang, except for Pete Dowling, who was traveling and couldn't find a flight that could get him to Washington in time, was there.

Morgan Wootten was shocked when Red greeted him as he came in the door and said quietly, "I'm really going to need my friends now."

"It was the first time in all the years I've known him that I ever heard Red say something like that," Morgan said. "That was the tip-off to how much he was hurting right then."

Rob Ades spoke briefly and so did I. But the clear highlight of the morning was Zang's eighteen-year-old grandson Robby, talking with great emotion about his doting grandfather, revealing a side of Zang few of us had ever seen.

When the service was over, Gertrude and the family let all the mourners know that they were invited back to the house for refreshments and to lift a glass one more time in honor of Zang. One by one, the lunch group asked Red if he was going to go to the house. Red shook his head. Clearly, he had seen enough grief for one morning. It was almost 11:00.

"Let's go eat," he said. "There's a real good place not far from here."

It was, of course, Chinese.

Everyone in the group agreed that going out to eat Chinese food at 11:00 on a cold, snowy February morning was the right thing to do. Zang wouldn't have wanted it any other way.

After all, it was Tuesday.

Afterword

THERE WAS SOME CONCERN IN the weeks following Zang's death about the future of the lunches. An unofficial committee was formed. Someone would check in with Red on Mondays to make certain all was well. We decided to go on the no-news-is-good-news plan: if there was no lunch, phone calls would be made. Otherwise, 11:00 — sharp — at the China Doll.

Initially, Zang's seat was left empty. But without anyone saying anything, it was apparent that the empty seat made Zang's absence that much more noticeable for Red. On the third Tuesday, Stanley Copeland began sitting in Zang's seat.

Red was quieter than usual in the days after his brother's death. Stories that might have gotten him on a roll didn't energize him the way they normally did. Everyone understood. The first signs of recovery actually occurred — not surprisingly — at a basketball game. On a sunny Saturday afternoon, the first time in weeks that the weather had been decent, Red went to see George Washington play LaSalle. Reid Collins and Nancy came with him, and Joe Greenberg, the professor emeritus at GW who showed up at lunch whenever he was back in town from his retirement retreat in Vermont, was there too. (Greenberg had first encountered Red at GW in the locker room one day after a workout. "You're Red Auerbach!" he yelled when he spotted him. "No kidding, really?" Red had replied. A friendship was born.) I brought Danny, knowing that Red enjoyed talking basketball with him.

It was midway through the second half of a tight game and several calls had gone against GW. Red doesn't often rail at referees these days, but he was squirming with frustration as the Colonials got into foul trouble and a comfortable lead began to disappear. Finally, when what looked like a clear charge on one of LaSalle's players was called a block, Red turned to Danny, hands out, palms pointed skyward, and said, "Why? Why do I even bother to come to these games?!"

Danny looked at him, clearly puzzled, and said, "What kind of a question is that? You come to the games because you love basketball!"

Red stared at Danny for a second and then cracked up. For the rest of the afternoon, he was his old animated self, critiquing not only the officials but the coaching, the players' shot selection, and the quality of the game. He had a satisfied smile on his face as GW pulled away late for the win.

314

As the weather warmed, the laughter returned to the lunches. Perhaps because he missed Zang, Red had widened the circle. Bob Ferry, the retired general manager of the Washington Bullets, became a regular. So did George Solomon, the equally retired sports editor of the *Washington Post*. Red was always at his best when new people came to the table. He argued at length with Solomon about Shirley Povich, the legendary *Post* columnist who had written for the newspaper from 1924 until his death — at the age of ninety-two — in 1998.

"Lemme tell you about your guy Povich," Red said to Solomon one day, wagging a finger. "He hated basketball. Didn't understand it. The only time he ever wrote about basketball was forty years ago when he wrote a story in *Sports Illustrated* calling basketball players 'pituitary freaks.' I'm not sure I've ever been angrier with a guy. He never went to games! He never once in all those years at the paper wrote about basketball. Not once!"

"Red, you're exaggerating," Solomon insisted. "You're right he didn't write much basketball, but he did it on occasion."

"Never!" Red said. "Not once! Look it up!"

Solomon, who had been very close to Povich and was putting together an anthology of Povich's best columns, accepted the challenge. "I will look it up," he said. "I'll bring you the columns."

A week later he showed up with a sheepish look on his face. "Couldn't find a single one," he said, suppressing a laugh. "I checked more than seventy years of clips. Nothing. Not one column."

Red was triumphant. "I told you," he said. Then he leaned

back in his seat and said, "Now, I'm not saying he was a bad guy. He was a good guy. He just didn't know a damn thing about basketball."

Red has always been gracious in victory.

There weren't very many victories for the Celtics during this period. Pitino's resignation had led to a renaissance under Jim O'Brien, his replacement. The players appeared to be relieved to be out from under Pitino's whip, and they performed for O'Brien. This isn't unusual in the NBA. Once players decide they aren't going to play for a coach, the coach, no matter how good he may be, has no chance.

The Celtics had two legitimate stars in Paul Pierce and Antoine Walker — especially Pierce. They reached the Eastern Conference finals in 2002 before losing a tough six-game series to the Nets. It is difficult to believe given the team's history, but had the Celtics won, it would have been their first trip to the finals since 1987 — the year after Len Bias's death. Talk about a turnaround. In Red's sixteen years as coach, the Celtics reached the finals ten times, winning nine titles. They won seven more titles and made one losing trip during the next twenty seasons, meaning they won sixteen titles and reached eighteen finals in thirty-six years (between 1950–86). Simple math tells you they were in the finals 50 percent of the time during that stretch. It has now been eighteen seasons since Bias's death and the Celtics have been back to the finals only once, seventeen years ago. In 2003 they lost in the conference semifinals to the Detroit Pistons.

The decision to hire Danny Ainge was a popular one in Boston at first but not nearly so popular by the end of last season. While Red kept insisting that only time would tell if Ainge's moves would pay off, the short-term results were disastrous. With Antoine Walker's departure by trade, followed by the almost-as-controversial acquisition from Cleveland of Ricky Davis — a talented but undisciplined guard (the move that led to Jim O'Brien's resignation) — the Celtics spiraled downward. Only the fact that the Eastern Conference was in shambles got the team into the play-offs. They finished 36–46. In the West that would have put them behind eleven teams. In the East it put them in the eighth and final play-off spot, meaning they were given the chance to be humiliated by the Indiana Pacers in four straight blowouts. None of the games, even the two in Boston, were remotely competitive. John Carroll, who had been named interim coach after O'Brien left, wasn't retained.

In the never-ending NBA world of revolving coaches, O'Brien landed in Philadelphia and Ainge hired Doc Rivers, who had been fired early in the season by the Orlando Magic. Red was pleased with the hiring of Rivers, whom he felt had been the victim of a string of injuries in Orlando. "He's a smart guy," Red said. "He knows what he's doing. I think it's a good start for us."

Of course the first thing Rivers did as coach of the Celtics was ruin one of Red's pet theories. "All these announcers, these guys who are supposed to be such basketball geniuses, are fired coaches," he liked to say. "If they're such geniuses, why are they all fired?"

Rivers had been hired by ABC as its lead color commentator after being fired by the Magic, making him a fired coach turned announcer. As part of his deal with the Celtics, he was allowed to finish his work for ABC during the play-offs. Which meant that he wasn't just a fired coach but also a *hired* coach. "I guarantee you one thing," Red said when the subject came up. "His replacement will be a fired coach."

Even with his eighty-seventh birthday looming in September, Red remained just as up-to-date and opinionated on basketball issues as he had always been. He was genuinely concerned about what would happen to the U.S. Olympic team in Athens during the summer. "Now Larry Brown [the U.S. coach] has a hell of a situation on his hands," he said one day. "Half the guys who should go don't want to go. They play into June and they're tired. They've got so much money that there's no amount you can pay them that's going to make it worth their while to give up the whole summer to play. But this time it's even worse because they're scared. They don't want to go to Athens with all the terrorist threats. What's more, we *have* to win. What happened two years ago [in the World Championships] was a terrible embarrassment to American basketball. Sixth place! Can you imagine that? Sixth place with NBA players! You can't have that."

He shook his head. "So much of it has to do with the coaching. All those years I traveled overseas and did clinics, I said to people, 'You know what? There's going to come a day when these countries are dangerous for us because these guys are *listening.*' You look at the foreign kids who come over and every one of them is solid fundamentally. Not our guys. No one can coach them because they all think they're stars now when they're fifteen. They don't think they need coaching because they get their butts kissed by so many people — college coaches; shoe salesmen; AAU guys; agents; their buddies, who want a cut when they get rich — everybody. It never stops. Then they come into the league when they're eighteen, nineteen and they don't know how to play. It must be like coaching in a developmental league at times.

"Those kids overseas, though, they learn how to play." He laughed. "Hell, I've had foreign coaches tell me they coach straight from my instructional book — the one I wrote back in 1952. It was all basic stuff, as basic as you can get, but those basics haven't changed. That's the biggest difference I see in international play today: the foreign kids aren't as talented as our guys — we've still got the best talent by far — but they know *how* to play. Our guys don't know how and they don't want to know how.

"Larry can't win. He gets the gold medal, everyone will say it was the talent. He doesn't get the gold medal, everyone will say he messed up. Lemme tell you something: we win the gold medal, he ought to get some kind of special medal of his own. Because I guarantee you it won't be easy."

Remarkably, after his health scare at the end of 2003, Red came roaring back. He had to skip lunch for a couple weeks and, again, there was concern about whether the era was ending.

But soon after his return from Boston, the lunches resumed and Red began dispensing stories and opinions as if he had been absent with a cold rather than heart and kidney problems.

"You know, if it weren't for the fact that getting in and out of my practice gear would wear me out, I'd almost like to coach again," he said one day when it was suggested to him at lunch that he should take over the team in the wake of O'Brien's resignation. He laughed. "Maybe I could just coach the home games and not go on the road. I'll tell you what, I'd be a lot different than most of these guys are today.

"Here's what they don't understand: you can't coach to try to keep your job. You have to coach to *win*. Half the time they can't even get their best guys to come to practice. You know how you solve that? Simple rule: you don't practice, you don't play. Maybe you get fired because the owner sides with the star. But you're gonna get fired anyway if you can't control him, so why not lay down the law? Maybe then, at least, the other guys will respect you. I always said you didn't win games as a coach during games, you won games as a coach before games. Choosing your team. Preparation. Practice. Knowing the other team's strengths and weaknesses going in. Once the game starts, if you haven't got all of that under control, you aren't going to win the game by being an X and Os genius. Players win during the games, not coaches."

The Lakers' march to the NBA finals and the looming possibility of coach Phil Jackson winning a tenth NBA title brought about another predictable round of Phil versus Red stories.

Jackson appeared to be going out of his way to be conciliatory toward Red. He was quoted as saying that he thought a lot of the animosity between the two of them dated back to the Knicks-Celtics rivalry of the seventies when Jackson played on very good New York teams, including one (1973) that beat a great Cowens-led Boston team in a seventh game in Boston for the Eastern Conference title en route to the Knicks' last NBA title. Red conceded that the Knicks-Celtics rivalry might be part of it. He also took note of Jackson's attempts to mend fences. But, in the end, he just couldn't bring himself to make nice with the Zen master.

He told ESPN, the *Washington Post*, the *Boston Globe* — anyone who asked — that he respected Jackson's abilities and that anyone who didn't think he was a hell of a coach was crazy. "But it bothers me that he never gives anyone else credit," he said repeatedly. "He never gave [former Lakers general manager] Jerry West credit for putting that team together and handing it to him. He never gives any of his assistants credit. I don't understand that."

When Jackson came up at lunch, Red just waved a hand as if to say he'd heard — and said — enough on the topic. And then he talked about it. "Lemme tell you a story on that subject," he said. "My junior college coach, Gordon Ridings, was a great coach. I mean, really a great coach. He went to NYU and built that program into a power. Then he got sick and died very young. Guy named Lou Rossini took his place. He takes all the players Gordon brought in and wins a lot of games. Guy was a good coach. But he *never* gave Gordon any credit, never once said he had been the one who built the program in the first place.

"I never forgave the guy for that."

He sat back as if he were finished, then leaned forward. "I know I couldn't have done what I did without a lot of people. I had a great owner, Walter Brown. I had great players. I got help from guys in the media, especially in the fifties before we had hit it big. When I was still coaching, after we'd won a game, I would only talk for a few minutes to the writers. When we *lost* I talked for as long as they wanted me to. I just believed that was the right thing to do.

"I still believe that's the way you should do things as a coach. Spread the credit when you win; take the blame when you lose."

On a warm June Tuesday, no fewer than eighteen people showed up for lunch, unofficially a record turnout according to unofficial record-keeper Aubre Jones. The only regulars or semiregulars missing were Morgan Wootten, away celebrating his fortieth wedding anniversary; Joe Greenberg, who had returned to his summer home in Vermont; and Aubre's dad, Sam, who was in Florida. Red sat in his usual seat, taking in the barbs flying back and forth across the table with a big smile on his face. Pete Dowling was in town, sitting in his old seat, repeatedly saying, "I can't tell you how good it is to see you guys." Hymie Perlo, completely recovered after a bout with cancer, was yelling at Pete about selling out and taking the money and wondering why I wasn't taking notes when Red talked. "Take notes!" he screamed. "He's not going to say a thing worth hearing, but you'll write it down anyway!"

Hymie's rants had everyone, including Red, laughing almost uncontrollably. "He's mellowed," Red said.

Arnold Heft, the ex-referee who had once been a part owner of the Washington Bullets, sat across from Red. "So what do you think? Can Smarty Jones win the Triple Crown?" he asked innocently.

"One more word about horses and you're never coming back," Red said.

He was kidding. Maybe. Heft took no chances and changed the subject. Herman Greenberg, Red's longtime friend from Woodmont, sat next to Chris Wallace and said, "Red wouldn't be happy if everyone wasn't arguing."

"Red's happiest when *he's* arguing," said Wallace, no longer the new guy. "Because he always wins the argument."

Lefty Driesell, the retired (should-be) Hall of Fame college coach who occasionally made the trip up from his retirement home in Virginia Beach, was sitting next to Red. The subject of college coaches came up and Lefty mentioned Norman Sloan, the longtime coach at North Carolina State and Florida. Sloan had died a few months earlier and Lefty had attended the funeral.

"There were almost no college coaches there," said Lefty, who had been friends with Sloan. "I was surprised."

"I'm not," Red said. "Not that many people liked him. I knew him pretty well. Used to play tennis with him. The guy was always mad about something. He won a national championship [1974] at North Carolina State and he was still mad because people said Dean Smith was a better coach than he was."

"Shouldn't that have made him mad?" Lefty said.

"Sure, I can see why it made him mad. Dean hadn't won a national championship then." Red smiled. "Of course Dean Smith *was* a better coach than he was, but that's not the point. The guy was always mad. I'm not sure I ever heard him say anything nice about anyone." He laughed. "I actually kinda liked him."

The previous night, Red had watched the final game of the Western Conference finals between the Lakers and Minnesota Timberwolves. At one point, after Shaquille O'Neal had committed a foul, referee Ed F. Rush had walked over to the scorer's table and asked how many fouls O'Neal had.

"That's an outrage," Red roared. "You can't do that. Officials are supposed to officiate the game — period. It's not their job to know how many fouls anyone has. The guy should be suspended. Of course he won't be. The league will defend him."

The next day the league announced no action would be taken against Rush — that he was simply doing his job because there had been confusion at the scorer's table about how many fouls O'Neal had. "Yeah, right," Red said. "Like there's a chance he would have committed his sixth and every single person on the Minnesota bench wouldn't have known he had fouled out."

The subject of O'Neal's poor free-throw shooting came up.

"How do you like that?" Red asked. "The guy [Jackson] has five assistants and he can't find anyone who can teach Shaquille how to shoot free throws. Great coaching, huh?" Then he turned serious. "You know why Shaq's a bad free-throw shooter? Same reason Chamberlain was a bad free-throw shooter and Russell wasn't so good either: their hands are too big. Imagine someone with normal-size hands trying to shoot a softball into a basket from fifteen feet away when the basket is only a little bit bigger than the ball. You ever try controlling a smaller ball like that? Well, that's what a basketball feels like in the hands of these guys. They just can't control it. Best big guy I ever saw shoot free throws was Ed Macauley. His hands were tiny for a big man, no bigger than mine. It's not a coincidence."

Even after the frustrations of the past few years, Red remained convinced he would see the Celtics win another championship. "We're three players away," he said. "Of course almost anyone in the league can say that. Danny [Ainge] has to make tough decisions. I've told him over and over again that the reason so many mistakes get made in the draft these days is that everyone gets their scouts in a room and they go around the room and *vote* on guys. You can't *vote!* This is not a democracy, it is a dictatorship! *You* decide! And then you live with your decisions. Danny will do that. He's got balls, which is what you need nowadays to succeed. You can get input from your scouts, advice even, but in the end you have to make the decisions."

The Celtics had the fifteenth pick in the draft and Red was

hoping that Jameer Nelson, the tiny St. Joseph's point guard, would fall to them. "I think he's going to be a hell of a player. He's tough, quick, makes big shots. I love him. *But* Danny has to decide." He smiled. "After he decides, I'll tell him whether he's right or not."

Ainge decided on Al Jefferson, a six-foot-ten-inch high school senior. Loyal as always, Red insisted he liked the pick. "He averaged forty-two a game," he said. "I don't care what league you're in, that's a lot of points."

It was a rainy, miserable Saturday morning and Red was getting a little work done — signing autographs for people who mailed requests to him; responding to letters (he still has the neatest handwriting on earth); returning phone calls — in his office. The building was virtually empty. He was in the news again because of Jackson's assault — unsuccessful as it turned out, thanks to the Detroit Pistons — on his record. The subject of coaching now versus coaching during his day came up again. What would he have to change to succeed as a coach today?

"Not much," he said, lighting a cigar. "You have to be more careful today about the kind of kid you take because if you make a mistake you can be stuck with a bad guy because of a guaranteed contract. But the rest doesn't really change. You have to get good players who want to win, not just make money. We've had players who became very wealthy guys while playing — Russell, Cowens, Bird, McHale, Parish —

and they never stopped caring about winning. If guys are just playing for the money, you don't win. I think one of the things we did well was identifying guys who wanted to win." He paused and his voice softened for a moment. "I thought Len Bias was that type of kid. I still think if he hadn't died we would have won a couple more titles before Bird, McHale, and Parish were done.

"Coaching, in the end, is about communicating. If you can't get your players to respect you and buy into what you're telling them, you don't win — with or without talent. If you can get through to them, you win — providing you have talent."

The subject of Allen Iverson came up. Could Red have coached him? "Are you kidding? I'd have loved to have coached that kid. First of all, he's as quick as anyone who ever played. But beyond that, he's a warrior. I'd have gotten along great with him. The [missing] practice thing would never have been a problem. I would just very quietly tell him, 'Look, you need to do this because it means something to me *and* to the other players.' What you have to do is let a guy know what's important to you and let him know that if he does right by you, you're going to do right by him. That's the thing: my guys always knew I'd take care of them if they played hard for me — while they were playing and after they were done playing."

He puffed on the cigar. "Iverson reminds me of a story. Few years ago, the NBA asked me to come in and coach in the rookie game on all-star weekend. I remember this because it was Iverson's rookie year [1997]. I walked in before the game and there's a TV guy putting a microphone on Kerry Kittles, who was playing for my team. I went over and said, 'No way is anyone going to be miked on my team during this game.' The guy says, 'Coach, it's just an exhibition game.' Then he says, 'Hey, how about if we mike you?' I said, *No way.* A few minutes later, I call the players together and I tell them I know this is an exhibition and they're here to have fun and they think that means they don't have to play defense. I say, 'You know what? You don't have to play defense. But if you don't, you aren't playing. Period.'

"The TV people were upset about the microphone and probably some of the players were upset because they had to play defense. But here's what I think, and if people don't like this, then too bad: if people are watching you play and you're out there on the court and you're keeping score, then you've got to play to win. We won the game. And when it was over, Iverson came over to me and said, 'Coach, it was an honor to play for you.'

"And you know what? He played good defense the whole game."

It was time to go to lunch and then to Woodmont for the afternoon card game. Red walked to the elevator and took it down to the underground garage where his car was parked. As he made his way to his car, a very attractive woman with blond hair, a short dress, and high heels sauntered past him. "Hi, Coach," she said, giving him a big smile.

"How are you?" Red responded with an equally bright grin.

He watched her walk away, nodding his head in admiration. "Pretty good, huh?" he said.

He opened the car door, then turned back. "Hey," he said, "did I ever tell you the story about the time a Hollywood producer wanted Dorothy to fly out there for a screen test? It was just before we got married. He offered her seventy-five bucks a day and . . ."

Acknowledgments

WELL, IT FINALLY HAPPENED. After writing sixteen books I have finally met someone who has more people to thank in his acknowledgments than I do. Of course, when one has lived for eighty-seven years and accomplished all that Red Auerbach has accomplished, there are bound to be a lot of people who have played an important role in your life. So, pull up a chair, light a cigar, and enjoy. Here's a list anyone would be proud to appear on:

Family: Hyman and Marie Auerbach; Victor Auerbach; Nancy Auerbach Collins; Reid Collins; Randy Auerbach; Julie and Eric Flieger; Peter Flieger; Hope Flieger; Noelle Flieger; Gertrude Auerbach; Johnny Auerbach; Edward and Sadie Lewis; Ed Lewis; Kitty Lewis; Inez Spencer; Sid Grossman; Stewart Grossman; Stanley and Ellen Copeland.

Celtics (past and present) who still stay in close contact: Bob

Cousy; Frank Ramsey; Jim Loscutoff; Bob Brannum; Tom Heinsohn; Sam Jones; K. C. Jones; John Havlicek; Jo Jo White; Bill Russell; Satch Sanders; John Thompson; Gene Conley; John Norlander; Wayne Embry; Dave Cowens; Larry Bird; Kevin McHale; Robert Parish; Dennis Johnson; Charlie Scott; Bill Walton; Rick Carlisle; Danny Ainge; Bill Fitch; Jim O'Brien; John Carroll; Doc Rivers; Leo Papile; Ed Lacoste; Paul Westphal; Ernie DiGregorio; M. L. Carr.

Owners, coaches, advisers: Walter Brown; Marvin Kratter; Don, Paul, and Paula Gaston; Harry Mangurian; Wyc Grousbeck; Steve Pagliuca; Bob Epstein; Alan Cohen; Mary Flaherty; Stanley Rosensweig; Ken Battles; Bob Richards; Jason Wolf; Eric and M. L. Wolf; Bill Reinhart; Gordon Ridings; Marty Glickman; Norman Knight; Bob Knight; Bill Friedkin; Will and Denise McDonough; Mike Gorman; Morgan Wooten; Ed Ornstein; Erv Lewis; Joe Gallagher.

Doctors and politicians: Roman and Ruth DeSanctis; Sean Dwyer; Murray and Brenda Lieberman; Mortimer Buckley; Carl Ollsson; Jerry Putnam; Harry Huang; Harvey Minnenberg; Max Fisher; Arnie Sheller; C. Hutler; Ted Kennedy; Ed Markey; Joe Moakley; Tip O'Neill; George Mitchell.

Friends, friends, and more friends: Jeff Twiss; Frank Bellotti; Jerry and Jan Volk; Steve Curley; Johnny Most; Eddie Andelman; David Stern; Russ Granik; Brian McIntyre; Zelda Spoelstra; Sam Cohen; Joe Fitzgerald; Dan Shaughnessy; Bob Ryan; Paul Sann; Ken Dooley; Ray Tye; Milt and Helen Kutsher; John Jennings; the Kowloon family and the Wang family; Emma Lee; Alan Dershowitz; Joe Greenberg; Bobby Orr;

Mark Wolf; Bill Reisfelder; Joe De Lorenzo; Steve Riley; Rich Pond; Tod Rosenzweig; Sam Kane; Hi Korzan; Steve Grayson; Arthur Becker; Jerry Cherner; Jerry Friedman; Jerry Silverman; Larry Silverman; Louis Glickfield; Mal Sherman; Harold Zirkin; Maury Lipnick; Steve Trachtenberg; Bob Chernak; Mike Gargano; Dom Perno; John Poppell; Si and Pop Wagman; Lloyd Lillie; Don Rodman; Herb Davidson; Pete Newell; Billy Cunningham; Steve Lipofsky; Eddie Donovan; Jack Diener; Herb Davidson; George Griffin; Doug Duncan; Chuck Thompson; Mike Lupica; Sany Tredinnick; Nick Del Nino; Jerry Colangelo; Bud Collins; Bob Rose; Red's youngest pal, Danny Feinstein.

From both of us, warm thanks to the China Doll gang — some past, most present and (we hope) future: Morgan Wootten; Hymie Perlo; Aubre Jones; Sam Jones; Rob Ades; Jack Kvancz; Joe McKeown; Stanley Copeland; Reid Collins; Pete Dowling; Bob Campbell; Arnie Heft; Chris Wallace; Stanley Walker; Erv Lewis; Herman Greenberg; Joe Greenberg; Alvin Miller; Johnny Auerbach; Stanley Walker; Mike Jarvis; Tom Penders; Karl Hobbs; Charles Thornton; George Solomon; Bob Ferry. Extra thanks to the long-standing members of the group who endured sitting down and telling stories to me.

And then there are my usual suspects: my long-suffering agent, Esther Newberg, and her two remarkable assistants, Andy Barzvi and Chris Bauch. Michael Pietsch, the best editor any writer could hope to have (all writers say this — I happen to mean it), and his staff at Little, Brown, notably Stacey Brody, Zainab Zakari, Heather Rizzo, Marlena Bittner, and

Heather Fain, the world's most patient PR person — who learned well from Holly Wilkinson.

Then there are my friends, most of whom would rather be on Red's list: Barbie Drum; Bob and Anne DeStefano; David and Linda Maraniss; Jackson Diehl and Jean Halperin; Lexie Verdon and Steve Barr; Tom and Jill Mickle; Jason and Shelley Crist; Bill and Jane Brill; Terry and Patty Hanson; Terry Chili; Tate Armstrong; Mark Alarie; Clay Buckley; Bob Zurfluh; Pete Teeley; Al Hunt; Bob Novak; Vivian Thompson; Wane Zell; Mike and David Sanders; Bob Whitmore; Andy Dolich; Mary Carillo; Doug and Beth Doughty; David Teel; Beth Shumway; Beth Sherry-Downes; Erin Laissen; Jesse Markison; Bob Socci; Pete Van Poppel; Frank Davinney; Scott Strasemeier; Eric Ruden; Billy Stone; Mike Werteen; Chris Knoche; Andrew Thompson; Joe Speed; Jack Hecker; the great Dick PetHall; Steve (Moose) Stirling; Jim and Tiffany Cantelupe; Derek and Christina Klein; Roger Breslin; Jim Rome; Travis Rodgers; Jason Stewart; Tony Kornheiser; Michael Wilbon; Mark Maske; Ken Denlinger; Matt Rennie; Mike Purkey; Bob Edwards; Jeffrey Katz; Tom Goldman; Mark Schramm; Ken and Christina Lewis; Bob Morgan; Hoops Weiss; Little Sandy Genelius; Jennifer Proud-Mearns; David Fay; Frank Hannigan; Mike Butz; Mike Davis; Mary Lopuszynski; Marty Caffey; Jerry Tarde; Larry Dorman; Marsha Edwards; Jay and Natalie Edwards; Len and Gwyn Edwards-Dieterle; Brian and Laurie Edwards; John Cutcher and Chris Edwards; Joe Valerio; Rob Cowan; Andy Kaplan; Chris Svenson; and Norbert Doyle, who first advised the Celtics to consider hiring Red.

My basketball people: Mike Krzyzewski; Gary Williams; Mike Brey; Tommy Amaker; Frank Sullivan; Doug Wojcik; Rick Barnes; Dave Odom; Jeff Jones; Jim Larranaga; Jimmy Patsos; Billy Hahn; everyone in the Patriot League. Also: the legendary Howard Garfinkel and Tom Konchalski, who remains the only honest man in the gym.

Swimmers (sorry, Red): Jeff Roddin; John Craig; Mark Pugliese; Mary Dowling; Carole Kammel; Margot Pettijohn; Susan Williams; Amy Weiss; A. J. Block; Danny Pick; Warren Friedland; Marshall Greer; Tom Denes; Peter Ward; Doug Chestnut; Bob Hansen; Paul Doremus; the gone-but-still-not-forgotten Penny Bates; and, of course, the FWRH club, Clay Britt, Wally Dicks, and Michael Fell.

The Feinstein Advisory Board: Keith Drum; Wes Seeley; Dave Kindred; Frank Mastrandrea. Not that I listen very much. *They* listen.

And, of course, my very patient family: Jim and Arlene; Kacky, Stan, and Ann; Annie, Gregg, Rudy, Gus, and Harry; Jimmy and Brendan. Also: Dad and Marcia; Margaret, David, Ethan, and Benjamin; Bobby, Jennifer, Matthew, and Brian. Danny and Brigid, who continue to grow up too fast, and, last but never least, Mary Claire Gibbons Feinstein. How she does it, I'll never know. But I'm eternally grateful.

— Red Auerbach and John Feinstein
July 2004

Index

About the Author

John Feinstein is the author of sixteen books, including *Caddy for Life, Open, The Majors, A Good Walk Spoiled, A Civil War, The Last Amateurs,* and *A Season on the Brink.*

He is a contributor to the *Washington Post* and *Golf Digest,* writes a column for America Online, and is a commentator for National Public Radio and Sporting News Radio. He lives in Potomac, Maryland, and Shelter Island, New York, with his wife, Mary, and their two children.